Jai Om Dave

SAMSĀRIK YOGĪ
Atman's Dawn to Samattva Yoga

BLUEROSE PUBLISHERS
U.K.

Copyright © Jai Om Dave 2025

All rights reserved by author. No part of this publication may be reproduced, stored in a retrieval system or transmitted in any form or by any means, electronic, mechanical, photocopying, recording or otherwise, without the prior permission of the author. Although every precaution has been taken to verify the accuracy of the information contained herein, the publisher assumes no responsibility for any errors or omissions. No liability is assumed for damages that may result from the use of information contained within.

BlueRose Publishers takes no responsibility for any damages, losses, or liabilities that may arise from the use or misuse of the information, products, or services provided in this publication.

For permissions requests or inquiries regarding this publication,
please contact:

BLUEROSE PUBLISHERS
www.BlueRoseONE.com
info@bluerosepublishers.com
+4407342408967

ISBN: 978-93-7018-299-8

Cover design: Ddeepika Om Sharma
Typesetting: Tanya Raj Upadhyay

First Edition: June 2025

प्रस्तावना
(An Offering of Intention and Grace)

What if I told you that you don't need to abandon your life to walk the path of the divine? What if the very chaos you are living in right now—the responsibilities, the burdens, the endless to-do lists—were not obstacles, but sacred tools for your spiritual growth?

I wasn't born a yogi. I wasn't even looking for the spiritual path. Like you, I was immersed in the world—working, striving, suffering, and constantly chasing the illusion of success. I thought that if I achieved more or had more control, I would finally be at peace. But life had other plans. It broke me. My body collapsed. My mind faltered. Even my hope slipped away.

And that's when something deeper stirred. A quiet refusal to believe that medications and numbness were my only future. That moment became the first step on a path I never planned to walk—the path of a *Saṃsārik Yogī*.

This book is not a grand spiritual treatise. It won't hand you enlightenment. It won't transform you overnight. I am not here to offer guarantees, formulas, or shortcuts.

What I offer is something simpler. Something truer.

A path. A path I walked. A path you, too, can walk.

This book is a companion for those who are willing to take that first step, not because they are perfect or pure, but because they are ready. Ready to stop surviving and start seeking. Ready to ask the deeper questions:

Who am I really? Why was I born? Is there more to life than just working, earning, and repeating?

If you've asked these questions, this book is for you.

But let me be clear: This is not a book for everyone. It is not for those looking for quick fixes or motivational slogans. It is not for those who want a spiritual checklist.

This book is for the seeker within the householder. It is for the mother, the professional, the teacher, the student, the parent, the caretaker—the one who lives in the world, but inwardly longs for the truth.

You don't have to quit your job, abandon your family, or wait for retirement. You don't have to be a saint. You don't have to be "worthy." You just have to begin.

This book is your beginning.

But it's not the whole journey.

When I began writing this, I thought it would be a single book. But as the pages unfolded, I realised something essential: this journey cannot be contained in one volume, not because of the number of words, but because of the depth it deserves.

That is why this offering is now in two sacred parts:

Part One – Atman's Dawn to Samattva Yoga
The Awakening, the Struggles, and the First Steps on the Path

Here, we explore:

- The eternal questions of identity and dharma
- The inner illumination of consciousness and self-worth
- The bondage of ego, illusions, and family karma
- The grace of Guru and Ishta Devata
- The transformative power of Bhakti and Karma Yoga
- The fourfold Yogic path that lays the foundation

This part is the *opening of the lotus*—the blossoming of awareness. But even the most beautiful awakening means little if it cannot be lived.

Part Two – Grihastha Sadhana to Adhyatma Rahasya
Living the Path, Integrating the Wisdom, and Embracing the Esoteric

This part will take you into:

- The discipline of daily sadhana while living in a family setup
- How Ayurveda, food, yoga asanas, silence, and simplicity purify us
- How time, death, and rebirth are not concepts—but living truths
- The gunas, Maya, humility, seva, and dharma in action
- The mysteries of manifestation, intuition, and Atma Yatra

This second part is where the *path becomes embodied*. It brings the teachings into your home, your kitchen, your workplace, your conversations, and your breath.

You cannot fully experience the essence of Saṃsārik Yogī without both. One shows you the mirror. The other teaches you to live what you've seen.

You may still wonder—Is this worth your time? I only ask you this: Don't read the whole book. Just read this *Prastāvanā* again. If it resonates, read the book; if it doesn't, walk away. But if something inside you feels stirred, trust it with faith.

I do not promise moksha. I do not claim sainthood. But I do offer you my truth. And I walk beside you.

With the grace of my Gurudev, Pujya Om Swami, and the blessings of Maa Jagadamba and Bhagavan Sri Hari, this book has come into existence—not as a destination, but as a dharmic offering.

May you walk this path not out of desperation, but out of devotion. Not to escape the world, but to realise the divine hidden in it.

And if you walk it with love… You will never walk alone.

ॐ असतो मा सद्गमय।
तमसो मा ज्योतिर्गमय।
मृत्योर्मा अमृतं गमय॥
ॐ शान्तिः शान्तिः शान्तिः॥

With folded hands and a heart full of surrender,
Jai Om Dave

Petals of The Path

Section 1: Atman's Dawn: Unveiling the Self 1

    1.1 Aham Brahmasmi – The Inquiry Within 2

    1.2 Dharma Sankalpa – The Soul's Purpose 7

    1.3 Chaitanya Jagriti – The Awakening of Consciousness 13

    1.4 Antarjyoti: The Illumination of Self-Worth 26

    1.5 Manushya Janma Rahasya: The Mystery of Human Birth 36

Section 2: Samsara's Leela: Navigating the World 45

    2.1 Ahankara Bandhan: The Ego's Entanglement 46

    2.2 Kula Dharma: Sacred Family Bonds 55

    2.3 Swapna Maya: The Illusions of Dreams and Expectations 72

Section 3: Moksha Marg – Paths to Liberation 88

    3.1 Bhakti Rasa: The Nectar of Devotion 89

    3.2 Guru Kripa & Ishta Darshan: Grace of the Guru and Divine Vision 101

    3.3 Ananda & Buddha: The Twin Paths of Bliss and Enlightenment 124

    3.4 Karma Sadhana: The Discipline of Action 134

    3.5 Chatur Yoga Marg: The Fourfold Path of Yoga 146

Section 4: Samattva Yoga: Balancing Dualities 163

    4.1 Shraddha & Samarpan: Faith and Surrender 164

    4.2 Trishna Mukti: Freedom from Desires and Attachments 179

    4.3 Dhriti & Karuna: Patience and Compassion 191

4.4 Adhyatmik Sampada: Spiritual Wealth vs. Material Abundance 204

4.5 Kshama & Kritagyata: Forgiveness and Gratitude 220

Acknowledgments.. **258**

SECTION 1:
ATMAN'S DAWN: UNVEILING THE SELF

1.1 Aham Brahmasmi – The Inquiry Within

"Who am I?"
It is not a question of identity or achievement.
It's not about your name, role, or occupation.
It is the ageless cry of the soul—the sacred inquiry that has echoed through seekers across all space and time.

This isn't about me, Jai Om. This is about *you*.
Who are you beyond the body, the name, the never-ending thoughts?
What is the eternal presence that links you to the infinite?

This question isn't meant to be answered but lived.
It is not a puzzle to solve—it is a flame to ignite.
A spark that awakens awareness and draws you closer to the Self.

In my early life, "Who am I?" wasn't something I consciously pondered. It didn't arise through books or debates. It came softly through experiences that cracked open my connection to the Divine.

As a child, I was immersed in the world of Gujarati Charan Sahitya. Padmashri Bhikhudanji Gadhvi, Ishardanji Gadhvi and Narayan Swamiji brought history and Bhakti to life through powerful Dayras. These weren't just performances—they were living scriptures in song.

I still remember one such performance vividly.
Ishardanji's "Anjani no Jayo" — a tribute to Hanumanji as Maa Anjani's son.
Each time it played, I cried. Not out of sadness but a deep spiritual stirring.
Hanumanji became more than a deity. He became my Guru, my friend, my guide. His devotion, strength, and unwavering faith pierced through me.

Years passed. Platforms like YouTube began offering similar bhakti programs. They weren't suggestions but sacred signals, leading me deeper into devotion. These weren't coincidences—they were divine breadcrumbs.

From the outset, my life has been shaped by uncertainty.
I was born on October 30, 1987, into a lower-middle-class Brahmin family. My father worked hard at the Municipal Corporation, and my mother devoted herself to our home and me.

We struggled financially.
My education was uncertain. I began with the Gujarati medium and then shifted to the English medium at my mother's insistence. Many in the family doubted I could adjust, but she stood by her decision. She gave me the foundation I didn't even know I would need.

Still, life felt unstable. Changing schools and colleges became routine. That instability followed me into my professional life—switching jobs, chasing stability, never quite arriving.

In 2020, I entered the digital marketing field and launched my agency.
Initially, it looked promising. However, by 2022, the weight of life had become unbearable.
Losing high-paying clients. Mounting bills. Family pressure. Mental exhaustion.

I reached a breaking point.

And then the deeper questions arrived—not as curiosities but cries of pain:

What am I doing?
Why is life so hard?
Why me?

These questions weren't philosophical. They were surviving.
And somewhere within that storm, a subtle voice began to whisper, "Who am I?"

Through it all, my devotion to Hanumanji and Mahadev stayed with me.

Even when I forgot to pray, they didn't leave.
I began to realise—these hardships weren't punishments.
They were karmic teachers.

Each loss, each moment of despair, was a spiritual nudge.
A divine redirection. A push toward awareness.

And in that space of exhaustion and surrender, the question "Who am I?" deepened.
Not to be answered in words, but to be walked as a path.

As you move through this chapter, pause—don't rush toward answers. Instead, sit with questions like:

"Am I happy?"
"Am I satisfied?"
"Am I complete?"

These aren't casual reflections. They may unsettle you, as they once did me. But this discomfort isn't a burden. It's a gateway, a sign that you're on the brink of something profound.

I've come to realise:
No one disconnected from the truth of who they are can find lasting peace.
We try to fill the void with achievements, possessions, or relationships, but they all fade.
True wholeness doesn't lie outside. It waits within, patiently.

This chapter doesn't hand out answers.
It helps you begin the inquiry.
Let your questions unfold like a lotus under the morning sun. There's no finish line—just the joy of beginning.

Perhaps now is the time to look beyond the surface and seek what lies within.

The Katha Upanishad offers timeless guidance:

आत्मानं रथिनं विद्धि, शरीरं रथमेव तु।
बुद्धिं तु सारथिं विद्धि, मनः प्रग्रहमेव च॥

"Know the Self as the rider in the chariot, the body as the chariot itself. Know the intellect as the charioteer and the mind as the reins."

This shloka reminds us:
We are not the body—it is our vehicle.
The mind, like reins, must be gently held.
The intellect is the charioteer, guiding us forward.
But above all, seated quietly within is the Atman—the true Self.

Most people confuse themselves with the chariot—the job, the body, the roles, the titles.
We say, *"I am a doctor," "I am a mother,"* and *"I am successful,"* as though these are our deepest truths.
But these are just waves—beautiful, but only ripples on the ocean of what we truly are.

The Upanishads tell us:
You are not your body.
You are not your ever-shifting mind.
You are not your ego, which clings, craves, and fears.

These are veils—temporary layers hiding the eternal light within.
Peel them back, and you will find the truth:
You are the Self, divine, timeless, unchanging.

A drop may think it's separate. But once it merges into the ocean, it realises it was always one. Likewise, the soul—the Atman—is never apart from Param Brahman. This truth doesn't dawn through intellect—it blossoms in the heart.

The ego—the false "I"—is the illusionist.
It whispers separateness. It builds identity.

But when even a sliver of this veil lifts, we begin to glimpse the Self. And in that moment, we realise—we were never separated.

The wave has no existence apart from the ocean.
The "I" has no existence apart from the Supreme.

Pause. Close your eyes.
Ask yourself softly, *"Who am I?"*

Don't chase the answer. Don't resist the thoughts. Let them rise and fall like waves. Just observe. Just be.

This question is not a riddle to solve. It is a seed meant to rest in your heart, quietly growing over time. The journey to the Self isn't a race. It unfolds at its own pace, shaped by your samskaras, your choices, and divine grace.

You don't need to rush. You don't need external validation. The honest answer lies not in words, but in being. And one day, in the silence of surrender, you may feel it—not as knowledge, but as presence:

You are not separate from the Divine.
You are the Infinite, embodied in this fleeting form.

Spend a few minutes with this question. Let it stir your heart, not your mind. Let the thoughts rise and dissolve. Let the silence teach you what words cannot.

Let each chapter from here be another step inward, deeper into the answer already resting inside you.

The question *"Who am I?"* is not a destination. It is the doorway.
The path.
Your path.

1.2 Dharma Sankalpa – The Soul's Purpose

What is the purpose of life?
Is it survival? Achievement? Legacy?
Or something deeper—a sacred purpose that transcends material success and awakens the divine within?

In the vast teachings of Sanatana Dharma, the life of Bhagavan Ram, the seventh incarnation of Maha Vishnu, shines as a beacon of purpose. Though divine, he lived as a human, facing exile, betrayal, and unimaginable loss. Yet, he upheld his Dharma with unwavering devotion and humility. His life reveals that purpose isn't about escaping hardships—it's about meeting them with grace and surrender.

In Uttar Kanda, Doha 45 of *Shri Ramcharit Manas*, Bhagavan Ram shares a profound teaching:

जौं परलोक इहाँ सुख चहहू। सुनि मम बचन हृदयँ दृढ़ गहहू॥
सुलभ सुखद मारग यह भाई। भगति मोरि पुरान श्रुति गाई॥

"If you seek happiness in this world and beyond, listen and hold my words in your heart. The path of Bhakti (devotion) is the simplest and most fulfilling, as declared in the Puranas and Vedas."

He continues:

ग्यान अगम प्रत्यूह अनेका। साधन कठिन न मन कहुँ टेका॥
करत कष्ट बहु पावइ कोऊ। भक्ति हीन मोहि प्रिय नहिं सोऊ॥

"Knowledge is difficult, obstructed by many hurdles. Other practices often fail to stabilize the mind. Without Bhakti, no one is dear to me."

And further:

भक्ति सुतंत्र सकल सुख खानी। बिनु सतसंग न पावहिं प्रानी॥
सतसंगति संसृति कर अंता। पुन्य एक जग महुँ नहिं दूजा॥

"Bhakti is sovereign, a reservoir of bliss. But without Sat-Sang (holy company), it remains out of reach. Sat-Sang alone ends worldly bondage—attainable only through great merit."

Finally, he shares a sacred secret:

औरउ एक गुपुत मत सबहि कहउँ कर जोरि।
संकर भजन बिना नर भगति न पावइ मोरि॥

"I bow and reveal one hidden truth: Without devotion to Bhagavan Shankara, no one can attain my Bhakti."

This declaration reveals the oneness between Bhagavan Ram and Bhagavan Shiva. Though an avatar of Vishnu, Bhagavan Ram humbly honours Shiva's grace as essential for Bhakti. This is not theology—it is divine poetry in motion. It reminds us that devotion is a gift, not an entitlement, and it flourishes through divine grace, the company of saints, and selfless service.

For me, this realisation came alive during my Masa Parayana of Shri Ramcharit Manas. These verses didn't feel like philosophy—they awakened something within me. I understood that Bhakti isn't just prayer or ritual. It is surrender, alignment, and a soul-level connection to the divine order.

Bhagavan Ram's words echo within me. They remind me that life's true purpose is not in what we acquire but in how we remember, serve, and surrender to what is higher than us.

Even though I've devoted an entire section later to explore Bhakti, this foundational revelation from *Ramcharit Manas* had to be here, because this is where it all began for me.

This chapter does not prescribe one universal purpose.
Instead, it invites introspection:

Why were you born a human?
What makes this life sacred?
What is the soul truly here to fulfil?

Life isn't just about surviving.
It's about waking up to your inner truth, your sacred dharma.

In my life, the search for purpose didn't arise during peaceful times. It came during storms—a financial collapse, emotional weight, and professional setbacks. I often asked:

"Why is this happening? Why now? Why Me?"

And then came the words of my Gurudev, Pujya Om Swamiji:

"The circumstances will never change. It is you who must change."

These words turned my world inside out.
I had been trying to change the external.
But fundamental transformation begins within.

When I began asking what truly brought me peace, the answers surprised me.
It wasn't money.
It wasn't recognition.
It was small, divine moments—bringing a smile to a child, comforting an elder, easing someone's burden.

That's when I realised—my purpose wasn't tied to applause or milestones. It was simpler: to serve with sincerity. In doing so, something higher moved through me.

Let these words be your mirror.
Let this chapter stir your heart.
The answers you seek may not come through logic, but they will come through devotion, reflection, and grace.

Humans today often treat material pleasures as life's highest pursuit. The race for wealth, recognition, and sensory satisfaction consumes most of our attention, leaving little space for self-inquiry or spiritual yearning.

Here's a simple reflection:
Compare the number of internet searches for *"how to make money"* versus *"how to live a meaningful life."*
This imbalance speaks volumes.
Humanity is stuck chasing survival, not purpose.

True fulfilment lies beyond wealth or fleeting joy.
It requires a shift inward to understand our soul's calling and connect with the divine.
Challenges aren't obstacles—they are opportunities, sacred nudges toward growth and alignment with dharma.

A common illusion is that life's purpose is gaining success, wealth, or approval. But such achievements, while momentarily satisfying, don't address the soul's deeper longing for meaning, connection, and truth.

Many see life as linear: birth, accomplishments, death.
But the Katha Upanishad offers deeper clarity:

श्रेयश्च प्रेयश्च मनुष्यमेतः,

तौ सम्परीत्य विविनक्ति धीरः।

श्रेयो हि धीरोऽभि प्रेयसो वृणीते,

प्रेयो मन्दो योगक्षेमाद् वृणीते॥

"Both the good (Shreyas) and the pleasant (Preyas) present themselves. The wise choose the good; the ignorant choose the pleasant for temporary gain."

This verse challenges us:

Are your choices rooted in ease or elevation?
Do they lead toward the eternal or just temporary comfort?

In the Bhagavad Gita (3.19), Bhagavan Krishna echoes this wisdom:

तस्मादसक्तः सततं कार्यं कर्म समाचर।

असक्तो ह्याचरन्कर्म परमाप्नोति पूरुषः॥

"Act without attachment. In doing so, one attains the Supreme."

Purpose doesn't demand withdrawal.
It asks for selfless action, done with a sense of surrender.
Even the simplest act, when done without ego, becomes a step toward the divine.

Dharma is not a rigid rule. It is the inner alignment with truth.
It varies depending on the time, role, and nature of the situation.
Bhagavan Ram's life reveals this.
As a son, he obeyed his father with humility.
As a king, he prioritised dharma over personal comfort.
Even in sorrow, he never lost sight of his path.

Purpose, like dharma, is not a destination.
It unfolds with each choice we make—each step of sincere action.

As you reflect, ask yourself:

What drives your actions—pleasure or purpose?
Are your decisions aligned with dharma, or do they serve ego or impulse?

Life's purpose is not something to find someday—it is something to *live now.*
Even daily life becomes sacred when we act in harmony with the divine will.

Reflective Practice: A Sacred Step Inward

Reflect on Your Joy
Sit silently. Ask yourself,

"When do I feel most aligned with my higher self?"

Journal Your Insights
Write freely, without judgment. Let your heart speak.

Take One Small Step
Choose an action today that reflects your joy—an act of kindness, gratitude, or silence. Walk it with awareness.

This is not about finding perfect answers.
It's about planting a seed—watering it with awareness.
And let it grow through surrender, one step at a time.

As Bhagavan Krishna (Gita 2.47) reminds us:

कर्मण्येवाधिकारस्ते मा फलेषु कदाचन।
मा कर्मफलहेतुर्भूर्मा ते सङ्गोऽस्त्वकर्मणि॥

"You have a right to perform your duty, not to the fruits of your action."

Let this wisdom guide you:
Perform your karma with love and surrender—not for reward, but for alignment.

As you close this chapter, ask gently:

"Am I living with meaning, or just existing?"

Let that question walk beside you.

The purpose of life is not an answer.
It is a journey—offered with love, shaped by karma, and guided by grace.

1.3 Chaitanya Jagriti – The Awakening of Consciousness

To me, Jagriti (awareness) means embracing the truths hidden beneath the surface—truths that only emerge when we choose to look deeper. It's the shift from seeing the world as it appears to seeing it as it truly is.

See, if you scoop a spoonful of water from the ocean and see no dolphins or whales, it doesn't mean they don't exist. Your spoon is simply too small to hold them.

This analogy shaped my journey into awareness. Just as the ocean holds unseen life, the universe holds divine truths. For me, Sri Hari and Maa Jagadamba are as real as the air I breathe. And above all, my Gurudev is the living embodiment of both.

Although I revered Mahadev and Hanumanji, I questioned the concept of Vyakti Puja. Vyakti Puja is a spiritual practice in which a person, often a saint or guru, is revered and worshipped as a representation of the divine. Saints inspired me, but I doubted their spiritual connection.

This perspective changed in my childhood when I got to know about Pujya Bhai of Ramanath Dham, Gondal—a saint deeply revered by my grandparents. He wasn't just devoted to Maa Jagadamba; he radiated divine grace. Despite having thousands of devotees, he never sought fame.

Pujya Bhai didn't live in isolation—he lived as a Saṃsārik Yogī, fulfilling worldly responsibilities while anchored in devotion. A Saṃsārik Yogī is a spiritual practitioner who balances their spiritual practices and worldly duties. Though I wasn't his disciple, his teachings became part of me. Even today, his photo sits beside my Gurudev's on my altar and in my wallet. I believe it was his grace that led me to Pujya Om Swamiji, whose presence became the light of my inner transformation.

Awareness, for me, is not just a concept. It's a way of living—with humility, kindness, and a quiet surrender to the unseen guidance of the Divine.

It has transformed how I think, feel, and act. Complaints turned to gratitude. Doubts turned into faith. It became the foundation of my spiritual path.

Awareness is the seed from which fundamental transformation grows, offering a beacon of hope and inspiration in personal and spiritual growth.

It is the first light that lifts the darkness of unconscious living, liberating us from the shackles of ignorance and leading us towards a path of empowerment.

Without it, we stay trapped in patterns—reactive, lost, and unaware of the deeper meanings behind our experiences. However, with awareness, we can break free from these negative patterns, fostering a sense of motivation and determination.

For much of my life, I lived in that darkness.

I wasn't an atheist—I believed in Mahadev and Hanumanji. However, it was a shallow faith, one lacking depth and meaningful dialogue. I didn't ask life any questions, and I didn't pause to hear any answers.

Challenges felt like punishments. If things went wrong, I'd ask: "Why me?"

I never considered that those moments held messages for me. I spent my days reacting rather than reflecting. Drifting—not walking. Surviving—not seeking.

The shift began with a struggle marked by financial instability, emotional burdens, and uncertainty about one's purpose. At first, these challenges overwhelmed me. But slowly, I began to pause and reflect on their deeper meanings.

And in those pauses, a pattern revealed itself. These weren't punishments. They were lessons. Each hardship was shaping me.

The moment I stopped asking, "Why is this happening?" and started asking, "What is this teaching me?"—my life began to change.

That question opened a new dimension of seeing. Pain became a teacher. Confusion became a compass. Struggle became a doorway. Awareness didn't come all at once—it was a slow unfolding. I had to revisit the painful chapters of my past and see them through new eyes. I saw how I had clung to negativity. I saw how often I overlooked blessings. I saw the recurring lessons that life patiently brought back again and again.

It became clear: the universe doesn't punish—it educates. And it repeats the lesson until we're ready to learn. With awareness came clarity. I saw how I was sabotaging my peace. I recognised the patterns I was trapped in. And with recognition came choice—the choice to change. But more than anything, awareness made me open to my Gurudev's teachings.

What once felt abstract suddenly became vital. Each word of Pujya Om Swamiji became a seed. Awareness became the soil. And slowly, something within me began to grow. His teachings no longer felt distant. They became intimate—echoes of the truths I was starting to remember for myself.

What awareness taught me is simple but life-changing: Life will offer the same lesson until you are ready to learn it. Struggles aren't random. They're precise. They arrive with intention. And their purpose is always to help you evolve. Life feels like a maze without awareness—confusing, endless, and exhausting. With awareness, the labyrinth becomes a map.

Each turn teaches you something. Each wall helps you reflect. Each path becomes a message from the Divine.

Transformation is the natural result of awareness. When we recognise our patterns, we can shift them. When we see our purpose clearly, we begin aligning with it. And when we sense the divine in our lives, surrender follows naturally.

Awareness is not just the key to change—it is the key to life itself. It helps us see beyond our human limits, discover meaning in struggle, and connect with the divine within and around us.

If there's one thing I've learned, it's that awareness is a gift—but one that we must cultivate. We awaken this inner light through reflection and a willingness to see ourselves clearly. Only then can transformation genuinely begin.

Awareness in daily life doesn't mean being hyper-alert, like a bodyguard always on edge. It's not about watching your every move. Instead, it's about approaching life with clarity and depth, tuning in to what's often overlooked in the rush of routine.

I'm not asking you to become a constant observer. I invite you to see the world with new eyes, reflect on your experiences without judgment, and let life's events teach you.

In my own life, I wasn't born with this awareness. Like most, I reacted to life without pausing to understand it. Caught in responsibilities and desires, I moved through life without examining its deeper meaning.

However, awareness doesn't necessarily demand an immediate change in circumstances. It begins with a shift in perspective. This shift occurred when I started to see events not as coincidences, but as messages—opportunities for growth.

You don't have to change everything. Just begin to observe—with compassion.

Notice how you react and how you respond. What choices are you making? What stories do you keep repeating?

Let me share a moment from my youth that only later revealed its deeper message.

I had a friend who loved video games, including Counter-Strike and Grand Theft Auto: San Andreas. We spent hours playing. When it was my turn, I would become completely absorbed. So much so that he often had to yell to get my attention.

Back then, I didn't understand his frustration. But now I see how that total immersion mirrors how most of us live—entangled in Maya, the illusion of worldly life.

We become so engrossed in roles, desires, and distractions that we miss the universe's whispers—the subtle invitations to awaken.

Awareness is the pause.

It's the moment you lift your head from the game and realise the world isn't just what's on your screen. It's a carefully woven story filled with meaning, lessons, and grace.

Maya, of course, can't be explained in a paragraph. In part 2 of Saṃsārik Yogī, I've devoted Chapter 6.1 to this topic. But here, I want to emphasise this—awareness allows us to see through Maya. It reveals that there is more to life than what meets the eye.

As you begin to live with awareness, external life may look the same, but something shifts within you. Your thoughts become more grounded. Your actions are more aligned. Your presence is more conscious. You don't escape responsibility. You engage with it more meaningfully.

This journey isn't about becoming perfect. It's about noticing when you're caught. Pausing. Realigning. And walking forward, again and again. Awareness is not a destination; it's a practice, not just of seeing the world clearly, but of seeing yourself.

I recently came across a drawing—simple in lines, yet infinite in meaning. It was the kind of picture that doesn't speak loudly, but whispers eternally to the soul. And as I looked upon it, I felt as though Sanatana Dharma itself had been illustrated with a brush.

Let me paint that picture for you in words.

A man hangs precariously from a branch of a great tree. Above him, a honeycomb drips sweet nectar—drop by drop—onto his lips. With all his effort, he stretches to catch each falling drop. Eyes fixed only on the honey, he is lost in its taste.

Beneath him, a pit of crocodiles awaits—mouths open, death certain. Two mice—one white, one black—gnaw steadily at the branch that holds his life. On the far end of that very branch, venomous serpents slither toward him. And below the roots of the tree, a mighty elephant repeatedly strikes its trunk against the base—shaking the entire structure.

And yet—just beside him, unseen by his honey-drenched eyes, the Divine Himself—Bhagavān Mahā Vishnu—extends a compassionate hand, patiently waiting for the man to notice, to awaken, to accept His grace.

Can you see the deeper truth here?

The man is you and me—entangled in the drama of existence. The white and black mice represent day and night—time itself—eating away at the limited span of our life. The elephant is karma, shaking us again and again through consequences we may or may not understand. The snakes are our fears, temptations, and uncertainties. The crocodiles represent death, loss, suffering, always just beneath the surface.

And yet… all we see is the honey—the fleeting sweetness of sensory pleasures, of Māyā. We ignore the danger, we forget the transience, and most tragically, we fail to see the outstretched hand of the Divine, trying to lift us into truth and freedom.

Close your eyes for a moment… and reimagine this picture.

Let the meaning sink in—not just in your mind, but in your life. For unless we awaken from this illusion, we too will remain hanging between suffering and sweetness, never truly free, even when freedom Himself stands by our side.

And to get out of this entire drama of Māyā, we don't need a thousand lifetimes or ten thousand scriptures—we need just one spark.

That first spark is what I call... Awareness.

For in that single moment of awareness, the illusion trembles, the grip loosens, and the journey home begins.

The Bhagavad Gita highlights this beautifully:

Chapter 6, Verse 5

उद्धरेदात्मनाऽऽत्मानं नात्मानमवसादयेत्।

आत्मैव ह्यात्मनो बन्धुरात्मैव रिपुरात्मनः॥

"One must elevate oneself by the self. The self alone is friend and enemy."

Our mind can lift us—or trap us.

Awareness is what helps us make the right choices.

Before we continue with personal reflections, let's pause to understand a common confusion:

Awareness vs. Mindfulness.

They are related but different.

Awareness:

Definition: Passive state of being conscious of your thoughts, sensations, or surroundings.

Mechanism: Engages the brain's default mode network, which monitors without focused effort.

Example: You're aware of the sound of birds outside while reading this.

Mindfulness:

Definition: Actively focusing attention on the present moment with intention and non-judgment.

Mechanism: Activates the prefrontal cortex (focus) and reduces amygdala activity (stress).

Example: Listening to the bird's song deeply—its pitch, rhythm, and feel—without distraction.

Both are valuable. However, awareness is the soil, while mindfulness is the seed you consciously plant.

Together, they allow us to wake up from the illusions of habit and ego—and live with intention, grace, and depth.

I believe awareness is a gift accessible to all, while mindfulness is a cultivated skill that requires tapasya—a deep spiritual discipline. This distinction has grown clearer as I walk my spiritual path. I strive to remain aware, but I humbly acknowledge that I'm still learning to live mindfully, moment to moment.

Awareness comes more naturally. I notice when my mind begins to wander and gently bring it back. But mindfulness—remaining fully present without judgment—demands more. It calls for inner steadiness, focus, and emotional balance. It's not just about returning to the moment; it's about staying there with surrender and clarity.

The human mind wasn't built for intense mindfulness without preparation. Trying to force it can bring fatigue, even burnout. Awareness, however, is gentle. It can be nurtured gradually without overwhelming the system. This realisation became clearer to me through the grace of my Gurudev, Pujya Om Swamiji, primarily through his book A Million Thoughts. While I can't claim to match the depth of his insights, his clarity has guided me more than any summary could.

Mindfulness is like climbing a steep mountain—it takes stamina, patience, and training. Awareness is like stepping onto the trail. It's manageable, intuitive, and essential. I share this not as a teacher but as a fellow seeker. I am still learning, growing, and making mistakes. I hope my journey inspires you to start yours—and perhaps even go farther.

Awareness initiates transformation. It opens the door to deeper practices, such as mindfulness.

Begin simply: when your mind wanders, bring it back. Not perfectly, but persistently. With time and grace, you'll move from awareness to mindfulness and eventually to the stillness of spiritual awakening.

We are walking this path together. With the blessings of my Gurudev, let us continue, one step at a time.

One day, Gurudev had shared a quietly profound story of Bhagavān Buddha that still echoes within me.

Buddha was once walking with a disciple when a fly began buzzing near his face. He instinctively waved his hand to drive it away. A few moments later, with no fly in sight, Buddha repeated the same hand gesture. The disciple, puzzled, asked, "Bhagavān, there was a fly the first time… but why did you repeat the gesture again?"

Buddha smiled and replied with deep simplicity:

"The first time, I acted unconsciously—driven by instinct. The second time, I did it with awareness. I do not wish to live even a moment unconsciously."

Now tell me—can you begin to see the subtle, luminous depth of this one small word called Awareness?

In a world ruled by habits and reflexes, to act with awareness is no less than a revolution—a return to your divine nature.

In Sanatana Dharma, awareness relates to recognising the eternal self, Atman, as one with Brahman. It's the realisation that we are more than mind and body. Mindfulness, on the other hand, grounds that awareness in everyday life. It ensures our insights are lived truths, not just fleeting thoughts.

Mindfulness trains the mind to be a friend. Awareness reminds us who we are beyond it.

Let me give you guided visualisation meditation instructions to help you understand these two.

(Please ask someone to guide you, or simply read and visualise.)

Sit comfortably in a quiet place, spine straight—either cross-legged or on a chair. Gently close your eyes and focus on your breath. Inhale deeply, exhale slowly. Allow tension to melt away. As you count from 10 to 1, feel yourself becoming centred and calm.

Now, visualise yourself standing in a place of extraordinary beauty—vibrant trees, soft clouds, birds singing in harmony. In the distance, sacred mantras hum through the air, their sound bringing peace and stillness.

You notice a radiant light shining ahead, unlike anything you've ever seen. It calls you forward. With each step, joy and wonder fill your heart. This light seems to carry the essence of divine grace. As you walk closer, burdens begin to dissolve. Worries fade. You feel lighter and freer.

You arrive at the base of a glowing staircase. Each step shines under your feet. You instinctively know that climbing this will bring you closer to the Divine. With reverence, you ascend, one step at a time.

At the top, the light expands. Before you stand, you will see the vision of Bhagavan Sri Hari reclining on Sheshnag and radiating divine stillness. Maa Lakshmi, graceful and serene, lovingly presses his lotus feet.

Tears well up. You fall to your knees. Not in sorrow but in the sacred overwhelm of love, surrender, and grace. At that moment, all struggles seemed small. In their presence, you feel whole, seen, and deeply loved.

You pour out your heart, sharing guilt, pain, and gratitude, and in that moment of surrender, Sri Hari and Maa Lakshmi smile with kindness. Their grace surrounds you, dissolving burdens you didn't know you carried. It feels as if every trial, every step of your life, was orchestrated to bring you to this divine encounter. Their blessings envelop you with light, love, and a renewed purpose. As their forms gently fade, their presence remains imprinted on your heart. You descend the glowing staircase slowly, carrying your grace within. You pause at the gate where your journey began, touched by an unshakable peace.

Now rub your palms together, place them over your eyes, and gently return to the present. You are no longer the same—you now carry divine awareness, ready to meet life with clarity, devotion, and compassion.

This transformation through awareness has changed my inner world. A recent experience showed me how much. When my mother was diagnosed with kidney failure requiring frequent dialysis, our entire family was distressed. One day at the hospital, I carefully parked my beloved motorcycle, a Bullet, in a designated spot. But when I returned, I saw someone had intentionally damaged it. The person I was a year ago would have chased CCTV footage, found the culprit, and demanded justice. But this time, I paused. A thought arose: "Perhaps this person is grieving or carrying unseen pain. Maybe life broke them, and this act came from that suffering." I said quietly, "May the Divine bless them and ease their sorrow." Awareness had done what once seemed impossible.

Meditation is the doorway to this awareness. While many look outward for peace, meditation draws you inward, toward a truth that already resides within. It's not always easy; it takes patience and perseverance without chasing mystical experiences. Science confirms meditation reduces stress and builds emotional resilience, but for me, its real gift has been a quiet stillness in the storm of life. I owe much of this understanding to 'A Million Thoughts,' a divine guide from my Gurudev, which helped me unlearn my misconceptions and walk the right path. I'll offer practical techniques for meditation in Chapter 5.2: Dhyana & Pranayama: Meditation and Breath Control in part 2 of Saṃsārik Yogī.

In my experience, people fail to cultivate awareness for two reasons. First, they don't realise awareness is a tool for transformation. Think back to childhood—how we casually chewed nails or skipped washing hands until we learned about germs. Awareness made hygiene a natural practice. Similarly, many are unaware of what awareness itself is. Second, even those who know its importance often ignore it, thinking, "Nothing will happen to me." That's okay. Everyone is on their path. We are not here to change others, but to transform ourselves.

One truth about awareness is that where it's absent, misunderstanding cannot exist. You can't hold misconceptions about something you've never touched. Until awareness arises, it's just not on the radar. But once it awakens, it becomes a light revealing your most actual path.

In today's fast-paced world, cultivating awareness begins with four essential values—kindness, empathy, compassion, and faith. When these are anchored in gratitude, they become the soil where awareness can grow. Gratitude, especially, transforms your inner climate. Practising these consistently shifts the mind toward higher awareness and a more focused life.

Awareness is not an overnight achievement. It's a slow, beautiful unfolding. It needs gentleness, effort, and a deep willingness to observe your mind in everyday moments. My life has changed not through grand awakenings but by these quiet, consistent shifts in awareness.

Years ago, I read The Magic of Thinking Big by David Schwartz. One sentence from that book lives in me: "When you tell your mind to do something, it automatically starts giving you the solutions and the ways to accomplish it." The mind, once given direction, becomes your most powerful ally. It will find paths, create space, and bring opportunities— often in ways you never planned.

If you feel lost or stuck, start with a simple intention. Reflect, speak clearly to your mind, and tell it what you want. You don't need a blueprint. You only need a spark of clarity and the courage to take one small step forward.

Transformation through awareness is not dramatic. It's subtle, like a sunrise—it reshapes everything without noise. You start aligning with your soul's higher calling by gently observing your thoughts, actions, and emotions. This is how you begin to live—not reactively, but consciously, fully, and in deep harmony with divine will.

Here's a simple yet powerful practice to help you take your first conscious step:

Choose one area of your life where you feel blocked—your career, a relationship, health, or spiritual growth. Set a clear intention about what you wish to shift or experience differently in this area. Write it down—clearly, honestly, and concisely.

Now, close your eyes and visualise your life beyond that block. Imagine how you will feel once you've moved past it. Let the emotions of peace, joy, and fulfilment settle in your heart. Don't rush—let yourself experience the shift, even if just in your imagination.

Today, take one small action toward this intention. It doesn't have to be big. Read a page from a book, call a trusted mentor, sit quietly for five minutes, or simply breathe with awareness. Small steps, when taken consistently, create significant transformation.

Most importantly, trust the process. Let go of the need to control every detail of your journey. Trust that the universe is aligning things in your favour. What begins with awareness must be followed by action, and both are nourished by patience and faith.

You are not as stuck as you think. Within you lies the power to shift your life's direction—gently, intentionally, and with grace.

As we move into the next chapter about Self-Worth, we'll explore how a deeper connection with your true value can accelerate and sustain your transformation. Awareness is the spark, but self-worth is the foundation that gives it strength.

Let us walk this path together—one mindful step at a time—with the grace of the Divine lighting our way.

1.4 Antarjyoti: The Illumination of Self-Worth

At first glance, the idea of self-worth might seem to contradict what I shared in Chapter 1.1—Who Am I?—where I expressed that "I am nothing, no one, merely an amsha (part) of the ultimate divine." If I see myself as an extension of the infinite, you may wonder why self-worth even matters. It's a valid question—and one that aligns with spiritual truth. But self-worth isn't about inflating the ego or clinging to identity; it's about recognising the infinite potential within each of us and honouring the gifts entrusted by the divine.

By self-worth, I mean an inner acknowledgement of the power and opportunity gifted to us through this human body and mind. It's about realising that to fulfil our divine purpose, we must first recognise our own value. How can we align our actions with the higher order without that recognition? Self-worth serves as the bridge between our spiritual identity and our worldly responsibilities. It's what gives our efforts meaning and our lives direction. While we may be mere specks in this vast cosmos, we carry the ability to serve, grow, and contribute in profound ways. Recognising that brings humility, not arrogance, and deep gratitude for the rare blessing of being born human.

True self-worth isn't about self-glorification. It's about discovering the potential that lies dormant within us. It begins with seeing ourselves through the lens of truth and choosing to act with sincerity, dedication, and faith.

Many aspects of self-worth aren't taught explicitly; our surroundings shape them. From a young age, we absorb the words and attitudes of the people around us—our parents, teachers, relatives, and peers. We're often told, "You're not good enough," "You're not capable," or "You're too immature." These seemingly casual remarks leave long-lasting imprints. I'm not a psychologist, but I've experienced the sting of these judgments firsthand. I wasn't a top student, an exceptional athlete, or an outstanding employee. I was average, and the validation

I longed for rarely arrived. Over time, these experiences etched patterns of self-doubt that still sometimes surface today.

Yet what kept me steady was faith—an unwavering trust in something greater than myself. That faith, even when shaken, always brought me back to myself. Slowly, it helped me reclaim my worth. I'm deeply grateful for that. In truth, faith became the light that pierced through the cloud of self-doubt.

Self-worth, self-esteem, and self-confidence often seem interchangeable, but they are distinct, much like awareness and mindfulness. Let me explain them as I've come to understand:

Self-worth is the deep recognition of our intrinsic value. It's not affected by how others see us or what we achieve. It is true that, by virtue of being human, we hold within us the capacity to transform, serve, and connect with the divine.

Self-esteem, by contrast, is shaped by how we view ourselves in the context of the world—our status, image, or the roles we play. When someone says, "He hurt my self-esteem," it usually means their identity or pride has been wounded. It often overlaps with ego and, if not kept in check, can lead to a distorted sense of self. Healthy self-esteem protects our dignity, but it must remain rooted in humility.

Self-confidence is our belief in our ability to do something, face a challenge, or learn a skill. It's action-based and often boosts our self-worth. Think of inspiring sports films like Bhaag Milkha Bhaag or Chakde India—stories that show how belief in one's ability fuels growth and purpose.

These distinctions may seem elementary, but they are foundational. Without clarity, it's easy to confuse inflated ego with confidence or external validation for inner worth. Before we dive deeper, understanding these terms sets the stage for everything that follows.

Self-worth is central to walking the spiritual path. When you begin this journey, doubts arise. Am I capable of understanding these deep truths?

Can I stay committed to such a path of discipline and surrender? These questions aren't signs of weakness—they're part of the process. But to keep going, you must believe you are worthy of the journey.

Spiritual progress requires that we trust not only in the teachings of the Guru but also in ourselves. We need to believe that we have the strength to endure, the courage to let go, and the wisdom to walk with sincerity. That belief is rooted in self-worth. When you understand your inner value, you stop seeing yourself as separate from the divine. You begin to experience your oneness with it.

This is why self-worth is not just personal—it is spiritual. It holds the power to carry you through doubt, hardship, and spiritual dryness. It reminds you that you don't need to be perfect—you just need to keep walking. Anyone with a sincere heart and unwavering faith can reach the goal. You don't need a perfect record. You just need the courage to believe in your own divine spark.

See how interconnected everything is? Self-worth isn't just about personal success—it's the soil from which spiritual growth takes root and inner peace blossoms. In Sanatana Dharma, self-worth stems from understanding the Atman—our eternal Self—and its inseparable unity with Paramatman, the Supreme Soul. The Bhagavad Gita, Upanishads, and Puranas all echo this truth: divinity lies within, and realising this truth is the key to authentic self-worth.

One of the most powerful teachings from the Isha Upanishad declares:

ईशावास्यमिदं सर्वं यत्किञ्च जगत्यां जगत्।

"The Lord pervades everything in this universe."

This reminds us that the divine isn't distant or exclusive—it dwells in every being, including you and me. Recognising this truth brings forth a sense of inner worth untouched by outer circumstances.

Understanding the Atman shifts our entire perspective. It lifts us from identifying with temporary roles or worldly accomplishments and connects us to something eternal and pure. The Atman is not affected by pain, failure, or judgment—it simply is. Embracing this truth gives rise to self-worth rooted in the divine, rather than external validation.

Reflecting on my own life—the burdens, expectations, and self-doubt—I realised how deeply I had been tied to the outer world. My worth felt dependent on how others perceived me. But something shifted as I deepened my understanding through my Gurudev's grace and the guidance of the shastras. I began turning inward. I stopped measuring my value by achievements and started recognising the divinity within.

The Chandogya Upanishad expresses this with the mahavakya:

तत्त्वमसि (Tat Tvam Asi) — "You are That."

This simple yet powerful revelation affirms that we are not apart from the divine. Knowing this silences doubt and strengthens our inner peace.

Another beautiful image comes from the Mundaka Upanishad:

द्वा सुपर्णा सयुजा सखाया समानं वृक्षं परिषस्वजाते।

"Two birds, close friends, sit in the same tree. One eats the fruit; the other simply watches."

Here, one bird represents the individual soul absorbed in worldly experiences, and the other represents the Atman—still, silent, and unchanging. When we become aware of the silent witness within, our sense of worth is no longer shaken by what we gain or lose. It becomes rooted in timeless truth.

One of the biggest misconceptions about self-worth is confusing it with ego. Many think projecting power, boasting achievements, or demanding respect is a sign of self-worth. But these often come from a place of insecurity. True self-worth is quiet and unwavering. It doesn't shout or seek applause. When ego pretends to be self-worth, it causes friction, distance, and eventually, spiritual stagnation. The ego creates separation from others, from truth, and from the divine, whereas true self-worth draws us closer to humility and grace.

Another misconception is linking self-worth to wealth, status, or social recognition. People often feel valuable only when they reach certain milestones, such as buying a home, earning a title, or receiving praise. But they feel empty and defeated when those are lost or never attained. This shows just how fragile externally driven self-worth can be. The antidote is introspection—realising that fleeting circumstances do not determine our value but our eternal Self.

Society reinforces this dependency on validation. From childhood, we're conditioned to measure our value through others' opinions—grades, appearance, and approval. Feedback isn't harmful in itself, but when we rely solely on others to define us, we lose touch with our inner compass. Many of those offering opinions don't even have the wisdom or awareness to understand our journey, yet we let their words shape our confidence. Why?

The root of this tendency is self-doubt. When we don't trust ourselves, we look to others to reflect our worth. But this dependence weakens our spirit and makes our peace conditional. Instead of living from within, we begin performing for the world.

My father once gave me a perspective I'll never forget. We were discussing missed financial opportunities, like Bitcoin. I asked, "What if we had invested early and become rich?" He smiled and said, "If we had millions, maybe we'd have lost our peace and closeness. Servants, not loved ones, might have surrounded us. What's the use of wealth if you lose your joy?" His words cut through the noise. They reminded me that success isn't what defines you—your values and relationships do.

And truly, had life been easier, I may never have felt the yearning that led me to seek my Gurudev. The struggles gifted me something no external success could—an inner awakening, a purpose, a path. The hardships became the fire that forged my devotion.

Ultimately, self-worth is about aligning with your inner truth, not the world's opinions. It's about trusting that you were born with divine potential and that your worth lies in recognising and living from that space. You don't have to chase it—it's already there, waiting to be remembered.

For much of my life, I didn't know this. Not because it wasn't true, but because I lacked awareness. I thought my ego was confident, but I undervalued my gifts because I didn't understand who I truly was. But once the truth began to reveal itself, there was no turning back. With awareness came reverence for oneself, the divine, and the extraordinary opportunity to walk this path with grace and dignity.

Growing up in an environment where constant comparisons—often even absurd, likening children to animals or insects—made developing a healthy sense of self-worth challenging. In such settings, doubting your abilities and internalising a limited view of yourself feels natural.

Realising my true worth didn't happen overnight. Once that awareness began to bloom, the real challenge was holding onto it, especially when those around me couldn't accept the change. For them, my shift seemed sudden, even unwelcome. They continued to see me through the lens of who I used to be. But for me, this transformation resulted from years of inner struggle, subtle realisations, and persistent growth. I learned to let them hold their perceptions while I continued walking my path. I never tried to change others; my sole focus has been on working on myself. And if this change came from giving a little, I often wonder what might unfold if I gave it my all.

This awareness freed me from the grip of external judgment. I realised that self-worth is not measured by validation from others but by how honestly we honour the divine potential within.

The foundation of self-worth lies in believing in yourself and acknowledging your inner strength. Earlier, I simply shared the differences between self-worth, self-esteem, and self-confidence. Now, let's explore how to strengthen your self-worth in practical ways.

Start each morning by affirming, "I am the best," and "Today, I'll give my best." These may sound basic, but they can have a profound impact on your mindset. They build resilience and confidence, which helps you face challenges without fear.

Consider real-life examples, such as actors and sportspeople. In the face of fierce competition and relentless obstacles, they held onto these affirmations and worked tirelessly to turn their beliefs into mastery. Their mantra was simple: "I am the best," followed by consistent effort. If you ever feel lost or discouraged, I encourage you to watch The Pursuit of Happyness. Will Smith's portrayal of struggle and perseverance serves as a reminder that belief in oneself is not a luxury—it's a necessity.

Believing in yourself doesn't mean skipping hard work. It means trusting that you can overcome what life throws at you. Every person you admire has faced moments of despair, failure, and fear. But their self-belief allowed them to rise again and again.

Before discussing faith in God or devotion in practice, it's essential to understand that you must first believe in yourself. Without this belief, even the most sincere spiritual practice will lack strength. This inner belief prepares you to walk the path of Sadhana while fulfilling your worldly responsibilities.

As Bhagavan Krishna says in the Bhagavad Gita, "The one who performs all duties with detachment while remaining devoted to me is indeed on the path to becoming one with me." There is no age or time limit to begin. I began my journey at 36—but you can start at any age, such as 63, 96, or even today. Self-worth and spiritual awakening are available to all, regardless of age or stage. Start today. Start now. Let belief become your foundation.

Gratitude and compassion are deeply transformative tools for strengthening your connection to self-worth. One personal practice I cherish is offering a heartfelt prayer before each meal. I thank Maa Jagadamba, saying, "Thank you, Maa, for lovingly taking care of me and my family. Thank you for this nourishing food that strengthens and heals us."

But my gratitude doesn't end with food. I offer thanks for every breath, every peaceful moment, and every small blessing. Each meal, each breath, each morning—these are gifts we often overlook. Many are not so fortunate. Let that knowing soften your heart, not with guilt, but with humble joy. Begin each day not with complaint, but with reverence for the ordinary.

Gratitude shifts your focus from a state of lack to one of abundance and from complaints to contentment. Likewise, compassion opens your heart to the divine in others. It reminds you that the spark of divinity lives in all beings, not just in saints and scriptures.

Now, ask yourself: When was the last time you thanked Maa, the universe, or life itself? If it's been a while, begin now. Say these words sincerely:

"I am thankful for everything you've given me. From this moment forward, I won't complain—just gratitude."

Feel the shift inside you. Let this practice of thankfulness anchor your days. When paired with compassion, it becomes a force that transforms your understanding of life—and your sense of self-worth.

The journey to self-worth begins with unlearning. Many of us unknowingly carry limiting beliefs passed down since childhood—doubts, fears, and internalised criticism. These hold us back. They need to be gently released to make space for healing and growth.

Self-worth is not something to master like a skill—it is a way of being. It is the dignity you carry even when life tests you, the quiet truth you stand by when everything else is uncertain. It helps you stay rooted, even when the world around you is shifting.

Challenges, especially the harsh ones, reveal your inner resilience. They are mirrors showing you who you are becoming. In my own life, I've faced many storms and still walk through some of them. Yet, through it all, I've discovered a source of strength I didn't know existed. That strength came not from others but from a growing faith—first in the universe and then slowly in myself.

Faith played a vital role in helping me recognise my worth. By trusting the divine intelligence of Prakruti, or Mother Nature, I began to see challenges as lessons and struggles as stepping stones. This shift in perspective led me to move from focusing on limitations to embracing possibilities.

Removing misconceptions is essential. Many of us hold false beliefs about who we are and what we're capable of. Once we begin clearing these, we open the door to discovering our true selves. Self-worth emerges naturally when we believe in our intrinsic value and align with the universal flow of life.

Living in harmony with the rhythms of Mother Nature deepens our sense of belonging. It reminds us that we're part of something far more significant, fostering both purpose and peace. Cultivating self-worth—especially in difficult times—is about embracing your infinite potential, staying rooted in truth, and trusting that every experience guides you toward growth. With awareness and faith, the path becomes clearer.

Understanding self-worth is crucial to fulfilling your life's purpose. You may already have clarity about your purpose, but without believing in your potential, that purpose remains distant. This isn't a linear formula; it begins with a decision—a commitment to yourself. Start by affirming that you are willing to learn and, more importantly, to unlearn. Let go of the mental baggage you've accepted as truth.

The moment you take that step, a shift begins. Every action and every decision feels more aligned. When you begin to view yourself as a medium for divine expression, your life takes on greater meaning. Recognising your role in this grand cosmic design is both empowering and humbling.

Being a channel for the divine is one of the greatest honours, but it requires faith in your worth. When your self-worth aligns with your purpose, the outcomes take care of themselves. Trust in the process, and you will see the path unfold.

Let me share my story if you ever feel unworthy of your dreams. As shared earlier, I've faced failure in nearly every area of life. I wasn't an exceptional student or employee. I tried building businesses, only to see them collapse. I struggled to meet my family's needs and often felt I had disappointed them.

There was a time when I wasn't even a good husband or father. I was consumed by selfish thoughts, neglecting the emotional needs of those closest to me. I often questioned whether I'd ever live free of fear, anxiety, or the pressure of unmet expectations.

I share this not with shame but to remind you that these feelings are universal. What changed my life wasn't perfection—it was awareness. I acknowledged my flaws and stopped labelling myself a failure. I began seeing each struggle as an invitation to grow.

Although I haven't yet fulfilled all my professional goals, I'm confident that I'm on the right path. My parents smile more now—not because I've provided everything they wanted, but because they see hope. A real, living hope that I am trying, sincerely and with faith, to create a brighter future.

This shift has transformed me from despair to hope, doubt to belief. And if I can change, so can you. Your worth has nothing to do with your achievements or mistakes. It rests in your effort, will to rise, and desire to walk the path with faith. Keep going, even when it's hard. Your worth will light the way.

Swami Vivekananda once said, "Talk to yourself at least once a day; otherwise, you may miss a meeting with an excellent person in this world." May you meet that person within yourself, and never lose them again.

1.5 Manushya Janma Rahasya: The Mystery of Human Birth

It is said that out of 84 lakh yonis (species), only one grants a human form. This truth alone is awe-inspiring. Imagine yourself in a vast, dark expanse with 84 lakh doors—only one leads to liberation, the rest to continued cycles of birth, pain, and death. Reaching this singular door isn't luck—it requires accumulated karma, divine grace, and deep merit.

But arriving at the door is just the beginning. Surrounding it are trials that test your humility, devotion, and perseverance: one wrong step, and the cycle resets. But if you remain steadfast, this rare opportunity becomes the gateway to merging with the divine, the source of all creation.

To realise that we've received this rare birth is breathtaking. Human life is not something to merely endure but to evolve through. It is a supreme opportunity to rise above ignorance and align with the truth of existence. Even amidst personal struggles, this realisation fills me with gratitude. Through my Gurudev's guidance and divine will, I walk this path. Despite life's trials, this human birth remains a priceless gift—a beacon leading us from darkness toward awakening.

The scriptures echo this reverence for human birth. From the *Skanda Purana* to the *Bhagavata Purana*, human life is portrayed not merely as physical existence but as a divine vehicle capable of liberation. The *Skanda Purana* calls it "a rare opportunity in the cycle of existence," earned through lifetimes of virtue. The *Devi Bhagavata Purana* states it is "a phase desired even by the gods," honouring its unmatched potential for devotion and moksha.

Adi Shankaracharya's *Vivekachudamani* declares:

दुर्लभं त्रयमेवैतत् देवानुग्रहहेतुकम्।
मनुष्यत्वं मुमुक्षुत्वं महापुरुषसंश्रयः॥

Three things are rare and given only by divine grace—human birth, the longing for liberation, and the company of a realised Master.

This verse is a cornerstone of spiritual life. Possessing a human body is not enough. Without the yearning for truth and the guidance of a living Guru, even this rare gift can be wasted.

The *Bhagavata Purana* emphasizes:

लब्ध्वा सुदुर्लभमिदं बहुसंभवान्ते
मानुष्यं अर्थदमनित्यमपीह धीरः।
तूर्णं यतेत न पतेदनुमृत्यु यावन्
निःश्रेयसाय विषयः खलु सर्वतः स्यात्॥

"Having attained this rare human birth after many incarnations, a wise one should strive immediately for liberation before death approaches. Pleasure exists in all lives, but the pursuit of eternal well-being belongs to human life alone."

This is a powerful reminder—sensual pleasures are available to all beings, but only humans can pursue self-realisation. Wasting this birth in pursuit of fleeting desires is to ignore its divine purpose.

Human birth is not merely a privilege—it is a sacred responsibility. Our intellect and self-awareness were given to guide us toward truth. Only in this form can we ask: "Who am I?" and "Why am I here?" and seek the divine consciously. Cherishing this life means fulfilling our dharma and walking the path of awareness, not because we are forced to, but because we are blessed enough to have the opportunity.

Throughout my life, I often felt weighed down by worries, financial pressure, debts, and responsibilities that left me feeling breathless. Life felt like a steep mountain climb, each step heavier than the last. Despite my faith in Mahadev and Hanumanji, inner peace felt elusive. My prayers were frequent, but they were more filled with frustration than gratitude. I couldn't see past my pain.

There were moments when despair swallowed me whole, so deep that I questioned whether I could continue. Thoughts of escaping life entirely haunted me. But even in those darkest hours, Mother Nature held me quietly. My prayers did not go unheard. The greatest blessing of my life arrived: the grace of my Gurudev, Pujya Om Swamiji.

Now, at 38, I see how deeply these experiences shaped me. For years, I was stuck with the question, "Why me?" Despite living with kindness, extending help to others, and causing no harm, I constantly faced setbacks. My attempts to do good went unnoticed, and I often felt invisible in a world that seemed to reward anything but sincerity.

The turning point came through the grace of my Gurudev. His teachings—through books, discourses, and videos—quietly transformed my perspective. Gradually, I stopped complaining about life's struggles and began surrendering to divine will. This shift wasn't deliberate—it was his grace unfolding the path before me.

As I embraced this surrender, the struggles I once saw as punishment became lessons—growth opportunities. They were not hurdles but steps toward self-awareness and spiritual alignment. Even after my initiation, I questioned why I had a Guru who felt so distant—someone I couldn't consult for every dilemma. But as I immersed myself in his wisdom, I discovered that the answers were already there, waiting within his words. With time, I realised they were also within me, revealed through faith and patience.

With this awareness, I began to see human life not as a burden but as a divine gift. Struggles were no longer obstacles; they became sacred invitations to evolve. Human birth is not just about survival or worldly success—it's a holy opportunity to align with the divine and live in harmony with dharma.

This rare life form is not random—it is the gateway to moksha. The scriptures repeatedly affirm that while pleasure is fleeting, the pursuit of truth is eternal. The human body, blessed with intellect, speech, and willpower, is a unique vehicle for inquiry into the nature of existence.

The *Chaitanya Mangala* likens this life to a precious gem, urging us not to waste it on transient desires. It describes the human body as a vessel for devotion and spiritual practice, reminding us to ask: Are we genuinely using this gift to explore our higher self? Are our actions aligned with dharma and the pursuit of truth?

Such questions make us reflect deeply. Human life is not an accident—it's a bridge between the material and the divine. This realisation calls us to cherish this birth and live with conscious intention, always moving toward liberation.

What truly sets humans apart is not just capability, but responsibility. We are equipped with tools no other species possesses, and with them comes the duty to fulfil our dharma and strive for freedom.

The human mind is capable of memory, imagination, and abstract reasoning. It allows us to learn, adapt, and reflect, making it a powerful tool for inner growth. Our ability to communicate thoughts and emotions fosters connection, learning, and collective evolution. The intellect (Buddha) helps us discern the real from the unreal, guiding us toward purpose. Intelligence helps us survive; intellect helps us transcend.

Then there is Intuition—the subtle guidance that comes from within—is a compass that helps us make choices aligned with truth. Free will is perhaps our most significant power. Unlike animals, we are not ruled by instinct alone. We can choose between love and fear, action and inaction, selfishness and sacrifice. This freedom holds us accountable for our karma and empowers us to rewrite our path.

We also possess self-awareness. We can ask, "Who am I?" and "Why am I here?" These are not questions of the intellect alone—they are the beginning of awakening. The capacity to consciously choose devotion, to align with dharma, and to walk the path of spiritual growth—this, too, is uniquely human.

You now hold the gift of a human body among millions of births. This is not just a blessing—it is a calling. Let this awareness guide your actions and decisions. Let it awaken your divine potential. Use it wisely. Walk toward liberation.

Despite these divine gifts, most of us lose sight of their purpose. Instead of rising above survival, we remain entangled in it. Conditioned from childhood to chase status, comfort, and material success, we forget the higher aim of life. The senses pull us into endless distractions, promising happiness but delivering only emptiness.

Uncontrolled desires are like salty water—the more we consume, the thirstier we become. This is the trap of the Maya illusion. It keeps us running in circles, blind to the immense opportunity this birth offers. Until we step back and reflect, we remain lost, forgetting that within us lies the power to awaken, choose, and return to truth.

The solution begins with awareness. If children are introduced to the truth of how rare human birth is early on, they will grow up with a deeper understanding of life's purpose. Imagine a world where children are taught not just to compete and accumulate but to reflect, inquire, and live with kindness and intention.

I spent much of my life unaware of anything beyond survival and worldly pursuits. Only by walking the path illuminated by my Gurudev's grace did I grasp the immense value of this human form. I often wonder who I would have become had I never found this path, if no one had guided or shown me the way.

That is why the root lies in what we are taught from an early age. We absorb the values and habits of those around us without questioning whether they align with our deeper life purpose.

When I became a father to my daughter, Rudri, I realised my responsibility—not just to provide or protect, but to guide. I chose not to lecture her about living a purposeful life but to live one myself. I changed who I was. I practised kindness, empathy, and compassion—not as teachings but as my way of being. When I helped someone, I did so quietly. When I spoke, I tried to ensure my words reflected the truth I lived.

Children aren't shaped by advice—they are shaped by example. They observe. They imitate. And this realisation became one of the most profound lessons of my life.

If we truly wish to honour the gift of human birth, we must build a culture where spiritual growth is not a luxury but a foundation. This begins at home, filters into education, and must flow into every interaction we have with the world.

In the next chapter, *Kula Dharma: Sacred Family Bonds*, I'll share more about how the family can become a sacred ground for spiritual growth. But for now, let us remember: our divine gifts—intellect, will, awareness—are wasted if misused or neglected. But when we align them with a higher purpose, they uplift us and all those we touch.

Life often feels like a labyrinth—uncertain, complex, and filled with moments of despair. But when I reflect on my journey, I now see these challenges as the stepping stones that led me to realise my purpose.

The struggles of financial hardship, overwhelming responsibilities, and emotional despair were not meaningless—they were perfectly crafted lessons. Had I remained lost in ignorance, unaware of the higher truths of existence, I may never have reached a point where I could receive the grace of my Gurudev. Awareness was the missing link—the key that turned obstacles into opportunities.

Our struggles and triumphs are not separate but threads of the same divine fabric. Every challenge, every moment of grace, has its place in the grand design.

Today, when I look back, I can see the divine hand that was always guiding me. And it's not just in hindsight. I feel that presence every day. Even as I write these words, I know they are not mine. This book, this effort, this message is the grace of my Gurudev, Pujya Om Swamiji, and the blessing of the Mother Divine.

I am merely a vessel—an instrument chosen to share this truth. This realisation humbles me and fills me with gratitude. To those who wonder if the divine truly walks with us, I say, pause and look. The presence is as real as the air you breathe, as sure as the rising sun.

And yet, had I not received this grace, I may never have recognised the value of this life. Only through awareness do we turn suffering into surrender and pain into purpose.

By understanding the significance of human birth, we begin to see joy and sorrow as sacred signposts—guiding us toward our dharma.

You don't need to abandon your life to walk this path. You only need to shift your inner vision. Change how you perceive. Change how you respond. When you begin to see human birth as the doorway to transcendence, dharma starts guiding your every step, and you'll find yourself gently walking in the footprints of the sages.

This shift transforms the ordinary into the sacred. Each moment becomes a chance to grow, each breath a prayer.

If you're searching for meaning, begin with faith. Faith is not blind. It is the invisible thread that binds us to the divine. Without it, we are adrift. Even our next breath is not guaranteed without grace.

Right now, as you read these words, countless beings across the world have not woken up. Many slept hungry. Others suffer in silence. Yet here you are—alive, breathing, and blessed with the chance to seek truth.

Isn't that a miracle in itself? The universe has conspired to place you here, at this moment, to help you remember your purpose. May this awareness open your heart to gratitude and inspire you to walk this sacred journey with sincerity and passion.

Human birth, in its rarity and significance, is a gift beyond comprehension. It is the culmination of countless lifetimes—a doorway to liberation and a divine opportunity to rise above the mundane and merge with the infinite. Each breath, each step, and each challenge is a testament to the extraordinary grace that has been bestowed upon us.

Throughout this chapter, I've shared personal reflections and scriptural insights on the essence of human life. From ancient wisdom to lived experience, the message is consistent: human birth is not a coincidence. It is a sacred calling.

But this gift comes with responsibility. It asks us to rise above mere survival, to align with our dharma, and to pursue the truth. The challenges we face are not burdens—they are catalysts. The joys we experience are not ends—glimpses of the infinite.

May this realisation inspire you to walk the path illuminated by the sages, guided by divine grace and the wisdom of our Gurus. This chapter is not a conclusion but a beginning—an invitation to undertake the most sacred journey: the journey within.

There is a beautiful story from the *Mahābhārata's Śānti Parva*, narrated by Bhīṣma to King Yudhiṣṭhira, that has deeply shaped my understanding of this truth.

It is the story of Kāśyapa, a devout but disheartened brāhmaṇa, whose faith had been worn thin by life's injustices. One day, while walking a village path, he was shoved aside by a wealthy vaiśya, drunk with pride, riding in a grand chariot. Humiliated and weary from poverty and neglect, Kāśyapa felt worthless. In despair, he resolved to end his life.

Moved by compassion, Indra, King of the Devas, took the form of a jackal and approached Kāśyapa with a message of deep truth.

"O brāhmaṇa," said the jackal, "you grieve over your suffering yet overlook the rare treasure you possess. The human body—with its hands to act, mind to discern, and speech to express—is a form I deeply long for. It is a privilege even gods revere. To waste this gift is a great mistake."

He continued, "As a jackal, I suffer immensely. I endure thorns, insect bites, and harsh conditions. I have no hands to build, no shelter to rest in. Even the basics of life are filled with pain. Yet, I do not despair, for

I know every struggle is an opportunity to evolve. Ending life out of anguish forfeits this chance for transformation and may lead to even lower forms of existence."

The jackal then revealed his own story. In a past human life, he had been arrogant, mocking brāhmaṇas, ridiculing the Vedas, and exalting logic above divine wisdom. That pride had brought him to his present state. Now, as a jackal, he longed for the very human life he once dismissed.

"O brāhmaṇa," he said, "your suffering is not a punishment but a doorway. Use this life to seek the Absolute Truth. That alone is the purpose of this precious birth."

Kāśyapa moved and awakened, saw beyond his pain. The jackal's words shattered his despair and rekindled his purpose. With renewed faith, he chose not death but devotion. He dedicated his life to meditation and spiritual practice, seeking liberation from the cycle of birth and death.

This tale reminds us that suffering is not the end—it can be the beginning. It is the lens through which we uncover purpose, transform pain, and embrace the divine.

As we close this chapter, let us carry this awareness forward: To live with intention, devotion, and gratitude for every breath. We must align our choices with divine wisdom, seeking not fleeting pleasure but lasting truth. To walk each step with the remembrance that human life is not an entitlement—it is a divine chance to awaken.

Let this understanding guide you as we move toward the next sacred step on this transformative journey.

SECTION 2:
SAMSARA'S LEELA: NAVIGATING THE WORLD

2.1 Ahankara Bandhan: The Ego's Entanglement

Before we begin to walk the spiritual path, we often believe we are the doers, achievers, and controllers of our destiny. But slowly, as we start to observe ourselves and life more deeply, we discover something hidden yet powerful—Ahankara, the subtle ego that quietly weaves itself into even our noblest intentions. It is not always loud or boastful. Sometimes, it disguises itself as humility, service, or even devotion. Often, it hides behind the masks of superiority or inferiority, making us feel either more important than others or utterly worthless. In both cases, the ego remains in command, distorting our true identity and clouding the purity of our spiritual pursuit.

In corporate, medical, or defence, hierarchies are essential for structuring responsibilities. However, in spirituality, these distinctions dissolve. From a spiritual viewpoint, there are only two identities: Bhagavan (the Divine) and Bhakta (the Devotee). In this sacred relationship, there's no comparison, only surrender. My Gurudev beautifully articulates this: "I do nothing. It is the Mother Divine who does everything through me." To me, my Gurudev is the most exalted being, but my reverence comes from devotion, not feelings of inferiority.

The concept of superiority or inferiority in daily life often stems from comparing achievements, appearances, or possessions with those of others. This constant evaluation can foster either pride or a sense of inadequacy, which can hinder personal growth.

Reflecting on a conversation with my daughter, Rudri, after one of her exams, I recall her distress: "Dad, my friends scored better than me." I responded, "Beta, everyone has their strengths. If this time didn't go well, work harder next time." Like any parent, I wish for her to succeed. But I also see that she excels in martial arts, music, and painting. She is not superior or inferior—just uniquely herself. Recognising and celebrating these unique strengths is key to fostering self-worth.

Sadly, her teachers often dismiss these non-academic talents, reinforcing the narrow belief that grades define worth. But this is where society goes wrong. We tend to box people into hierarchies, ignoring the diverse brilliance within them. When we let go of these labels, we start to see the value in individuality and nurture our true self-worth.

The comparison begins early in life and lingers into adulthood. While it can occasionally inspire improvement, it more often breeds insecurity, jealousy, and a broken sense of confidence. Let's go back to Rudri. If she continues to feel inferior to her classmates, this belief may grow into adulthood, quietly undermining her professional life, relationships, and emotional resilience. Imagine her starting a business but hesitating because deep inside, she doesn't feel "good enough."

Suppose she marries into a family seen as "superior"—more educated, wealthier, or more accomplished. Without inner self-worth, she may constantly try to prove herself or suffer silently in comparison.

This is not just her story. Many people live under the burden of inferiority, constantly measuring themselves against others and always feeling they fall short in their own eyes. The outcomes?

They doubt themselves endlessly, fear failure, avoid risk, and struggle in relationships due to internal inadequacy.

Comparison is a trap. Inferiority breeds resentment, helplessness, and withdrawal. False superiority breeds arrogance, isolation, and illusion. Both are destructive.

The root of comparison lies in our conditioning. We're judged by grades, sports, and even appearance from a young age. Social media only magnifies it, showing curated lives that make others feel lacking by comparison.

Let me give you a real-life example I'm sure you'll relate to.

Imagine standing in a long queue at your favourite temple. You've waited for hours, hoping for a momentary darshan of your Ishta Deva.

The crowd is dense, and the wait is endless, but your shraddha holds you steady.

Suddenly, a VVIP arrives and is taken straight into the garbha griha. They perform their rituals peacefully, while the temple staff, who were stern with regular devotees, now offer them their finest hospitality.

When your turn comes, you're rushed, barely able to absorb the moment. You catch a distant glimpse of the deity before being ushered out.

Let me be clear—this isn't about bitterness. I respect everyone's devotion, even that of the VVIPS. But what unsettles me is this: in the divine's eyes, there are no VIPs or commoners. My Bhagavan makes no such distinctions. Yet society imposes them, even in the one space meant to dissolve them.

Now, let's look at a more ordinary scene: a peak-hour traffic signal. You're on your bike, helmet on, sweating in the 48–50°C heat, waiting for the light to turn green. The road is packed, and the journey is slow. Suddenly, everything halts because a VVIP is about to pass. Roads are blocked, security lines the streets, and ordinary citizens are left to wait in the sun while the "important" ones glide by.

From temples to traffic signals, society reinforces the illusion of superiority. These aren't just moments of inconvenience; they reveal how deeply ingrained these divisions are in our collective mindset. From childhood, we're conditioned to accept them through respect for authority, admiration for wealth, or simply accepting the hierarchy.

These ideas create a false sense of superiority in some and undeserved inferiority in others. The result is disconnection, resentment, and a loss of unity. But the divine makes no such distinctions. Bhagvan's grace flows equally to all who seek it. Recognising this truth is the first step in dismantling societal ego and embracing our shared divinity.

We must transcend these artificial labels and cultivate unity and compassion in all aspects of life.

The human ego is subtle yet powerful. It shapes how we view ourselves and others. Let me share how it's played out in my own life. I've always been introverted, naturally inclined toward silence and reflection. I avoid small talk and crowded social settings, even when networking is part of my professional work.

My mother often sees this as a sign of ego. "You don't talk to people—you act superior," she says. But it's not pride; it's just my nature. I prefer meaningful conversations over surface-level interactions.

This was especially clear at a business event I attended in Goa. Surrounded by influential entrepreneurs, I quietly observed rather than joined the buzz. The goal was to network, but my reserved nature held me back. I wondered—was I hiding behind my introversion, or was it ego in disguise?

This reflection prompted me to explore the ego more deeply, particularly in a spiritual context. Unlike worldly ego, which feeds on accomplishments or status, spiritual ego is the belief that "I" am the doer.

Earlier, I discussed self-worth—our recognition of our divine potential. The ego is its distorted twin. Self-worth inspires growth; ego demands credit. Ego says, "I did this," "I deserve that," and "This is mine." It clings to identity, seeks validation, and separates us from the source.

When I began writing this book, I reminded myself constantly: this isn't mine. The grace of my Gurudev and Maa Jagat Janani flows through me. I am just a medium. Even in my daily practices—sadhana, puja, or seva—I silently say, "This is not my doing. It is being done through me."

There is one truth that has anchored me through every path I walk, and it is this: I know nothing.

Whether I sit for pūjā, chant the Divine Name in japa, flow through āsanas, breathe mindfully in prāṇāyāma, or dive into silence through meditation, I never claim that I know what to do. Instead, I bow my head and whisper within:

"He Gurudev... please guide me. Let your wisdom flow through me in this moment. Let me not act from ego, but from surrender."

This feeling of inner emptiness is not ignorance — it is an invitation. It has kept me rooted, free of pride, and aligned with my dharma. The moment we believe we know, we block what the Divine wants to reveal. But when we accept that we don't, He walks in, silently, completely.

This bhava, this feeling of surrender, is crucial for every seeker. The ego is easy to fall into—it often wears the mask of confidence or independence. However, on the spiritual path, it is a significant obstacle. It blinds us, feeding the illusion of separation from the divine.

The only way to transcend ego is through humility, surrender, and self-reflection. We must continually remind ourselves that we are not the source—we are instruments of the source.

As I have explained earlier, ego, self-respect, and self-worth are often mistaken for one another. Though they may appear similar on the surface, they emerge from entirely different roots and lead us to different destinations. Let's understand this more clearly with an example.

Consider a police officer. Their authority loses weight if they lack self-respect or don't embody a sense of duty. People won't listen to them—not because of external failure, but internal uncertainty. This principle applies to soldiers, teachers, parents, and leaders. They uphold their roles with dignity and earn respect when grounded in self-respect.

In my journey, when frustration consumed me. I kept asking, "Why is this happening to me? Why am I not getting what I deserve despite all my efforts?" These thoughts spiralled into self-pity, leading to unhealthy habits, addictions, and eventually a dark phase of anxiety and depression.

Looking back, I now see how the universe repeated situations to teach me what I refused to learn. Every setback was a gentle reminder to reflect on my actions and intentions. It wasn't until I surrendered completely to my Gurudev that clarity began to emerge.

My initiation became the turning point. His teachings made me realise I had been chasing validation, not alignment. My ego closed my eyes to the importance of surrender, humility, and faith.

Today, though financial hurdles remain, I no longer resent them. I see them as consequences of past choices made in ego and confusion. Now, I walk with awareness, guided by trust in the divine and anchored in surrender.

This journey has shown me that success without direction is empty. The ego can motivate, but unchecked, it becomes destructive. When we surrender, we find peace and purpose, free from the chains of ego.

The difference between healthy pride and arrogance is subtle but profound. Pride grounded in effort and humility uplifts; arrogance, born of superiority and entitlement, isolates and blinds. Let me illustrate this with two examples.

A rickshaw puller's daughter becomes an IPS officer—a triumph forged through years of her father's sacrifice. His pride isn't boastful; it's a quiet joy rooted in her success and his unwavering support. This is Garva—healthy pride that inspires without diminishing others.

Contrast that with a cricketer who scores a double century and begins to believe he's untouchable. Ignoring poor performances and dismissing his team's support, his pride morphs into arrogance. Where healthy pride grounds us, arrogance disconnects us from reality and others.

The Bhagavad Gita (16.4) defines arrogance as a demonic quality:

दम्भो दर्पोऽभिमानश्च क्रोधः पारुष्यमेव च।

अज्ञानं चाभिजातस्य पार्थ सम्पदामासुरीम्॥ (16.4)

Hypocrisy, arrogance, pride, anger, harshness, and ignorance—these traits lead to spiritual decline.

Key Differences Between Pride and Arrogance:

- Root: Healthy pride arises from genuine effort and sacrifice. An inflated ego and a misguided sense of self-worth fuel arrogance.
- Relationships: Pride builds admiration and bonds. Arrogance breeds distance and conflict.
- Failure: Pride learns and adapts. Arrogance denies and deflects.

Healthy pride celebrates effort and growth, but must always be tempered by humility. True success is a blend of personal effort, divine grace, and support from others. Grounded in gratitude, we can honour achievements without falling into arrogance.

If you've read this far and felt a deep connection, perhaps you carry the same questions I once did when my perspective-shifting journey began. Let me offer clarity on these questions.

How does believing in one's superiority affect spiritual growth?
It blocks surrender. Superiority breeds pride, preventing reflection and humility—essentials on the spiritual path. Scriptures remind us of the Asuras, whose downfall came not from a lack of power, but from their refusal to walk on the path of the divine.

How does feeling inferior limit potential?
Inferiority shackles the spirit. It traps the mind in a state of survival, suppressing aspirations. Thoughts like "Spirituality isn't for me" keep people from ever realising their worth or capacity.

How can one balance strength and humility?
Balance comes through practice. The key is cultivating Samarpana Bhava—the spirit of surrender.

To develop this, focus on four pillars:

- Kindness – Be gentle in thought and action.
- Empathy – Understand the emotions and needs of others.
- Compassion – Care without attachment.
- Faith – Trust in the divine flow of life.

All these are anchored in one unshakable foundation: Gratitude.

I remember when my Mama (maternal uncle), whom I lovingly call Bapu, is a priest at a Shivji temple in Rajkot. I've respected him deeply since childhood for how he lives his life. Once, he shared a simple yet profound philosophy with me: "If you live by these four words, you'll never experience unhappiness—Chalshe (I'll accept whatever comes), Favshe (I'll adjust to any situation), Gamshe (I'll like whatever comes my way), and Bhavshe (I'll eat all food with gratitude)." Even today, I follow this wisdom with complete acceptance, which has brought me immense peace and a sense of humility.

Ego and pride are like veils that dim the light of our true selves. They trap us in illusions of superiority or inferiority, creating separation from our divine essence. Spiritual teachings consistently remind us that overcoming these veils is key to finding clarity, contentment, and inner freedom. The moment we begin labelling our actions as "I" or "mine," we enter the cycle of attachment and suffering.

The first step to dissolving the ego is awareness. Watch for subtle signs—when you crave praise, feel stung by criticism, or compare your life to others. These moments aren't failures; they're invitations to grow. Pause and ask, "Am I acting from ego or humility? Is this pride or a genuine desire to serve?"

Gratitude is one of the most powerful tools to soften the ego. When you begin each day with sincere thankfulness, your focus shifts from what's missing to what's already abundant. I've made this a personal habit. Whether I'm eating a simple meal or reflecting on my day, I offer thanks silently. This practice grounds me in humility and reminds me that everything I receive is a gift of divine grace, not just a result of personal effort.

Rather than trying to crush our ego, we can gradually transform it through spiritual practices, such as meditation, chanting, and selfless service (seva). These disciplines purify the mind and heart, allowing humility to flourish. When our actions are rooted in devotion, the ego loses its grip, and a quiet inner strength takes its place.

Comparison is another form of ego in disguise. Instead of measuring yourself against others, ask, "Am I growing from who I was yesterday? Am I learning? Am I walking my path sincerely?" This inward focus frees you from needing external validation.

A short daily reflection can deepen this humility. At the end of each day, sit quietly and ask, "Did I act with kindness? Was I patient? Did I truly listen?" These small moments of introspection anchor you in self-awareness and help you realign with your values.

Overcoming inferiority also requires a shift in perspective. View your struggles as part of your personal growth and evolution. Celebrate small victories, no matter how modest they may seem. Every expert began as a novice. Trust that the divine has equipped you with all you need to face life's challenges gracefully.

The essence of all transformation lies in samarpana—surrendering to the divine will. When you recognise yourself as a channel for the sacred, pride and insecurity dissolve. You no longer need to prove your worth or hide your imperfections. You simply walk your path with quiet strength rooted in devotion.

Letting go of ego and pride is not a one-time effort but a lifelong practice. It's about finding the delicate balance between self-worth and surrender, knowing your strengths yet remaining humble. True greatness doesn't come from being above others but rising above your limitations. In that transcendence, you move closer to the divine and to the freedom that lies in spiritual liberation.

2.2 Kula Dharma: Sacred Family Bonds

For me, family is far more than shared blood or memories. Like anyone, I cherish my loved ones, but through a spiritual lens, family becomes a sacred responsibility—a beautiful duty entrusted by the divine.

It never feels like a burden. It's a blessing to have my parents' shelter, my wife's support, and my daughter's pure love. This sense of completeness feels divinely orchestrated—a cosmic arrangement meant to be nurtured and honoured.

On a deeper level, I have been given this role by Sri Hari and Maa Jagat Janani. They have entrusted me with the care of their reflections—my family. Each one is an *amsha*, a spark of the divine. Serving them with love is, in essence, my service to the divine itself.

This understanding transforms daily life into spiritual practice. Acts of love, support, and care are no longer routine—they become offerings, moments of *seva* woven into my journey with sacred intent.

Isn't it humbling to view family this way—not just as relationships but as sacred forms of divinity? This awareness fills me with deep gratitude, and it makes every moment a part of my spiritual journey.

Earlier in life, before I encountered these spiritual teachings, family responsibilities often felt like pressure. The weight of expectations and duties was overwhelming. I saw it as an obligation, not an opportunity.

But as I began walking the spiritual path, this perception shifted. Through reading the *shastras* and the words of my Gurudev, I came to understand the immense significance of the four *āśramas*—*Brahmacharya* (student life), *Grihastha* (householder life), *Vanaprastha* (retirement), and *Sannyasa* (renunciation).

Among these, *Grihastha* stood out as the most crucial. It's more than raising a family or managing a home. It's the foundation of all other life stages—supporting the young, sustaining the elders, and enabling renunciates. It teaches how to balance worldly duties with inner growth, turning even mundane tasks into acts of devotion.

It took me years to grasp this, but my entire view changed once I did. Family was no longer just a set of roles—it became a spiritual foundation. Every act of care now carried a divine purpose. How could I remain the same after realising this? With this new awareness, every moment with my family became meaningful and filled with love.

This understanding changed everything. What once felt like a burden now brings peace and joy. My family became a sacred school where I continue to grow into a better version of myself.

As I've shared earlier, my journey has had its share of ups and downs, including financial struggles, failures, and moments of uncertainty. Yet, one steady pillar remained through it all: my family, especially my parents. Their support never wavered. Even when I failed, they continued to believe in me. Their love wasn't rooted in scriptural understanding but in the purest form of human kindness.

Their simple words—"Don't worry, everything will be fine. Just keep doing your work." It lifted me countless times. Every time I stumbled, their faith gave me the strength to get back on my feet. That moral support became the foundation of my resilience.

Their sacrifices were many, and I've always been aware of them. It wasn't just about meeting needs—it was about the emotional ground they built for me, a space where I always felt safe and guided.

I know this isn't unique. Every parent sees their child as a hero, and every child sees their parents as their world. But that's the sacred beauty of family—the love we receive shapes us, and we pass it forward.

As I walk deeper into spiritual life, this cycle feels even more divine. The love my parents gave me flows naturally back to them as they age. This rhythm of support is eternal. It's not just human—the divine expressing itself through love and care.

My family didn't just shape who I am—they gave me the strength to walk this path with faith and resolve. Every part of me is rooted in their love. And for that, I remain eternally grateful.

When we reflect on the spiritual essence of family, our thoughts often return to the foundation laid by our parents. My father, for instance, embodies duty, selflessness, and quiet resilience. Born into hardship, he carried the weight of his siblings and his family without a word of complaint. Even at 73, he continues to work tirelessly. Through his actions—not his words—he taught me a lesson no scripture could convey more effectively: family is a sacred responsibility entrusted by the divine.

His life wasn't about fulfilling duties but about embodying them with grace and devotion. These values shaped my spiritual journey more deeply than any teaching ever could. Watching him dedicate himself completely inspired me to embrace my family not as an obligation but as a blessing.

When I got married in May 2009, life shifted dramatically. With marriage came not only companionship but a growing list of responsibilities. My father retired that same year, and I wondered if I could rise to his level of commitment. This marked the beginning of my true spiritual trials. I faced instability and failure, doubting my abilities more than once. Yet, my parents never judged me. Their silent support became the force that strengthened my resolve and solidified my understanding of family as a spiritual school—a sacred training ground for growth, humility, and love.

In *Sanatana Dharma*, marriage holds immense spiritual significance. The *Saptapadi*—seven sacred steps taken around a fire—is not just a ritual, but a spiritual commitment. Each step carries meaning, guiding the couple toward mutual growth and divine partnership. Let me share these vows in my own words, preserving their timeless relevance:

First Step: Nourishment and Prosperity
A vow to support one another in happiness and financial well-being.

Second Step: Strength and Protection
A prayer for mental and physical strength and the promise to protect and uplift each other.

Third Step: Wealth and Loyalty
A commitment to loyalty and shared efforts toward building a prosperous life.

Fourth Step: Joy and Respect
A pledge to bring joy and mutual respect into the relationship.

Fifth Step: Noble Children and Welfare
A joint prayer for virtuous offspring and universal well-being.

Sixth Step: Lifelong Companionship
A vow to walk together through all life's phases in happiness and sorrow.

Seventh Step: Eternal Love and Friendship
The final affirmation—eternal fidelity and sacred companionship in the presence of the divine.

These vows are a framework for a dharmic life. I must admit that I didn't fully grasp their meaning during my wedding. Whether the *panditji* explained them or not, I wasn't in the space to receive it. Years later, as I delved into their spiritual depth, my understanding of marriage—and my connection with my wife—transformed. It became clear that these vows are not merely symbolic gestures, but anchors for a spiritual partnership.

Family, then, is not just a network of roles. It is a divine structure—a *microcosm* of universal order. Every member plays a sacred role, contributing to the whole's emotional, moral, and spiritual development. My father's example and the truth behind the *Saptapadi* helped me reframe my perspective: family is a spiritual path in itself.

This awareness has been deeply transformative. It changed how I saw responsibility and helped me approach it with love, patience, and reverence. I now see my family not just as support but as my greatest spiritual classroom.

Of course, no family is perfect. Disagreements and misunderstandings are part of every household; mine was no exception. In the early days, overwhelmed by financial instability and career struggles, I often wondered how to manage both personal and professional responsibilities. The frustration sometimes left me disconnected, even bitter.

But by the grace of my *Kuladevi* and *Ishta*, nothing in our family ever broke beyond healing. The tensions remained on the surface and, over time, resolved naturally. A big reason for this was my wife. Her ability to "let go and move on" brought peace when I clung to anger or disappointment. She gently reminded me that holding onto grievances only makes the present darker. Her forgiveness inspired mine and slowly shaped a more harmonious family life.

None of us is perfect, but we've learned to focus on one another's strengths. That mutual acceptance has built a foundation strong enough to weather any storm.

On May 5, 2012, our daughter Rudri was born—a divine blessing that brought a new light into our home. Financial challenges remained, but something within our family shifted. Her presence brought warmth, laughter, and a sense of peace. Despite the outer struggles, we felt more connected, more whole. Rudri's birth felt like divine reassurance that we were on the right path.

This doesn't mean that disagreements no longer arise. Tensions still persist, but my response to them has shifted. I now approach such moments calmly, understanding that family bonds matter more than winning any argument. Sometimes, I let things go; other times, my family members do. This mutual willingness to yield is a blessing from God.

The most profound change in me began on the sacred morning of Diwali, November 12, 2023, when my Gurudev initiated me. That moment marked a quiet but powerful transformation. Day by day, I began to view family challenges not as burdens but as invitations to love, growth, and understanding.

The journey hasn't been easy, and this shift didn't happen overnight. But I'm certain that divine grace, coupled with my Gurudev's guidance, is what continues to shape me into a more compassionate and aware family member. These lessons continue to unfold, deepening my understanding of love, patience, and unity.

Honestly, I often feel I fall short of my family's expectations, not regretfully, but with the quiet awareness that they deserve more than I can currently offer. My energy is consumed by work I love, but whose outcome remains uncertain. Imagine standing at a crossroads, filled with passion yet burdened by the unknown. It's a blend of profound purpose and relentless questioning.

Balancing personal growth with family responsibilities has always mattered to me. I once managed this well, but now the urgency and scope of my work have tipped that balance. Still, I don't see this as neglect but as a conscious, temporary phase. I've chosen to give my all to the path I believe in. To me, this isn't just work—it's seva, selfless service. I've surrendered the results to Sri Hari, trusting He will care for what lies beyond my reach.

My current lack of family attention may not align with His wishes. Yet I believe He sees my heart and intention. In this surrender, I find both strength and solace.

The journey of balancing personal ambition with family devotion is still unfolding. What sustains me is faith—faith that sincere action, born of passion, will restore balance in time through His grace.

I was born into a Brahmin family, blessed by God's grace, but we were never steeped in karma kanda or elaborate rituals. Even my grandfathers, as far as I know, didn't follow such practices. But that didn't mean we lacked spirituality. Ours was simple: temple visits, bowing before vigrahas, and reverence for our Kula Devi and Ishta Devata, Mahadev.

For many years, my temple visits were filled more with complaints than gratitude. Only after meeting my Gurudev did I understand the power of thanking the divine for what we already have. Although my conscious spiritual journey began there, the roots of kindness and compassion had already been planted, quietly watered by my family's way of living.

Though not a traditional spiritual guide, my father taught me priceless lessons through his actions. One of his core beliefs was never to bargain with small vendors, such as vegetable sellers, shopkeepers, or street hawkers. He would say, "How much profit do they make? If we, too, start haggling, how will they survive?"

That stayed with me. He would add, "We never bargain in malls or restaurants. Then why do we do it with those who earn so little? If it fits your budget, go ahead and buy it. If not, take less or don't buy it at all." His words weren't just advice—they became a lens through which I saw the world.

He taught me empathy, not by preaching it, but by living it.

When I was 10 or 11—I can't recall the exact year—my parents planned a birthday celebration I'll never forget. Instead of a typical home party, they arranged a visit to an orphanage. There were over a hundred children. We cut cake, shared a meal, and laughed with children who, despite their hardships, radiated joy. I didn't fully grasp the meaning of gratitude that day, but something within me shifted. The happiness in that room left a lasting imprint.

That moment wasn't an isolated gesture. My parents lived this way—feeding stray animals, offering food to those in need, and treating everyone with dignity, regardless of their background. They never instructed me to be kind. They simply embodied it.

From a young age, I've believed that animals deserve the same respect and compassion as humans. While society often treats them as lesser beings or means to an end, I've always felt a responsibility to protect their well-being. This belief isn't abstract—it's something I practice every day.

One of the first ways I aligned my life with this value was through milk consumption. I ask my milk vendor a simple yet essential question: "Have the calves been fed first?" If the answer is no, I won't buy the milk. I cannot accept nourishment that was unjustly taken from a calf. Milk is nature's gift, and it is meant for the young ones first. In my view, taking it before they're satisfied is a serious violation of nature's balance.

This might seem like a small act, but to me, it's a spiritual discipline—a daily practice of empathy that reminds me to honour the interconnectedness of all life.

Another reflection of this principle is my refusal to use animals for transport during pilgrimages. Whether at Vaishnodevi or trekking uphill, I choose to walk instead of burdening ponies or mules. I've witnessed them overloaded, exhausted, and beaten, enduring suffering simply so others can reach a sacred place with ease. If the path is spiritual, how can it be paved with cruelty?

Walking the path ourselves, bearing the discomfort and effort, brings far more spiritual merit than riding on the pain of another being. There is no divinity in reaching a holy place through the suffering of the innocent.

We live in a world that primarily caters to human convenience, often at the expense of other species. From factory farming to habitat destruction, animals face daily torment in a world they didn't create. I try to reduce this harm in whatever small ways I can.

I ensure that the stray dogs in my area have food and water, especially during extreme weather conditions. I've encouraged my daughter, Rudri, to carry this value forward. Watching her feed birds in our yard or offer biscuits to strays—without being told—fills me with hope. These acts of kindness, though small, have the power to shape generations.

Sanatana Dharma teaches us that all living beings are divine manifestations. In the Bhagavad Gita, Lord Krishna says:

सर्वभूतस्थमात्मानं सर्वभूतानि चात्मनि ।
ईक्षते योगयुक्तात्मा सर्वत्र समदर्शनः ॥

"One who is united with the Divine sees the Self in all beings and all beings within the Self."

This teaching is a constant reminder: every creature holds the same divine spark, no matter how small. Hurting them disrupts not only their lives but the balance of the cosmos.

My path is grounded in Ahimsa—non-violence in thought, word, and action. This means choosing not to harm, even if the harm is indirect. Allowing a calf to drink first, feeding a stray dog, or refraining from exploiting an animal for convenience are all ways to practice this principle daily.

These simple acts have deepened my patience and compassion. They've taught me to move with awareness, to cherish life in all its forms, and to accept the responsibility that comes with being human.

I inspire others to pause, reflect, and reconsider their everyday choices by walking this path. True spirituality, to me, lies in extending our love beyond our species, to all creatures who share this world with us.

Looking back, it's clear my first spiritual teachers were my own family. They didn't preach or quote scriptures. They just lived with kindness, simplicity, and empathy.

These experiences taught me that true spirituality begins at home. It's in how we speak to one another, support the vulnerable, and uphold compassion even when no one is watching.

There were many times when family responsibilities felt crushing, especially while juggling financial instability, career pressures, and unspoken expectations. But during these very hardships, I uncovered something vital: strength doesn't always come from outside. Often, it rises quietly from within, built upon a foundation of love, faith, and growing awareness.

In times of overwhelming responsibility, I leaned heavily on my spiritual practices and trust in the divine. When the weight of providing for my family felt overwhelming, I reminded myself that I was merely a conduit. My duties, though they appear mine, are entrusted by the universe. I told myself, "This, too, is a form of seva (service) to the divine." That shift transformed the burden into a blessing.

I also drew strength from my family's unwavering support. Even in my setbacks, they stood by me with quiet encouragement. This mutual love became the foundation of my resilience. I learned to break down big problems into smaller steps, facing each with faith.

This journey taught me that while challenges are inevitable, divine grace also exists. Surrendering to that grace while doing our best is the only way I've found to carry life's heaviest loads.

The difference between fulfilling duties with love and being entangled in attachment is subtle but vital. I've understood that it all lies in our bhava—our inner attitude. When I serve my parents, wife, or daughter with devotion and gratitude, I see the divine in them. As my Gurudev says, "Every act done with love and selflessness elevates the soul."

But attachment creeps in when we seek validation or control over the outcomes—when I want my daughter to excel just to feel proud, or when I crave immediate success at work. That's no longer seva; it's expectation. Expectations often bring frustration.

This awareness has changed my approach. I do my duties wholeheartedly, remembering that results are not in my hands. Loving my family deeply, yet without attachment, is a spiritual practice. They are part of the cosmic design, walking their journey just as I walk mine.

It's about loving without clinging, serving without expecting anything in return, and living with gratitude while letting go of control.

Souls come together across lifetimes. Family relationships, in my view, reflect deep karmic ties. This isn't just a spiritual theory—it forms the basis of how I see life.

Years ago, I watched a video titled *"There is a reason behind everyone you meet in life."* It beautifully echoed what my father often said: that a child born into a family may be a returning ancestor or a soul from a past life, arriving to repay or reclaim a karmic debt.

I believe these karmic connections extend far beyond ancestry. Souls reunite as a family due to unfinished spiritual contracts. Without these karmic links, there would be no reason for us to reunite like this in this life.

Another concept that resonates deeply with me is that a soul chooses its womb. Based on its prarabdha karma—its destiny accumulated from past lives—it selects the family most aligned with its evolution. This choice isn't random. It's intentional and deeply sacred.

Yet I've also come to realise that understanding the details of past-life bonds isn't necessary to live with love and devotion. Whether or not we recall the karmic story behind our family members, we can still serve them with a whole heart. Seeing each one as a divine form is enough.

For me, this change in perspective has been transformative. My family is no longer just a group bound by blood. They are a gift—a sacred field where I can practice devotion, patience, and selfless love. What if every interaction with a loved one felt like seva to Bhagavan himself? How rich and beautiful life would become.

These karmic ties may remain a mystery, but their purpose is always meaningful. Everything unfolds for a reason, which is tied to our growth. Whether we understand the cause or not, our role is to love, serve, and evolve together.

Perhaps someday, I'll dedicate an entire book to exploring these karmic relationships. I now invite you to cherish your family as a sacred gift, trust in the divine plan, and let each moment with them be a blessing. When we live with this awareness, even the simplest moments become jewels on our path to liberation.

Modern family structures have a profound influence on an individual's spiritual growth. My intention here isn't to criticise changing lifestyles but to offer a spiritual lens through which we can view them.

Today, nuclear families—small units of parents and children—have replaced the joint systems of earlier times, where multiple generations lived under one roof, sharing love, guidance, and emotional support. While the modern setup offers convenience, it often comes at the cost of losing the wisdom and nurturing presence of our elders.

The root of this shift aligns with the nature of Kali-Yuga, described vividly in *Srimad Bhagavatam*:

ततः चानुदिनं धर्मः सत्यं शौचं क्षमा दया ।

कालेन बलिना राजन् नङ्क्ष्यत्यायुर्बलं स्मृतिः ॥

"As the age of Kali progresses, dharma, truthfulness, purity, tolerance, compassion, longevity, strength, and memory will decline due to the influence of time."

What we witness today—fragmented families and weakening values—is just one symptom of this age.

Children may grow up without learning patience, humility, and compassion if they lack the guidance of elders. The emphasis shifts from inner growth to external success. I'm not here to prescribe how one must live but to remind you that family is not a burden—it's a sacred opportunity. The sacrifices of our parents are beyond measure. Ignoring their value creates an imbalance and also sets a precedent for future generations. Karma is impartial—what we give, we eventually receive.

But this isn't about fear. It's about transforming our mindset. Why sow seeds of regret when you can serve with love now? Family duties, when seen through the lens of *dharma*, become spiritual practices. Every act becomes *seva*, and even routine interactions gain depth and meaning.

Ultimately, family is a spiritual school—a space where we learn patience, humility, love, and surrender. When you embrace family as a divine gift, you're not just nurturing others; you're also evolving your soul.

Another critical influence is the role of technology in modern life. We live in 2025, surrounded by tools meant to simplify our lives, but this convenience often distances us from the very relationships we cherish the most.

I would like to share a profound insight from Vedic astrology: Rahu, the North Node of the Moon, is said to govern technology and innovation. While Rahu blesses us with advancement, it also brings a shadow—a "technology curse." This duality is visible in how we use devices: meant to connect, they often have the opposite effect.

Think about it—how often do we instinctively check our phones in the morning? How much of our day is spent scrolling, even during meals or just before sleep? Instead of simplifying our lives, these gadgets overwhelm our minds with noise and pull us away from meaningful connections.

You've likely heard this before. But just as people ignore tobacco and alcohol warnings on their packages, many of us overlook how screen time eats away at family bonding. The real issue isn't just lost time—it's the missed depth of presence, the unspoken words, the silences we never share.

Our minds, bombarded with constant input, grow restless. Social media, binge-watching, and endless notifications leave us mentally depleted, with little room for reflection or connection.

Let me be clear—I'm not advocating that we abandon technology or entertainment. Balance is essential. My wife, Charmi, and I enjoy watching a movie or series together on weekends. Two hours a week is enough to unwind without letting it dominate our lives.

This arrangement helps preserve our bond. It's not a perfect formula, but it works. Change, after all, is gradual. I didn't shift my habits overnight, either. What helped was replacing mindless scrolling with more meaningful tasks. Slowly, the urge faded.

When used mindfully, technology can beautifully support spiritual growth and family bonding. My Gurudev has gifted the world something genuinely transformative: the Sadhana App by the Vedic Sadhana Foundation. It offers a treasure trove of spiritual tools—chanting, meditations, and guided practices—all available for free, accessible anytime, anywhere. I introduced the app to my daughter Rudri, and to my joy, she now enjoys it more than any other app on my phone. Isn't that remarkable?

This is why I revere my Gurudev as a modern saint—he shares eternal wisdom in ways that resonate with our times, helping us integrate spirituality into our daily lives. I'll explore this further in Chapter 3.5, Chatur Yoga Marg, but I wanted to mention it here because it illustrates how technology, when used with intention, can become a doorway to higher awareness.

Another simple but powerful practice we've adopted is the "no screens at the dining table" rule. This slight shift has transformed mealtimes into moments of connection. We sit together, laugh, share stories, and offer thanks to Maa Annapurna for nourishing us. The joy and unity that arise from simply being present during meals are immeasurable.

Practices like these may seem minor, but they have a profound impact. They carve out space for presence, reflection, and gratitude—qualities often lost in our fast-paced lives. These small rituals have become anchors for me, helping me balance the demands of modern life with a sense of spiritual grounding. Indeed, the results have been truly transformative.

I'm not here to preach or impose—just to share what's worked for me, hoping it may inspire reflection. This isn't about giving up entertainment, but about ensuring it doesn't eclipse what matters most: time with family and spiritual growth.

This is about using technology as a tool, not a crutch. When we live with this awareness, conversations deepen, relationships flourish, and life becomes more meaningful.

If one principle sustains family harmony, it is respect for each person's choices, space, and individuality.

I emphasise respect over love because love, while beautiful, can sometimes carry expectations or possessiveness that strain relationships. But respect allows space—it honours another's journey without trying to control it.

Let me share a few personal reflections.

I deeply respect my father, not just for his achievements but for his lifelong commitment to our family. We've sometimes disagreed, but I always remind myself that he's my father. My role is not to win arguments but to honour his journey and give him the freedom to be himself. That is my expression of love.

My mother's strength shaped me. Despite having limited education, she supported us during financial hardships—travelling town to town, selling dresses, and working as a postal small savings scheme agent, collecting small deposits for modest commissions. More than financial support, she defied social norms to prioritise my education. In an era when English-medium schooling was rare, she insisted I have it, so I could one day write this book and connect with hearts worldwide.

Today, as she grows older and more dependent, I care for her, not out of duty, but with deep gratitude. Her temperament can be challenging, sometimes creating friction, especially with my wife, Charmi. Initially, things went smoothly, but over time, disagreements began to surface. Friends told me such issues were common, but living through them taught me otherwise.

Back then, I chose to stay neutral, not taking sides. My father often handled it better. But the tension lingered until I finally sat with Charmi and shared my heart. I said, "This is our reality. We can't expect Mom to change at this stage. But we can change how we respond. Let's see this as our sadhana. Are you with me?"

That conversation changed everything. Over time, Charmi's perspective softened. Complaints faded, and harmony slowly returned. Yes, occasional frustration still arises—we're human—but the foundation of mutual understanding now holds us steady.

I don't claim to be the perfect son, husband, or father. I've made mistakes. I've had habits I'm not proud of. Yet Charmi never judged me. Her patience taught me to offer that same compassion back. She accepted me as I was and, in doing so, inspired me to become better.

There have been many times I've let go of personal preferences to preserve family harmony. As a lifelong vegetarian, I've long wished to follow a more *Satvik* diet—avoiding onions and garlic and eating dinner before sunset, as recommended in Ayurveda. But insisting on this would mean Charmi cooking separate meals at different times, which would place unnecessary pressure on her. So, I stepped back, trusting that we may naturally align with such practices in time.

My spiritual practices also demand specific timings and solitude. However, living in a shared home often means making adjustments. Guests sometimes arrive during my meditation time, and I'm unable to use the altar in the living room. Rather than feeling frustrated, I remind myself that countless others don't even have the quiet space or resources I'm fortunate to possess. Bhagavan sees the devotion, not the setting. What matters is the intention behind the practice, not the perfection of the environment.

Even small, conscious choices make a difference. For instance, my father loves bringing chocolates or biscuits for Rudri. While I prefer she avoid processed foods, I've learned to let it be. His happiness in nurturing her and her joy in receiving his love matter more than my nutritional concerns. These are moments of connection, and honouring them adds to the rhythm of our family life.

Right now, my mother undergoes dialysis twice a week due to her kidney dysfunction. My father, despite his age, takes her to the hospital, lifts her into a wheelchair, and stays by her side through hours of treatment. At times, I accompany them and see other families in the waiting area, each carrying their burden with quiet strength. These glimpses of silent devotion deeply inspire me.

Such experiences have shown me that one can pursue spirituality while living entirely within the embrace of family. Harmony isn't the absence of tension but the presence of mutual care, respect, and flexibility. If I can navigate these responsibilities and still feel connected to the divine, then so can you.

2.3 Swapna Maya: The Illusions of Dreams and Expectations

When I first began planning this book, I hadn't intended to dedicate a chapter to dreams. My focus was on expectations and the struggles they bring. But then I asked myself—where do expectations begin? The answer became clear: they start with dreams. To truly understand expectations, we must first understand the nature of dreams spiritually and practically.

From a spiritual lens, there are two types of dreams. I'm not referring to scientific interpretations here, but rather what I call Divine Dreams and Illusory Dreams—so you can recognise the difference and stay anchored in what truly matters.

Divine Dreams

Divine Dreams are blessings that often arise as one progresses spiritually. These are not imagined or manufactured; they come uninvited yet feel unmistakably sacred. When your devotion to your *Ishta Devata* or Guru deepens, such dreams connect you directly to the divine presence.

They contain no need for dialogue or instruction. I've had dreams where I was at the lotus feet of my Gurudev or in the radiant presence of Sri Hari. They bring stillness, joy, and a sense of completeness that stays with you forever. These dreams defy logic because *Bhakti* begins where logic ends. They are grace itself, free from the noise of interpretation.

Illusory Dreams

Illusory Dreams, by contrast, are shaped by our subconscious churn—restless thoughts, emotions, media, and daily experiences. Watch an intense movie or worry deeply; fragments from your dreams may appear in your sleep. These dreams are noisy, fleeting, and spiritually hollow.

In today's world, bombarded by social media and constant mental input, our dreams often become reflections of overstimulation. Yet people still rush to assign meanings to every symbol: "A snake means this, a cliff means that." These interpretations are often baseless and only stir confusion or false hope. Let such dreams pass. They're just clouds—acknowledge them and move on.

And then there are Waking Dreams: Aspirations.

Beyond dreams of sleep, we carry another kind—our waking dreams. These are the aspirations and longings that guide our choices. And like sleep dreams, these too can be constructive or destructive.

Constructive dreams align with your higher self. They emerge from an inner call and inspire growth, learning, and service. Destructive dreams, on the other hand, stem from ego, societal pressure, or fleeting desire. They may appear shiny, but they drain energy and lead to frustration.

I've chased such illusions—driven by validation and ego, not soul. I didn't question if my dreams served my deeper purpose. The result? Exhaustion, setbacks, and a nagging void.

Only after receiving wisdom from my Gurudev did I realise the need to align my dreams with dharma. The hurdles didn't disappear, but I stopped seeing them as barriers. They became teachers.

How to Discern

Ask yourself:

- Does this dream bring me closer to my higher self?
- Is it aligned with my spiritual values?
- Is it rooted in love, surrender, fear, competition, or insecurity?

These questions help illuminate which dreams are worth nurturing. Follow the guidance within. Your soul always knows the way.

Ignore the noise. People will advise, judge, or project their fears. Not every dream will manifest, and that's okay. What matters is who you become in the pursuit.

Dreams, whether in sleep or life, reflect our inner landscape. Some guide us, others mislead. But with clarity, discernment, and devotion, we can walk through this dreamscape with wisdom.

Let Divine Dreams inspire you. Let Illusory Dreams dissolve. Let waking dreams serve as a catalyst for your highest evolution. Trust that each dream, fulfilled or not, has its place in the divine unfolding.

Expectations are born from dreams, but they often become chains that bind us. When reality doesn't meet our imagined outcomes, pain creeps in. On this path, I've come to see that *suffering arises not from circumstances but from attachment to how things should be*. Letting go of expectations frees us.

And then there's the pace of progress. The wait can feel endless when you pour your soul into something and see no results. But the universe doesn't follow our clock. Its rhythm is sacred, interconnected, and perfectly timed.

Imagine planning a simple two-day family trip—just some time away to relax, connect, and create memories. On the surface, it seems straightforward: pack your bags, refuel your car, and hit the road. But in truth, even this short trip sets off an unseen chain of events, touching many lives and elements of nature.

Before leaving, you stop at a small shop for snacks. This isn't just a transaction—it's a lifeline for the vendor. The few hundred rupees you spend may allow him to bring something home for his children or buy groceries. Your purchase spreads joy in his home, and that money flows to his suppliers, creating a ripple of sustenance and support.

At the fuel station, filling your car supports a chain of workers, attendants, transporters, and refinery staff. Each drop of fuel has passed through many hands before reaching your tank. The wages earned support families you'll never meet, yet your one action contributes to their well-being.

Driving down the road, you might unknowingly take the lives of tiny insects. It may feel insignificant, but even their brief lives fulfil a karmic role in the grand design. Their death might nourish soil or feed another being—part of nature's delicate balance.

When hunger strikes, you stop for a meal. The vegetables were sown by farmers, harvested by labourers, and transported by others. The meal you eat was prepared and served by people working tirelessly to make a living. A simple plate of food carries the effort of so many.

Checking into a hotel brings the same awareness. The clean sheets, warm water, and working lights are all thanks to the hands of housekeepers, cooks, receptionists, and technicians—people whose silent labour makes your comfort possible.

What seemed like a quick getaway was a symphony of unseen contributions. From the vendor's counter to the insects on the road, every moment of your journey is intersected with countless lives, each thread carefully woven by the universe.

This understanding helps us soften our expectations. We often become impatient when things don't move at our pace. But even fulfilling a small wish involves aligning countless variables. When progress feels slow, remember that life is orchestrating something vast and unseen behind the scenes. The delay isn't a denial—it's the unfolding of a more fantastic plan.

I've come to believe that everything happens for a reason at the right time. My role is not to control the timing but to surrender to it. When life feels unfair or stagnant, I remind myself of the interconnectedness of everything. There's a greater choreography that I may not yet understand, but it always moves in perfect harmony.

This perspective anchors me during moments of restlessness. What looks like stagnation is often preparation. The universe isn't late—it's precise. I've learned to embrace this pace with gratitude, trusting each step is divinely timed.

In my earlier years, I was burdened by others' expectations and the unrealistic ones I placed on myself. My career path was scattered and restless—running a travel agency, selling mobile phones, opening a men's fashion store, and eventually trying my hand at digital marketing. I wasn't failing because the ideas lacked merit. I failed because I wasn't listening to my inner voice. I was chasing what I thought I was *supposed* to do rather than what I was *meant* to do.

Swamiji once said, "People who dig small, shallow holes in many places will never find water. Only the one who persistently digs deep in one place, with patience and unwavering determination, will eventually reach the water beneath."

Hearing this was a revelation. It felt as if Swamiji was addressing me directly, highlighting the scattered, directionless efforts I had made for years. His words became a mirror, revealing the futility of constant switching and the wisdom in unwavering focus.

That was when I realised personal freedom lies not in chasing every opportunity but in listening to the quiet guidance within.

The universe often speaks to us through subtle signs—recurring messages, symbols, or everyday encounters that seem to carry hidden meanings. These signs became increasingly clear to me through Swamiji's discourses, books, and silent moments of reflection. Once I began noticing them, my inner voice grew louder and more certain.

That voice had always guided me gently, but societal expectations and self-imposed pressure often drowned out its sound. Only when I paused and reflected did I genuinely hear it. And it didn't speak of material success—it led me to what I genuinely love: the occult sciences, such as Numerology, Astrology, Yoga, Meditation, Pranayama, and energy healing.

For the first time, I felt aligned—not just with a career, but with my dharma. This wasn't just ambition; it was purpose.

Even now, I'm only beginning this journey. I've just started digging the well, hoping to draw water from the depths of divine wisdom. But this time, I'm committed. No matter how long or hard it gets, I'm not leaving this path.

The weight of expectations doesn't feel heavy anymore. It's a reminder to trust my inner guidance and stay anchored in faith. I've learned that the universe moves with you when you align with your true calling. That alignment is the key to absolute freedom.

Until I began walking this path under the grace of my Gurudev, my dreams felt distant and vague. They weren't spiritual aspirations, but materialistic desires, and they laid the groundwork for many of the challenges in my life.

Let me confess something—those dreams are what led me to financial strain. I kept chasing illusions: a dream house, sleek cars, branded clothes, a steady income, luxuries. I convinced myself these would bring success. Each small growth in business became an excuse to take on more EMIs, believing the rise would continue.

But I never planned for uncertainty. What if my steady client stopped calling? What if an emergency arose? One EMI turned into another, and before I knew it, I was drowning in debt.

Here's the truth: financial institutions thrive on lending and interest. They offer appealing loans and easy approvals, but they're structured to stretch you thin. They sell instant gratification and hide the long-term consequences.

Even today, when my father asks, "Jai, where did all that money go?"—I have no answer. The truth is, I don't even know. It vanished into heavy interests. This is modern-day Maya—a web of illusions spun by ego and consumerism.

I share this not to discourage dreams but to offer a heartfelt warning. Dreams rooted in materialism carry hidden costs. They're tempting, but if not pursued with awareness, they can lead to cycles of suffering.

This doesn't mean you shouldn't aspire for a better life. Comfort and growth are not wrong, but awareness is essential. Understand the risks. Don't chase dreams mindlessly.

I've realised that today's financial system often mirrors the Asuras of ancient times—offering glittering rewards while pulling you into entrapment. It creates an illusion of success while tightening the grip of debt.

To anyone walking a similar path, I say—pause. Reflect. Be mindful. Ask yourself: Is this dream aligned with your soul, or is it feeding your ego? Are you chasing fulfilment or running from fear?

Even now, I remain entangled in the consequences of these choices. I carry financial strain, but I walk forward, grounded in truth, guided by spiritual light. This part of my life is not a chapter I hide but one I share so others may walk more mindfully.

Let my experience serve as a light. May it help you dream wisely, stay rooted in your truth, and pursue aspirations not as slaves to Maya but as seekers walking the path of conscious growth.

By now, you know my struggles—the setbacks, sacrifices, and hurdles that weren't theoretical but deeply personal. Fear? Of course. These failures left scars on me and my family. I've made choices, taken risks, and paid the price. And yet, here I am, digging a new well again.

This time, though, it feels different. I'm not driven by material desires or societal pressure. I'm fueled by something deeper—love, faith, and surrender. When you've lost so much, there's a strange freedom in having nothing to lose.

That freedom has shifted my mindset. I no longer obsess over outcomes. I plant seeds with trust and leave the harvest to the divine.

I'm learning to let go of control, to surrender to a greater wisdom that knows far more than I do.

Surrender isn't about giving up—it's offering everything, including your fears, at the feet of the divine. My Gurudev's presence anchors me. His grace protects me from paths I shouldn't take and nudges me forward when I hesitate. Even this book feels like a product of that divine flow. Could I have written this alone? Absolutely not. I know these words aren't mine—they're his.

Honestly, I no longer follow a step-by-step method to overcome fear. I've tried that route. Now, my only practice is to let life unfold. I trust the universe knows what it's doing. My role is simply to show up, do the work, and offer it as Seva—selfless service. If even one life is touched, it's worth it.

There's also the truth of time. I have the energy now to give my best, but that won't last forever. Age catches up with us all. If not now, then when?

This urgency doesn't overwhelm me—it focuses me. It reminds me that now is all I truly have. Despite the fear and uncertainty, I continue walking, step by step, guided by faith.

Failure has been my greatest teacher. It's taught me humility, patience, and trust. Real progress isn't about how fast you move but how sincerely you walk. Fear may still whisper, but it no longer steers me. I move with conviction, knowing I'm exactly where I need to be.

Hope and faith are like a climber's harness—they steady you when the terrain turns steep. Life, especially the spiritual path, is like scaling a towering peak. From afar, it's majestic. But once you begin, every step tests your resolve.

One story that beautifully reflects this is that of Arunima Sinhaji, the first female amputee to climb Mount Everest. Her journey wasn't just about reaching the summit—it was about reclaiming strength, turning pain into purpose, and showing the world the power of unwavering belief.

I share her story because it mirrors the essence of hope and faith. She didn't let her circumstances define her. With each painful step, she trusted her purpose more than her limitations.

Spiritually, the climb toward self-realisation is no different. The path can be steep and slow. At times, doubt creeps in. But as I shared earlier, the aim isn't just the summit—it's cherishing the journey. That's where hope and faith shine. They whisper that even small steps matter; even stumbles serve a purpose.

In challenging moments, I draw strength from the tools I've come to trust:

- Astrology and Numerology for understanding life's patterns and timing.
- Yoga Asanas, to attune myself to the cosmic rhythm.
- Pranayama and Dhyana are used to quiet the mind and bring you back to the present.
- Reiki and healing practices bring balance to the subtle body.
- Daily Study of Spiritual Texts to stay connected to timeless wisdom.
- Mantra Japa is to align with higher vibrations.
- Tantra Sadhana and Nitya Puja are to express gratitude and devotion.

These aren't mere rituals but the pillars of my spiritual foundation. They've helped me stay grounded, navigate storms, and gracefully approach life's steepest slopes. In Chapter 3.5, I'll share how I gradually adopted them and how you can do the same.

Even now, there are days when discipline wavers. I've said, "Maybe tomorrow," or "Let's skip today." But then I ask—does my breath pause? Do my needs take a day off? If not, why should I skip my sadhana?

Discipline, for me, is a form of devotion. When I think of my Gurudev, disappointing him steers me back. This inner dialogue shifts everything. I remind myself, "Get up, Jai. This isn't just a task—your offering, your path."

No matter how late I sleep, I rise at 5 AM, honouring this sacred time before the world stirs. These early hours ground me, anchoring my day in stillness and purpose.

The mind naturally seeks comfort and tends to avoid effort. The challenge isn't in silencing it but gently guiding it—retraining it to embrace discomfort as part of growth. Over time, I've learned to befriend my mind, steering it toward higher pursuits rather than fleeting pleasures.

Hope and faith don't just sustain—they transform. They turn the steep path into a sacred one, where every obstacle becomes a lesson, every stumble a step forward.

Through discipline, devotion, and faith in the divine plan, I climb. The summit may be far, but each step brings me joy, reminding me that the real beauty lies in the ascent.

I've come to believe that everything we face in life is shaped by karmic forces—Sanchita, Prarabdha, and Agami (or Kriyamana) Karma. These are the subtle threads weaving our destiny.

- Sanchita Karma is the vast pool of accumulated karma from all our past lives.
- Prarabdha Karma is a portion of Sanchita Karma that has been selected for this life, is already in motion, and is beyond alteration. It's like an arrow mid-flight.
- Agami (Kriyamana) Karma is the karma we generate now, through our thoughts, words, and deeds, shaping future experiences in this life and beyond.

Understanding this interplay has reshaped how I respond to life. While I can't undo my Prarabdha, I influence my present (Agami) and the latent (Sanchita). By living with awareness, compassion, and spiritual effort, I can purify past impressions and plant seeds for a better tomorrow.

When Prarabdha brings unavoidable trials—such as financial stress and emotional tension—I respond with patience and faith. In doing so, I'm not just enduring karma but transforming it.

The scriptures give us living proof that karma is not fixed. Look at Valmiki, once a bandit who transformed through devotion into the sage who composed the *Ramayana*. His story reminds us that no karma is beyond redemption when met with surrender and effort.

I've stopped seeing hardships as punishment by aligning my daily actions with dharma. They've become gateways to purification and self-discovery, part of a cosmic order that unfolds with divine precision.

Letting go of a dream is often misunderstood as a failure, but it depends on the nature of the dream. When a dream aligns with divine timing, it unfolds without struggle. But those born from ego or illusion must sometimes be released to make space for clarity.

I've had to let go of dreams I clung to—goals I once believed would bring joy or stability. It wasn't easy, but it was essential.

In my digital marketing work, I sometimes had to accept clients who paid far below what I deserved. It felt like compromising my values and self-worth. Yet survival, EMIs, and family responsibilities left me no choice.

Life doesn't always permit ideal circumstances. But even in compromise, I tried to keep my attitude intact. I treated every client with the same care and respect, regardless of their pay. Why? Because resentment only poisons the soul. By maintaining a seva attitude, I protected my peace of mind.

These experiences taught me humility and patience. They helped me detach from the ego's need for validation and find fulfilment in service.

Releasing old dreams gave me clarity. The fancy car, lavish home, and high-status lifestyle I once pursued only led to debt and stress. Letting go of those illusions freed me to focus on what truly matters: my family, my spiritual practice, and my life's purpose.

Through these experiences, I've learned that letting go of a dream doesn't mean giving up—it means creating space for the right dreams to emerge. Even in moments of compromise, I found joy in small things: serving clients wholeheartedly, fulfilling my duties as a son, father and husband, and growing in my spiritual practices.

Letting go brought me closer to myself. It reminded me that my worth isn't tied to external accomplishments but to my ability to remain grounded, to serve with love, and to find peace in the present, regardless of circumstances.

In truth, life is not a straight path. Some dreams guide us briefly before fading, making room for deeper growth. The treasure lies not in achieving every dream but in evolving and staying faithful to our inner truth.

Balancing motivation and perfectionism is delicate. I've learned how easy it is to cross that line. Expectations—external or internal—can be overwhelming, turning ambition into anxiety and inspiration into frustration.

Healthy motivation drives growth and learning. But perfectionism, rooted in the need for approval or fear of failure, creates pressure that suffocates. It shifts focus from progress to impossible standards, often leading to burnout.

I fell into this trap, trying to mould myself into the archetype of an aggressive, high-converting digital marketer. I chased strategies built around persuasion, "closing," and performance metrics. But that wasn't me. My strength lies in honesty, transparency, and building genuine relationships, rather than using high-pressure sales tactics.

I invested time, energy, and money into these models, but they never felt authentic. In chasing these ideals, I drifted from my true nature—and paid the price in peace of mind and purpose.

The hard lesson: not all paths are meant for you. Following trends without alignment only leads to disillusionment.

Client experiences reinforced this truth. I delivered quality work and exceeded expectations, yet some clients left, chasing cheaper agencies or building in-house teams. Initially, I doubted myself. But with reflection, I saw it wasn't personal. It was the nature of the industry and of people who value cost over quality.

These lessons taught me that forcing yourself into roles or systems that are misaligned with your values only deepens your suffering. I stopped chasing clients. Instead, I serve fewer, more aligned individuals who value what I offer.

In business, losing clients is inevitable. Not every effort bears fruit; not all relationships are meant to last. But I won't compromise on values just to survive.

The key to navigating the line between motivation and perfectionism is to stay anchored in your truth. External advice may offer insight, but should never override your inner compass. I've learned to overcome unrealistic expectations, embrace imperfections, and focus on making meaningful progress rather than just achieving hollow performance.

Life isn't about chasing every dream—it's about honouring who you truly are, learning as you go, and walking forward with faith and resilience.

Along this journey, I've been guided in miraculous ways—through books, synchronicities, and my Gurudev's grace. These weren't coincidences but divine affirmations of an unseen order shaping my path.

One such instrument of divine guidance is the Ram Shalaka from the *Sri Ramcharitmanas*. When approached with sincerity and devotion, it is a sacred matrix that offers clarity to the most perplexing questions. It has been my spiritual compass—subtle yet precise, speaking through silence when logic fails.

But the most profound guidance has always come from my Gurudev. His teachings extend beyond the physical realm, connecting me to the divine in seen and unseen ways. Though I may not approach him directly, his presence surrounds me.

I turn to his books or videos whenever I'm lost or uncertain. I simply open a random page or play a discourse. Astonishingly, almost every time, the message speaks directly to what I'm going through. It's no coincidence. It's the result of complete bhava—devotional surrender—through which I see him as a Guru and an avatāra of Sri Hari.

For sceptics, this may sound implausible or irrational. But as I often remind myself, true spirituality begins where logic ends. To experience divine guidance, one must move beyond intellectual reasoning and surrender to the wisdom of the heart.

This book itself is an example. When I first started writing, I was flooded with self-doubt. Who would read it? Why would anyone care? I wasn't a celebrity, a best-selling author, or someone with a spectacular success story. And I never had a Ferrari that I sold. What could I possibly offer?

Those doubts lingered for months until a visit to my Gurudev's ashram changed everything. For three days, I immersed myself in his discourses; each word felt as if it were meant for me. Every teaching became a personal message, an invitation to embrace my dharma.

Even now, when I watch his videos or read his books, I feel he's speaking directly to me. That connection gave me the courage to begin, realising that my flaws and failures weren't limitations but my strengths.

Unlike books written by monks or high achievers, this is a conversation between two ordinary seekers. It's a testament to resilience, surrender, and the quiet faith that the divine is near even amidst life's storms.

This awareness—that my life, imperfect as it may be, holds value—transformed how I see myself and my purpose. With each word I write, I carry the blessings of my Gurudev and the grace of the Divine Mother, trusting that this offering will reach whoever needs it most.

To you, dear reader: never dismiss the quiet nudges of grace. The divine always speaks, whether it comes through scripture, intuition, or the stillness within; we just need to listen with our heart.

As I shared earlier, I now feel I have nothing left to lose—strangely, this has brought peace. I've chosen a different path rooted in seva, where fulfilment doesn't depend on success but on presence, surrender, and service.

It's this surrender that allows me to find joy even when weighed down by uncertainty. Knowing that the divine is present in every breath keeps me anchored.

Recently, I asked myself, 'What if I had never faced these struggles? ' What if I had continued my earlier life of financial ease, career progress, and material comfort?

At first, it sounded ideal. But when I looked deeper, I realised I might never have felt the call to seek the truth. I might never have known the love I now feel for my Gurudev or the transformative power of his presence.

Without hardship, I may have remained who I once was—trapped in ego, habits, and distractions. My struggles weren't punishments—they were divine interventions. My Gurudev often says, "If you don't learn the easy way, life will teach you the hard way." That's what happened to me.

Every failure, every doubt, and every fall has led me closer to the truth. And for that, I'm grateful. So, where do I find joy in chasing my dreams now? I know that every step I take is sacred. I'm no longer chasing illusions but walking a path of dharma, devotion, and service.

The absolute joy lies in the journey—the stillness of a chant, the offering of sadhana, the quiet gratitude that fills me as I bow before the divine. That connection is my light, my strength, and my compass.

Looking back, the challenges I once resented have become the very blessings that shaped me. They stripped away my false sense of control and gave me the gift of faith.

Now, I see my life, every up and down, as a divine gift. A journey designed not to break me but to bring me back home to myself. And for that, I am eternally grateful.

SECTION 3:
MOKSHA MARG – PATHS TO LIBERATION

3.1 Bhakti Rasa: The Nectar of Devotion

For me, devotion is not just an act or practice—it's a state of being. It's not about rituals or structured disciplines. It's an inner bhava, a natural connection to the divine that flows effortlessly, like breath.

I wasn't always devotional. Though I revered Mahadev and Hanumanji, it wasn't through rituals but through what they represented—Mahadev's Vairagya, and Hanumanji's unwavering devotion. To me, they were ideals rather than deities to be ceremonially worshipped.

That was reverence, not yet devotion. True devotion awakened when I met my Gurudev, Swamiji. The path that led me to him had grace-filled turns, which I'll share later. But once that connection formed, everything shifted.

Devotion isn't about remembering someone out of discipline—it's about their presence becoming inseparable from your being. Whether walking, eating, or working, my Gurudev's presence accompanies me. His words, his actions, even his laughter—they all live within me. That is devotion.

Over time, I've seen that devotion isn't something you create—it awakens within. It begins quietly, maybe with admiration or inspiration, and deepens into something far more sacred.

This journey wasn't planned. It began with love for divine virtues, and grew into a bhava—a surrender to the sacred, nurtured under my Gurudev's grace. It taught me that devotion doesn't need structure. It requires only an open heart.

To those reading this: devotion isn't about what you do on the outside. It's about who you are on the inside. When your actions, thoughts, and emotions begin flowing from love for the divine, you no longer "practice" devotion—it becomes who you are.

Love itself is divine. Divine love is not an emotion—it's a state that defies logic. I experienced this during my visit to my Gurudev's Ashram.

I've always seen myself as emotionally guarded, hardened by life's demands. Crying never came easily. But as I stepped into the Sri Hari temple, something shifted. I felt enveloped in an invisible embrace, a presence beyond words. For me, Sri Hari and my Gurudev are the same grace in different forms. Without warning, tears streamed down my face. Not tears of joy or sorrow—but of something far deeper. A soul-level recognition of divine love. I didn't even realise I was crying until I left the temple.

Since then, that love has never left me. I feel it for Sri Hari, Maa Jagat Janani, Mahadev, Hanumanji, Sri Ram, Sri Krishna, and of course, my Gurudev. Each is a unique facet of the same infinite truth, reflecting my inner bhava and capacity for divine perception.

Each form reveals something distinct, guiding us based on what we're ready to receive.

Bhagavad Gita 9.22:

अनन्याश्चिन्तयन्तो मां ये जनाः पर्युपासते।
तेषां नित्याभियुक्तानां योगक्षेमं वहाम्यहम्॥

"To those who are constantly devoted and worship Me with love, I provide what they lack and preserve what they have."

This shloka captures the essence of divine love. When a devotee approaches with ananya bhakti—undivided devotion—Bhagavan takes personal responsibility for their well-being. Such love requires nothing in return except the purity of surrender.

I feel this love whenever I sit in sadhana, perform nitya puja, or simply reflect in silence. It asks for nothing. There is no exchange, no request. It is simply the merging of soul with source—a quiet, blissful state where no words are needed.

To describe divine love is nearly impossible. Words can only point toward it—they can never contain its essence. It's like describing the scent of a blooming jasmine flower to someone who has never smelled a flower in their life. No matter how poetic the words, the fragrance must be experienced to be truly known.

What I can say is that divine love has transformed me. It's shown me that beyond the mind and body lies a deep connection that dissolves barriers, heals wounds, and awakens the soul. This love isn't just something I feel—it's who I've become. Living in it, I know I am aligned with the divine.

Reverence, I've come to realise, is the foundation of devotion. It begins with a deep, unshakable respect and opens the door to a divine connection. When I was seeking a Guru—unknowingly forgetting that it is the Guru who chooses the disciple—I stumbled upon *If Truth Be Told*, the memoir of my Param Pujya Gurudev, Swamiji.

I didn't merely read that book; I absorbed it. Every word felt divinely directed, as if Swamiji were speaking to my soul. Through those pages, my heart shifted. Reverence bloomed—pure, complete, and unconditional. I surrendered to Swamiji's lotus feet without ever having seen him. A connection was forged that transcended time and space.

Bhagavad Gita 12.13–14

अद्वेष्टा सर्वभूतानां मैत्र: करुण एव च |
निर्ममो निरहङ्कार: समदु:खसुख: क्षमी ||
सन्तुष्ट: सततं योगी यतात्मा दृढनिश्चय: |
मय्यर्पितमनोबुद्धिर्यो मद्भक्त: स मे प्रिय: ||

"He who bears no hatred, is friendly and compassionate, free from ego and selfishness, patient in pain and pleasure, forgiving, content, self-disciplined, resolute, with mind and intellect surrendered to Me—such a devotee is dear to Me."

This shloka reminds us that true devotion is not transactional. It flows through compassion, detachment, contentment, and surrender. Divine love transcends the limits of worldly relationships. It is not rooted in gain or reciprocation—it is pure being.

Reverence changed me, but it was just the beginning. Devotion took me deeper. While I revered Swamiji wholeheartedly, I hadn't yet tasted the bhava of love that flows from surrender. That love came through the words of Sadhviji (Sadhvi Vrinda Om) and Swamiji's other disciples. Their writings revealed Swamiji as a teacher and a nurturing, divine force.

Sadhviji's books bridged the gap between reverence and devotion. Her words unveiled Swamiji's tenderness, unconditional grace, and deep care for seekers like me. Through her, I didn't just admire him—I began to love him. Spiritually, deeply, silently.

That love was the missing link. It turned respect into surrender, and reverence into devotion. I understood that while reverence honours the divine, devotion merges into it. Reverence sees from a distance; devotion dissolves all separation. And love—selfless, unwavering love—makes that merging possible.

Today, my journey is carried by all three: reverence for my Guru, love for the divine, and devotion that fuels every breath. It's not a goal—it's a state of being I return to, again and again, with gratitude.

I also want to reflect on a soul who walked this land a few years back—Sri Aurobindo. His life continues to inspire generations. He found realisation not in an ashram, but in prison. Through intense sadhana of the *Bhagavad Gita*, he received such profound grace from Sri Krishna that he began to see Krishna in everyone: the prisoners, the guards, the lawyers, and even the judge.

This wasn't poetic symbolism. It was a literal vision. For Sri Aurobindo, Krishna became the only reality—the one divine presence manifest in every form around him.

Yet here I am, walking this path, writing these words, living with devotion. I haven't witnessed any grand miracle that erased my problems. Externally, nothing has changed "magically," yet everything has changed internally.

How? Because I no longer view challenges as enemies. They are waves in the ocean—inevitable, beyond control, but temporary. Devotion has taught me not to wait for life to become perfect but to remain anchored in faith, no matter how turbulent the sea.

This understanding unfolded slowly, through consistent practice, reflection, and surrender. I've learned that time won't always favour us, nor will circumstances align perfectly with desire. The universe moves by its divine rhythm, not ours.

Sanatana Dharma is more than a religion—it's a way of living that embraces the full spectrum of life. Planning and effort are in our hands, but outcomes are not. So why exhaust energy on what's not ours to control?

Instead, I focus on what is—my sadhana, my work, and my intention. I offer my best not for results, but as an offering to the divine. Distractions will always exist, but deep-rooted devotion becomes your anchor. It steadies you when life tries to sway you.

Even challenges have become stepping stones—placed not to hinder, but to shape and guide. This shift in perception sustains my devotion more than any ritual ever could.

So, if you ask how to remain devoted amid distractions and difficulty, remember: faith, acceptance, and surrender. Accept what life brings, trust in the divine design, and let go of your attachment to results. In doing so, devotion becomes unshakable—even in life's fiercest storms.

As I've shared earlier, true devotion isn't something you *do; it's something you are*. It arises naturally, like a seed growing once it's planted in fertile soil. To explain, let me offer an analogy.

When we eat, we are fully aware of chewing and tasting. But once swallowed, the rest is unconscious. Digestion, absorption, and elimination all happen without our active involvement. The body takes over.

Devotion is like this. It begins as a conscious decision—seeking, connecting, and surrendering. But once rooted in faith and love, it grows on its own. It becomes effortless, woven into your being.

This unconscious bhava is what makes devotion so profound. It doesn't require reminders. It simply flows—like breath, like the heartbeat. Once established, it becomes a constant presence, subtly influencing every action and thought.

Yet even this grace requires readiness. Although devotion may arise spontaneously, the opening must be prepared through conscious effort, such as chanting mantras, prayer, and meditation. Over time, these dissolve into surrender and love.

Eventually, devotion transcends the mind. It's no longer tied to action but becomes identity. It's not what you practice—it's what you are. Devotion reaches its purest form when each breath, thought, and gesture becomes an offering to the divine.

It begins with effort, but its ultimate flowering is grace. And when that grace descends, the need to strive falls away. What remains is love, presence, and divine flow.

I believe at the heart of spirituality lies one truth—pure love. Beyond all concepts, this love is the essence of all existence. Love is truth, and truth is love.

Spiritual love isn't transactional. It asks for nothing, expects nothing, and offers everything. It knows no form, label, or boundary. It transcends ego, time, and space.

When this love arises, you don't approach the divine to gain or to fix. You surrender—not to receive, but because surrender itself becomes the expression of love. It's not devotion seeking reward. It's devotion that *is* the reward.

This love is a connection to something infinitely greater than myself. It defies emotion and definition. It's the purest vibration of being, a bridge between the self and the source. It is both the beginning and the end—the alpha and omega of the journey home.

I often pray to God and my guru not to test me, because I know I'm not strong enough to bear intense trials. I'm soft-hearted and easily shaken by difficulty. Yet, in spirituality, I've understood that tests are inevitable. They don't come to harm or derail us but to deepen our faith and refine our path. They show us where we falter and gently push us toward greater resilience.

The phase I'm currently in feels like one extended, continuous test—financial uncertainty, emotional strain, and the challenge of balancing worldly life with spiritual discipline. I don't know if I'm passing or failing, but one thing is clear: my faith hasn't wavered. Like the Sun behind clouds or storm winds, my devotion remains steady.

When doubt creeps in, I return to my sacred bond with my Gurudev. It's not built on fear or duty, but pure surrender. I trust he knows what I need, even when I don't. And that belief gives me strength.

I've learned that surrender is the key. Divine tests are not about winning—they're about letting go. Every obstacle, every pause, is a part of a greater plan. I try to meet each one as a divine lesson, knowing that nothing happens without purpose, and every trial carries me closer to truth.

My faith is my anchor. My devotion, my compass. My love, my strength. These are not fragile—they are as eternal as my connection to the divine. And this bond is what carries me through every storm.

Each carries inclinations from birth—silent callings that draw us toward certain aspects of life. For me, one such pull has always been toward sacred texts, such as the Vedas, Puranas, and Upanishads.

Though I felt drawn to them, I never truly explored them until I began my Sadhana. They sat on my wishlist for years, waiting. But something was missing: grace.

Without grace, scriptures remain beautiful but lifeless. You can read them endlessly and remain untouched. Grace brings them alive. It opens the heart and allows wisdom to move from the page into your being.

Once I began Sadhana, that grace arrived. The dormant desire became a living practice. I started not just reading but absorbing. I undertook purushacharana—structured recitation and disciplined study—not to memorise, but to internalise. Slowly, the texts became guides. Their words felt alive, offering just what I needed at the exact moment I needed it.

Books written by my Gurudev and Sadhviji are no different. For me, they are as sacred as any ancient scripture. They hold the same grace and clarity, serving the same purpose: to light the path, deepen devotion, and reveal the divine within.

I've realised that reverence for sacred texts or spiritual tools isn't about blind worship—it's about humility and openness. These texts become mirrors and compasses. They reflect who you are and point to who you can become.

They are bridges between the mundane and the divine. With reverence and practice, they elevate your thinking, shape your actions, and align your being to truth. They don't just guide—they transform.

The world God created is beautiful and straightforward. Everything rooted in divinity reflects this clarity. It is we who complicate life. We pile on expectations, fears, structures—turning what is instinctive into something burdensome.

An excellent book that illustrates this is *Who Moved My Cheese* by Spencer Johnson. It shows how our resistance creates complexity. The same is true for devotion. We've wrapped it in layers of ritual and rigidity when, in truth, it's meant to be natural, flowing, and free.

Devotion is not something we're taught—it's already within us. It's a primal instinct, a thread in the very fabric of our being. Think of ancient tribes. Before a hunt, they offered prayers—not because of scripture or pressure, but from heartfelt trust in their Ishta Devata. Their devotion wasn't formal—it was real. They believed because they had faith, and they had faith because they loved.

Why did they pray? Not because of custom. They prayed because they felt a sense of the divine. And that feeling, that inner pull, is the root of devotion.

Devotion is like the heartbeat—natural, continuous, and essential. It doesn't need elaborate practice to awaken. It requires only the willingness to strip away doubt, ego, and distraction. Once we do, it flows.

It's not something to be earned or acquired—it's already here, waiting patiently beneath the noise, ready to lead us home.

Consider your heartbeat. You don't make it happen, yet it sustains you. Devotion is much the same—a soul rhythm, flowing naturally like breath. It only ceases when the body does. But even beyond the body, the soul remains eternally connected to its divine source.

Is devotion accessible to all? Absolutely. It knows no boundaries of religion, caste, status, or role. It is universal, a unifying force beyond all divisions. The moment we stop questioning its simplicity and embrace it as our natural state, we realise it was never something to be attained—it was always within us, waiting to be remembered.

Devotion is not about doing—it is about being. It flows not from effort but from openness, surrender, and love. Once you recognise this, it guides you in ways that words cannot explain.

For me, Hanumanji has always embodied devotion. As a child, I admired him—not just for his strength, but for his seva bhava towards

Bhagwan Ram and Sita Maiya, and his love for his mother. He was my ideal. I used to tell friends I could talk to him, and I believed it. It wasn't for attention; it was simply the truth of a child's heart, pure and untouched by doubt.

But as life unfolded and Maya pulled me into its grip, I drifted. The connection faded, buried under worldly desires, pleasures, and expectations. I stopped feeling his presence. And yet, even now as I write, the memory of that bond stirs love, gratitude, and yes, a quiet sorrow for having let it slip.

Still, I know it's okay. Life is a journey; sometimes, we lose something precious to understand its value.

The grace of my Gurudev and the teachings of Sanatana Dharma brought me back. The scriptures reminded me: devotion doesn't demand perfection. It asks only for sincerity, the courage to surrender, and the humility to let the divine purify you over time.

Through my Gurudev's kindness, I began reconnecting with Hanumanji. Though I still carry impurities, I know I'm on the right path. Gurudev's love filled the void I had created. He reminds me that devotion doesn't require worthiness even when I feel unworthy. It involves the truth of the heart.

Hanumanji's story continues to inspire me. His unshakable love for Ramji shows that accurate service and surrender are the highest forms of devotion. Gurudev's teachings helped me bring that same spirit into daily life through discipline, gratitude, and unwavering faith.

This rediscovery of devotion hasn't been a moment—it's been a quiet, ongoing return. A return to what was always there. The divine never left. It waited patiently.

Devotion is bhava—the emotional essence behind every act. When Bhagavan says he sees your bhava, not your rituals, he means that sincerity matters more than form. Bhava is the bridge between your soul and your Ishta. It is your truth laid bare.

Why pretend before the one who knows your every thought? Bhava is raw openness. It is shedding all masks and saying, "I am yours"—as I am.

A beautiful Gujarati stuti of Maa captures this essence:

પાપે પ્રપંચ કરવા બધી વાતે પૂરો,
ખોટો ખરો ભગવતી પણ હું છું તમારો,
જાડ્યાંધકાર દૂર કરી સદ્ બુદ્ધિ આપો,
મામ્-પાહિ ૐ ભગવતી ભવ દુ:ખ કાપો

"O Bhagavati, forgive my flaws and illusions. Though I may be false, I am still yours. Dispel the darkness within me. Protect me, Maa, and free me from the sorrows of worldly life."

This bhava of surrender is the purest connection to the divine. It asks nothing, yet offers everything.

In my sadhana, this bhava isn't always steady. It ebbs and flows, like tides. But when it comes, it silences everything else. The world fades, and only divine presence remains. I know sustaining this requires practice and grace. I've only just begun, but I trust that with time, this bhava will root itself deeply within me.

Just start.

It may sound simple, but that's the beauty of devotion—it doesn't demand grand rituals, ideal circumstances, or elaborate preparation. All it asks is a single step, however small.

Begin with whatever feels natural: lighting a diya, chanting a mantra, or sitting silently with your thoughts turned toward the divine. Even if you don't know how to start, that first step opens a door—and divine grace, always waiting, begins to flow in.

You don't need to be perfect to begin. Devotion isn't about perfection—it's about sincerity. Come as you are, with all your flaws, fears, and doubts. Offer your true self, and the divine will meet you there, cleansing, guiding, and awakening the love already within you.

Take small, consistent steps. Read a few lines from a sacred text. Listen to a bhajan. Sit quietly in prayer. Over time, the path that once felt unfamiliar will begin to shape you. What was once an effort will become joy. What was once discipline will become devotion.

Most importantly, trust the process. Once you begin, the divine takes care of the rest.

3.2 Guru Kripa & Ishta Darshan: Grace of the Guru and Divine Vision

I never imagined I'd one day become a disciple. For much of my life, I resisted surrendering to a Guru. This hesitation came from seeing false gurus exploit the innocent for fame and wealth. The scandals I heard only deepened my scepticism.

Still, my spiritual leanings were strong. I was devoted to Mahadev and Hanumanji, though without structured sadhana. Every Shravana Month, I observe fasts with faith, and Mahadev never fails to bless me with something meaningful. My trust in His grace was unwavering, even if I didn't see that this was just the beginning.

In Shravana 2022, a simple moment became pivotal. While buying *puja samagri*, the shopkeeper casually suggested a 30-day *purushacharana* of the Panchakshari Mantra: "Light a diya, offer incense, chant—nothing more. Visit a Shiva temple if possible, but it's not necessary." His words struck a chord, and I committed to it fully.

For the first time, I undertook structured sadhana. It deepened my bond with Mahadev and awakened a thirst for spiritual knowledge. Yet, at that time, the idea of needing a Guru hadn't crossed my heart.

That changed through a podcast on The Ranveer Show, hosted by Ranveer Allahbadia, where an enlightened guest from one of the episodes, Rajarshi Nandy, spoke about Shivatva, Bhairava Tatva, and the necessity of a Guru. His words about Bhairava Sadhana, practised without expectations, stayed with me. I began the sadhana, and something shifted within—a quiet but firm desire for a Guru emerged.

In my ignorance, I started searching for one, not realising that the Guru finds the disciple, not the other way around.

I explored many well-known spiritual paths—each guided by enlightened beings, each offering profound teachings that have transformed countless lives. I attended programs, practised the techniques, and immersed myself in their philosophies with an open heart. Their wisdom touched me, and I could feel the sincerity of the masters who had shaped those movements. And yet, something within me remained quietly restless. It wasn't dissatisfaction or judgment—it was simply the absence of that intimate, soul-deep connection I was seeking. My heart whispered that my Guru was still waiting for me, somewhere beyond the boundaries I had yet to cross. And so, I continued walking—not away from those teachings, but toward something that felt destined and deeply personal.

During this search, one book that truly moved me during this search was *Autobiography of a Yogi*. Its pages carried a fragrance of deep devotion, miracles, and divine grace. Like millions around the world, I felt uplifted by its words and inspired by the life it portrayed. And yet, despite the inspiration, my heart still longed for a more personal connection—a presence I could surrender to, not just admire from afar. My soul kept whispering that my Guru was still waiting, hidden in the sacred silence of destiny.

Then came another podcast episode. Parakh Om Bhatt, a disciple of Pujya Om Swamiji, was the guest this time. I had tuned in hoping for another Rajarshi session, but I nearly skipped it. But as Parakh Om spoke of Swamiji, something stirred.

Midway through, I paused the episode and searched for Om Swamiji online. As I read his writings, watched his videos, and browsed the ashram's site, I recalled an old video where he explained the *Sri Yantra*. At the time, I hadn't thought much of it. But now, it felt like a divine thread connecting us across time.

The more I explored, the stronger the pull became. That quiet desire became surrender. I received my first *diksha* from Swamiji, and everything changed that moment. He became my Guru, my Bhagavan.

His mantra—*Love, Live, Laugh, Give*—became the compass of my life.

Looking back, I was naive. I imagined a Guru who'd always be available, respond to emails, solve doubts, and offer guidance whenever needed. Influenced by stories of ancient Gurukulas, I thought the modern-day version might come with Zoom calls and personal replies.

After my *diksha*, I wrote a heartfelt email with pressing questions, expecting a personal reply. A few days later, I received a response from the ashram team. It was kind but clear: Swamiji doesn't handle emails due to the sheer volume from thousands of disciples.

I was heartbroken. I couldn't understand how a Guru could be so distant. Wasn't he supposed to be there for me? The disappointment was real, but so was the lesson.

A faithful Guru teaches in silence, through presence, not constant contact. My perspective changed as I immersed myself in Swamiji's books and discourses. I realised how immature my expectations were.

An honest Guru doesn't create dependency. He empowers. He turns your gaze inward, so you seek the divine, not just the human form of the teacher. He breaks your illusions so you can stand alone, grow in your sadhana, and walk with strength and clarity.

Though not delivered to me personally, Swamiji's teachings began to work their quiet magic. I understood that my Guru's role wasn't to respond to every request, but to awaken the strength, wisdom, and devotion already within me. His grace wasn't in his accessibility but in his power to make me inwardly free.

When I reflect on my initial expectations, I feel only gratitude for the journey, the transformation, and the love I've developed for my Guru. Today, my devotion is without conditions, rooted in deep reverence for the path he illuminated for me.

Isn't it beautiful how a faithful Guru doesn't just change our life, but our understanding of what it means to walk a spiritual path?

I've seen people whose Gurus are always within reach—actively involved in their disciples' daily affairs, offering guidance, comfort, even blessings in real-time. I share this with complete respect. Every disciple-Guru bond is sacred, and these Gurus' work is invaluable.

But I've come to understand that physical proximity isn't the essence of grace. There are disciples whose Gurus have left their bodies, yet their bond remains alive through a photo on an altar, a mantra, or a moment of remembrance. A faithful Guru's consciousness transcends the body. Their guidance and presence are not bound by time or space.

I share this not to defend my experience, but to help others avoid the mistake I once made—believing that the Guru's role is always to be physically available. The Guru's purpose is to awaken our divine potential, not to feed our dependency. Even unseen, their presence can be the most potent force in our lives.

As I've shared earlier, I saw my Guru in person nearly two years after receiving initiation from Swamiji.

That moment was beyond words. He was just a few steps away. I could have touched his lotus feet if I had stretched my hand. It felt as though all my longing had crystallised into that one moment.

But what stays with me most is his gaze. His eyes were slightly red, and the way he looked at me went far beyond the physical. It felt like he saw through me—all the layers, all the masks. I couldn't hold back my tears. I wept like a child, not from sadness, but from something so deep, so raw, that only the soul could understand. In those few seconds, it felt like he looked only at me, even though many others were around.

That gaze wasn't ordinary—it was a fire. It felt like he burned away all that was impure, all that wasn't me. A purifying, consuming grace that wiped away my past and gave me a new birth. The only comparison that comes close is the fierce, loving gaze of Maa Mahakali. In that moment, Swamiji's eyes held the same divine intensity—a powerful love that purifies everything in its path.

I left that moment transformed. I felt small and infinite, vulnerable and safe, broken and whole. That single darshan felt like the culmination of lifetimes. Even now, when I recall it, the memory carries me back into that sacred space.

It wasn't just a meeting—it was the initiation. A silent transmission that redefined me and filled me with humility. The most divine moment of my life.

My Gurudev is everything—my Ishta Devata, my Sri Hari, my Maa Shakti, my Shiva, and my Ved Mata Gayatri.

Please don't mistake this for blind faith. My faith doesn't depend on seeing—it comes from deep knowing. I share this not to convince but to offer the truth of my heart.

Only by the grace of my Ishta did I find my Guru in this life. No amount of effort could have led me to him without that divine blessing. And that fills me with reverence and gratitude. Through him, I feel the living presence of all that is sacred.

Sanatana Dharma holds this truth beautifully: the divine, though formless (*Nirakara*) and beyond attributes (*Nirguna*), manifests in countless forms to meet the yearning of each devotee. That which is infinite takes form so that we, the finite, may find a way to reach it.

This is where the true beauty lies: I see the Nirakara—the formless ultimate—reflected in my Guru. It's not just belief; it's a living experience. In him, I feel the compassion of Sri Hari, the nurturing power of Maa Shakti, the strength of Shiva, and the wisdom of Ved Mata Gayatri.

This realisation transformed my journey. My devotion to my Ishta and reverence for my Guru are not separate—they are the same. Through my Guru, I experience the divine. He is both the channel and the embodiment of that which is infinite and eternal.

Without this oneness, the deep, unshakable bond essential for spiritual growth would be impossible to achieve. This bond is the foundation, seeing the Guru not just as a guide, but as a living reflection of the divine.

When I revere my Guru, I honour my Ishta. When I bow to my Ishta, I feel my Guru's presence. This sacred loop sustains me.

Among the countless lessons my Gurudev has given, two in particular have become cornerstones of my life:

1. "Your world shifts only when you do."

These words awakened something profound in me. For years, I believed my struggles—financial instability, emotional strain, professional hurdles—were due to external situations. I waited for life to improve before I could be at peace.

But Gurudev shattered that illusion. The outer world is rarely under our control. What we can change is within our mindset, our reactions, and our inner strength.

This single teaching made me turn inward. Instead of waiting for calm, I learned to find balance in the midst of the storm. I stopped resisting challenges and began to see them as invitations to grow. Whether it's family life, career struggles, or spiritual practice, this lesson continues to guide me.

2. "Become one with Mother Nature, and you will become one with Mother Divine."

This teaching redefined my relationship with life itself. Gurudev helped me understand that nature is not separate from the divine—she is the holy, in form.

This shifted how I live. I chose sattvik food, embraced simplicity, and began practising sustainability—not out of moral duty, but out of reverence. Waking up for sunrise, planting trees, walking barefoot—each act became sacred.

Even more than external habits, this lesson created inner harmony. I began to feel nurtured by the earth, held by her rhythm. My restlessness softened into peace. In nature, I began to feel the embrace of the Mother Divine herself.

These two teachings—'change yourself, not the world' and 'connect with nature to connect with the divine'—are not just concepts for me. They are living truths. They shape how I make decisions, how I face pain, and how I stay grounded.

When a storm arises in life, I don't ask, "Why is this happening to me?" I ask, "What do I need to shift within me?" And when I feel disconnected, I return to nature—because I know she'll return me to God.

These lessons gave me resilience and faith. They deepened my surrender and strengthened my relationship with my Guru. For this, I am endlessly grateful.

It's also important to say this: a Guru is not an absolute necessity for spiritual growth. Some seekers walk their paths through inner faith, intuition, and divine grace alone. Many have reached great spiritual heights without ever meeting a physical Guru in this lifetime.

The divine becomes their teacher for such souls, guiding them inwardly through introspection and surrender. If pure and attuned, the inner voice becomes their greatest light.

For someone like me—an ordinary person with countless imperfections and distractions—having a Guru is like holding a compass in a vast, uncharted ocean. Without that compass, the journey becomes an uphill battle, full of uncertainty, missteps, and unnecessary detours.

I often compare it to solving a complex mathematical equation. Imagine trying to crack it using only faded memories of old formulas. Even after work hours, you're left unsure, questioning every step you take. Now imagine having a calculator—a tool that gives you instant clarity. Why would anyone ignore such guidance?

Walking the spiritual path without a Guru feels the same. It's not impossible, but far more difficult. The journey is filled with subtle nuances; without guidance, it's easy to get caught in ego, pride, or illusion. A true Guru has walked this terrain. He knows the pitfalls, the illusions, the inner storms—and how to pass through them.

For me, my Guru is my anchor, my lighthouse, and my mirror. He shows me the beauty and the blind spots within. He helps me see the subtle traps I might miss—pride, laziness, or self-deception. He doesn't just give answers; he shows me how to unlearn.

Above all, he reassures me. With his guidance, I no longer second-guess every decision. His presence offers clarity and confidence. With him, I have the tools to stay grounded and the love to keep walking—even when the road feels dark.

Let me be clear—I'm not saying this to glorify my Guru or to claim that everyone must have one. My Guru doesn't need validation. But if someone even slightly ahead of you offers guidance, why not receive it? Why not learn from someone who can help you avoid unnecessary suffering and direct you toward your spiritual goal?

For me, having a Guru has been transformative. With his hand on my head, I feel secure, purposeful, and never alone. His teachings are the greatest gift I've received.

A true Guru won't do your sadhana for you. He won't hand you realisation or create a shortcut to the divine. His role is to guide, not to carry the load. Because this path is meant to be walked with your own feet, only then will the journey shape your soul.

The Guru doesn't impose a connection with the divine. He equips you to build it yourself. He ensures your practices align with the scriptures, dharma, and the eternal truths of Sanatana Dharma.

My Guru taught me to approach my sadhana with bhava, not as a mechanical duty, but as an offering of love. Initially, I followed rituals mindlessly. But under his guidance, everything changed. He helped me understand that inner feelings bridge you to your Ishta, not the outer ritual.

Once I internalised this, my sadhana transformed. Rituals became joyful. Mantras became conversations. My bond with my Ishta Devata deepened—not because I was doing more, but because I was feeling more.

Without a Guru, spiritual practice can become a forest of confusion. Which mantra? Which path? How to approach the divine? A Guru brings clarity, shining light on the way forward.

A Guru simplifies the spiritual journey. They guide us according to our temperament, capacity, and growth stage through wisdom and compassion. They help peel away the layers of doubt, fear, and confusion that cloud our bond with our Ishta Devata. The Guru reveals that the divine is not distant or unreachable—it resides within, waiting to be realised.

With the Guru's guidance, our connection to the Ishta Devata becomes more than just belief or imagination. It evolves into a living relationship—intimate, trusting, and surrender-filled. The Guru helps us see the Ishta not as a deity in some celestial realm, but as a presence within and around us—a source of love, strength, and guidance.

In my journey, I've learned from my Guru that this connection isn't something we manufacture. It unfolds naturally when approached with humility and sincerity. My Guru helped me realise that the divine isn't separate—it's within my heart, waiting to be recognised.

While our effort deepens this bond, the Guru accelerates the process. Their blessings and presence remove obstacles we might not even recognise. They keep us aligned, focused, and steady, ensuring our effort is not scattered or wasted.

This makes the connection so personal and transformative—it's born from our devotion and surrender, refined by the Guru's grace.

This journey is never identical for any two disciples. Each relationship with the Guru and Ishta Devata is shaped by karma, personal effort, and divine grace. Yet, what remains constant is the Guru's unwavering presence, ensuring we never feel lost or alone on this sacred path.

Through my Guru, I've come to see my relationship with the divine as a connection and a realisation of oneness. It is the awareness that the sacred is not separate from me but the core of who I am. For this gift, I remain forever grateful.

I believe the sacred bond between Guru and Shishya transcends lifetimes. It is not a temporary tie of this birth but one rooted in the karmic web of many incarnations. It unfolds with divine timing, orchestrated by a wisdom far beyond our understanding.

Nothing in life is accidental. Every encounter serves a deeper purpose. And so, the Guru-Shishya bond—one of the most sacred of all—continues a connection forged across lifetimes.

I've often reflected on this in my journey. I remember wondering, 'Why did I meet my Guru at 36?' Why not earlier, when I was lost in struggle and confusion? Why wasn't I among the blessed few who met him just after his tapasya, when his teachings began to spread?

Sometimes, these thoughts would stir gentle envy, not out of bitterness, but longing. I wonder if early guidance saved me from inevitable missteps or pain. I yearned for those moments when his satsangs were small and intimate, when the access felt closer.

Recently, I found deep solace in a book by Sadhviji, *Bhagavan and Bhakta*. As it often happens, when I sincerely seek, the universe answers through books, videos, or unexpected moments. That book spoke directly to my heart and shifted my perspective.

In it, she shared two profound lessons that helped me understand the nature of divine timing and the timelessness of the Guru-Shishya bond.

Sadhviji shares a story that deeply moved me. A dog from her building had gone missing, and her heart ached for the family's pain. She wrote to Gurudev, asking for his help. Swamiji replied simply: "Is this important for you, Sadhviji?" She replied with a heartfelt yes.

The next day, the dog returned safely. While it felt like grace, Swamiji later explained that such outcomes aren't as simple as they appear. He described the intricate workings of the universe—how even one small change requires a vast alignment of energies, actions, and circumstances. Every ripple affects the cosmic balance, and even well-meaning interventions have consequences.

This teaching resonated deeply with me. We often demand instant results, unaware of the countless unseen forces at work. It reminded me of my earlier reflection on how even a simple family trip creates an invisible web of interconnected events. Swamiji's words helped me see how surrendering to divine timing is an act of deep spiritual maturity.

The second lesson from her book etched itself into my heart. She spoke of her fortune in serving Gurudev and Sri Hari in this lifetime, but she also acknowledged that this privilege wasn't born of a few years of devotion. She wrote that it may have taken her fifty lifetimes, or more, to reach this point. Her humility opened my eyes to the magnitude of karmic effort that precedes grace.

It reminded me of the story of Dhruva from the *Srimad Bhagavatam*. When saints questioned why young Dhruva had attained Darshan of Sri Hari while they had not, Narada Muni led them to a mountain of bones, remnants of Dhruva's previous lifetimes of Tapasya. Narada explained, "These are the lifetimes of effort that brought him divine grace in this one."

This truth is both humbling and beautiful. What appears as divine favour is often the fruit of countless births of devotion, effort, and surrender. It deepened my reverence not only for my Gurudev but also for the divine's patience and the slow, sacred unfolding of Bhakti.

Sadhviji's words reminded me that the Guru doesn't merely guide us in this life. Their presence plants seeds that blossom across lifetimes. The bond between Guru and disciple is timeless. Even in silence or struggle, the disciple is never alone.

That realisation fills me with gratitude. To know that my connection with my Gurudev transcends time gives me strength and responsibility—to walk this path with integrity, to serve with love, and to surrender with trust.

Now, you may wonder—if I see all gods as one, why do I speak so intimately about my Ishta Devata? If I believe in the formless, infinite Nirakara, why do I offer such reverence to certain forms?

Let me share from the heart.

I've always been drawn to Mahadev and Hanumanji. They were the pillars of my early devotion. Now, I speak often of Sri Hari and Maa Jagatjanani. But this isn't a shift—it's an unfolding, a natural evolution of grace guided by Sanatana Dharma.

As I shared earlier, it is said in the *Sri Ramcharitmanas* that only through Mahadev's grace does one attain Bhakti of Sri Hari. That has been my lived truth. When I say "Sri Hari," I don't mean just Vishnu—I mean Bhagavan Vishnu and Maa Lakshmi together.

Sri, the divine consort, embodies compassion, grace, and the abundance that nurtures life. Hari, the preserver, offers refuge and unconditional love. Together, they are wholeness—the giver and the protector, the mother and the father, the breath and the rhythm.

I cannot imagine one without the other. Their union is the completeness of existence, and my ability to perceive them this way is Shiva's grace.

I see no separation between Hari and Har, Mahadev and Maha Vishnu. They are one. Mahadev embodies Vairagya (detachment) and supreme renunciation, while Maha Vishnu radiates Prem (love), compassion, and the readiness to uplift his devotees. And in both, the divine feminine—Maa Adi Shakti and Maa Maha Lakshmi—eternally flows.

Hanumanji, for me, is the perfect devotee—my eternal teacher of surrender and humility. He shows what it truly means to serve and love the divine. There's a beautiful *chopai* from the *Sundarkand* of the *Sri Ramcharitmanas* that pierces my heart:

राम दूत मैं मातु जानकी।
सत्य सपथ करुनानिधान की॥

When Hanumanji met Maa Sita in Ashok Vatika, she asked, "Who are you?" And he replied, "I am the messenger of Sri Ram. I swear by the ocean of compassion."

That one line shifted something deep within me. Imagine—Hanumanji, an *amsha* of Lord Shiva, powerful enough to destroy the universe, introduces himself not by his name or strength, but as a humble *duta* of Sri Ram. His identity was rooted not in power, but in service. This is the heart of *Bhakti*—pure surrender.

Could he not have destroyed Lanka or Ravana by himself? Of course, he could. But he chose not to. With one leap, he crossed the ocean; with one roar, he shook Lanka. Yet he waited for Sri Ram's command. That is the extraordinary beauty of his devotion—not just strength, but restraint. His greatness was not in power, but in obedience to divine will.

Hanumanji teaches us that true devotion isn't about what we can do but how selflessly we align with the divine's purpose. I love him not for his might but for his humility, for dissolving himself completely in Ram Bhakti. Through him, I've come to understand that real service is never about recognition, but about love and surrender.

The presence of my Ishta—Sri Hari and Maa Jagajanani has transformed me. They've taught me to love selflessly, to walk in kindness, and to stay anchored in truth. Their grace sustains me, and their presence gives me the strength to rise again and again.

But the reason I even recognised their presence is only due to the grace of my Gurudev. Without his guidance, I would have remained lost in ignorance.

The bond with one's Ishta doesn't come by planning—it awakens by grace, at the right time. And when it does, everything changes.

Let me be completely honest. I am not pure—neither in thought nor in action. I still carry many inner impurities, and I say this without shame but with awareness. This is a part of my journey, one I continue to work through.

There are karmas I deeply regret, especially from my youth. Even today, I sometimes get caught up in Maya, in thoughts and temptations that no seeker should indulge in. These moments make me question, "Why can't I rise above this? Why is it so hard to live by the teachings of my Guru and the scriptures?"

But the truth is, we're all made up of *vrutis* (mental patterns), *prakruti* (nature), *gunas* (qualities), *maya*, *svabhava* (temperament), and *vikaras* (distortions). These deeply embedded traits influence everything—thinking, acting, and stumbling. For ordinary souls like me, rising above these isn't easy.

It's not impossible but demands grace, discipline, and relentless effort. And yet, guilt often creeps in. "Why did I fall again? Why wasn't I stronger?" That guilt can be crushing. Sometimes, I feel unworthy of my Guru's teachings or Ishta's love.

In those moments of guilt, I impose quiet self-discipline. It may sound unusual, but I stop myself from looking at my Gurudev's face or my Ishta Devata's image. I lower my eyes, refusing to meet their gaze—not because they've turned away, but because I feel unworthy of beholding them until I've purified my heart.

This self-imposed distance is temporary but profoundly compelling. It reminds me how precious their presence is and reignites my commitment to rise above my shortcomings. It becomes a turning point—a call to return to sincerity, purity, and discipline.

Oddly enough, this very act deepens my devotion. It reminds me that I carry a sacred responsibility—not just as a seeker, but as someone blessed with their grace. The idea of letting them down, even for a moment, is unbearable. That pain keeps me anchored, even when I falter.

Yes, there have been moments when I doubted myself and wondered if I could live up to my guru's teachings. But every time I've slipped, I've reminded myself of one truth—they don't expect perfection, only sincerity. I know I'm still walking their path as long as I remain honest in my effort.

Now, I'm at least aware. I can sense when my thoughts stray or when my actions fall short. Sometimes I let my mind get the best of me; sometimes I stumble. But even in those moments, a voice inside whispers, "Jai, this isn't who you truly are." That awareness doesn't always stop me in the moment, but it plants a seed that keeps growing slowly but surely. And I genuinely believe this awareness will one day help me transcend these patterns. It's what holds me steady when Maya tries to pull me away.

Surrender has been the most transformative part of my journey. It isn't just a concept—it's the ground I stand on. For a long time, I was stuck in a loop of effort, constantly trying to fix things on my own. My ego whispered that I could handle it all. But I was going nowhere, just circling the same pain.

The turning point came when I finally said, "I've done everything I know. I give up. Sri Hari, it's all yours now." That one act of surrender lifted a heavy weight. It didn't solve every problem overnight, but something within shifted. There was peace. There was movement.

I remembered a story from Gurudev's memoir, where he spoke about his Guru, Pujya Naga Baba. His response was unwavering whenever he received an instruction: "Ji Babaji, Hanji Babaji, Thik hai Babaji."

It wasn't blind obedience but trust born of deep love. For him, his Guru's words were sacred.

I feel the same. When Gurudev speaks, I listen as though Sri Hari himself is guiding me. There's no analysis, no mental debate—just surrender. Not because I lack understanding, but because I trust the one I've accepted as my spiritual compass. As Gurudev once wrote, *"Jab hamne unko Guru maan hi liya, to bas fir sochna kesa?—there is nothing beyond it."*

That line has become my own. For me, surrender is the highest form of strength. It's what silences doubt, melts fear, and opens the door to grace. It's not about weakness—it's about finally stepping out of the way so the divine can take over.

This surrender has given me clarity, purpose, and peace I never imagined. And as long as I stay in this space of faith, I know I'll never be lost on this path.

My guidance for those who haven't yet found their Guru is simple: stop searching—just begin your spiritual journey with faith. Make Mahadeva, the Guru of all Gurus, your first guide. Surrender to his wisdom and grace. Start your sadhana with devotion to him or your Ishta Devata, and trust that everything else will unfold in time.

Let me share a light moment from my early journey. After my initiation by Gurudev, I was flooded with questions and insecurities. As I began to experience the beauty of the path, I developed a childlike possessiveness toward my Guru. I avoided sharing his name, thinking, *What if others also become his disciples? What if one day there's no space left for me in his heart?*

Looking back, I smile at how limited that mindset was. And now, I am writing an entire book singing his glories. That shift—from possessiveness to expansiveness—is the Guru's magic. They don't just guide; they transform how we think, feel, and love.

On a serious note, don't rush to find a Guru just to fill a void or check a spiritual box. I lived 36 years without a Guru, navigating many painful lessons. Yet, my faith in Mahadeva never wavered. I surrendered to him and prayed to be guided to my Guru—and with his grace, the moment arrived. My Guru found me, not because I was worthy, but because I was ready.

So if you're still waiting, don't despair. Begin with your Ishta Devata or the divine form that resonates with your soul. Offer your prayers, do your sadhana sincerely, and ask for their blessings to guide you. Many saints have found their Gurus through the grace of their chosen deities.

Here's what matters most: you don't choose your Guru. Your Guru chooses you. And when that moment comes, you'll know. There will be no doubt, no hesitation. Your soul will recognise them instantly. You'll feel an overwhelming urge to surrender completely—words will fall short, but your heart will understand.

And you don't need to rush this. When the time is right, the universe will align to bring this connection into your life. Until then, walk your path with trust, sincerity, and an open heart.

While the Guru is the guiding presence, another sacred force silently shapes our journey—the Ishta Devata.

The concept of an Ishta Devata—your deity—is central in Sanatana Dharma. In my experience, it's predetermined and dynamic, evolving with your inner journey.

Ishta means "the one you love", who calls you home. When I speak to Maa in my heart, I often say, "Maa, however flawed I am, I'm still yours." For me, this manifests as Maa Mahakali, Maa Lakshmi, Maa Durga, or Maa Jagadamba—each form holding a unique vibration that supports me through different phases of life.

In masculine energies, Sri Hari is my eternal anchor. But I also revere Mahadeva, Hanumanji, Brahmaji, and Kaal Bhairava. Each represents a facet of the divine. Kaal Bhairava's fierce grace clears negativity, while Mahadeva teaches supreme detachment.

Does this mean I lack a central Ishta? Not at all. Sri Hari is my focal point. But my love for others doesn't diminish that devotion. It enriches it. All deities are expressions of the supreme reality, appearing in forms that guide us based on our nature and needs.

Early in my journey, I wrestled with a familiar doubt: *If I pray to one deity, will the others feel neglected?* Over time, I realised how misplaced that fear was. The divine doesn't operate through jealousy or competition. Each form complements the other. They are all rays of the same sun.

Swamiji beautifully explains in *The Ancient Science of Mantras* that any sadhana should begin with Ganapati Bhagavan. He is the remover of obstacles—*Vighna Harta*. Even if he isn't your Ishta, invoking him creates alignment and clears your path.

This understanding changed everything for me. I came to see that loving my Ishta doesn't require excluding others. It means embracing all forms as sacred, while remaining centred in the one that feels most like home.

This realisation freed me from all fear or confusion about doing sadhanas for different deities. Each sadhana simply aligns us with a particular energy and supports our growth. It doesn't imply disloyalty to one's Ishta; on the contrary, it enriches our connection with the divine.

So, is your Ishta Devata predetermined, or can it change? I believe both are true. At the soul level, your Ishta is destined. But as your consciousness evolves, your connection with other forms of the divine may deepen. That doesn't mean your Ishta has changed—it means your heart has expanded. You're not replacing one with another; you're seeing the divine through broader lenses.

This is what I've come to understand. I hope it clears any confusion about devotion to multiple deities. The divine isn't divided. Whether you love one or many, the destination remains the same—the infinite, the eternal, the one.

To me, my Guru transcends identity. He is not just a person—I see him as my living Sri Hari, divinity embodied in human form. This isn't poetic sentiment; it's the truth of my relationship with him. He chose me because I needed him the most.

I often wondered, *Why me? What good had I done to deserve such a great Guru?* Looking back on my life, I found nothing extraordinary—no great karma, no noble deeds. But deep down, I realised it wasn't merit. It was his boundless compassion. He saw a soul entangled in worldly illusions and thought, *This one needs me.*

Though I see him as divine, I also see his human side—how he walks, smiles, jokes, and teaches. And yet, it is through these very human expressions that his divinity shines even more. His gaze during my first darshan felt like Maa Mahakali herself looked through me, dissolving all that was unworthy. And then, in the next moment, he would laugh and speak so simply. This contrast doesn't confuse me; it deepens my reverence. It shows me that the divine doesn't need to stay distant—it can live among us, teaching through presence.

For me, surrender is key. I don't question him. His words carry the same authority for me as the Gita. His guidance is sacred. Even his silence speaks volumes. I don't try to interpret or judge his humanness—it's just another layer of his grace.

His duality has never been a conflict because I see no duality. His form is a doorway to the formless, his humanness a vessel for divine will. It is his grace that has transformed me. I am no longer the same. His presence has shaped my life, so I bow with endless gratitude. He is not just my Guru—he is my eternal Sri Hari, in whom I've found meaning, peace, and my true path.

Recently, someone asked me if I follow any daily rituals to deepen this bond with my Guru and Ishta Devata. If I'm honest, I don't follow anything rigid or structured. And the reason is simple: we humans don't *do* anything significant by ourselves.

Every sadhana, every mantra, every remembrance—none of it happens because of *us*. It is only by their grace that anything flows through us at all. Without their blessings, even the most perfect ritual bears no fruit. To think *I'm* doing something to deepen this connection would be egotistical. It is not I who remembers my Guru; I even think of him by his grace. It is not I who clings to my Ishta—*their* love holds me.

That said, there are certain things I do not consider formal practices, but as a natural way of living with awareness:

Remembering Them in Every Breath
This is the most powerful practice for me. I try to remember my Guru and Ishta Devata with every breath, thought, and action. Before I act, I ask, *Would this make my Guru happy? Would my Ishta smile upon this?* This inner dialogue becomes a living meditation.

Surrender in Every Action
Whether it's a small household task or spiritual practice, I offer it as seva. I'm not the doer—my Guru and Ishta are working through me. I simply act as their instrument.

Absorbing Wisdom
I often find answers through my Guru's books and teachings. But this ability to understand is itself a gift. Rajarshi Nandyji once said that even the capacity to grasp spiritual knowledge is a grace. Without their will, scriptures remain just words. It is their grace that turns knowledge into wisdom.

The Sadhaka Mentality
Rajarshi Nandyji also said, "If someone asks me who I am, I would say, 'I am a Sadhaka.'" This line grounds me. I am not the achiever—just a seeker, a vessel. My Guru and Ishta are the true forces behind everything.

So, when I say I've found guidance through teachings or texts, it's not due to personal capability. It's only because *he* wishes me to learn. My understanding and my growth all come through his will. My role is simply to remain open, humble, and aware.

If I had to describe my Gurudev in one word, it would be Sri Hari.

I've said this before, and I repeat it with even deeper conviction: my Gurudev is Sri Hari. He is the living embodiment of that infinite love, kindness, and divinity. When I think of Sri Hari, I think of someone who looks past your flaws, lifts you through storms, and gives you strength when you're lost. This is precisely what my Gurudev has done for me.

This isn't a metaphor—it's my truth. His words, presence, and silence have nourished me like amrit.

By now, you might feel I've repeatedly praised my Gurudev throughout this book. And you're right—I have. But I say this with intention and honesty.

First, these aren't just praises—they are heartfelt truths. Words born not from naive belief but from lived experience. They may not make logical sense, and that's okay. Some things in this world transcend logic.

Second, no amount of praise will ever be enough. I wish for you not to idolise *my* Guru, but to hold the same love and surrender toward *your* Guru. Your Guru may not be mine, but the *bhava*—the feeling—must be just as deep. That is what makes this path meaningful. Without this love, even the presence of Mahadeva as one's Guru may not bear fruit.

So, now you understand why I speak about my guru the way I do. It's not exaggeration—it's reverence. Just that. Nothing else.

Let's now shift briefly to something more grounded.

There was a recent incident, seemingly minor, but for me, it was a divine intervention.

As I've shared earlier, I've struggled financially for the past few years. Despite this, I never shared the burden with my family. Not out of secrecy, but from a genuine place of love—I didn't want to worry them.

My parents are ageing, and I didn't want to burden them with my struggles. I couldn't bear the thought of hearing questions like, "Why did this happen? How did it get so bad?"—questions I had no satisfying answers to. More than anything, I didn't want them to feel obligated to help me financially, especially when they had already done so.

In my heart, this was my karma, my cross to bear. I told myself, "I created this—I must face it alone." But despite this resolve, silence grew heavier with each passing day.

Eventually, my parents sensed something was wrong. They gently asked, "Is something troubling you?" Again and again, they urged me to share. At first, I deflected, changed the topic, and avoided their gaze. But their concern only deepened.

Then came the moment when I could no longer hold it in. Trembling, I surrendered. With a heavy heart, I told them everything—the financial setbacks, business losses, the mounting debts.

As I spoke, I felt a release I hadn't felt in years. It wasn't easy, but it was liberating. I had nothing to hide. I hadn't lived carelessly or dishonestly. My pain was born of circumstance, not wrongdoing.

And in that moment of vulnerability, I felt my Gurudev's presence. As if his grace silently carried me through the fear and confession into freedom. It was his unseen strength that helped me open up.

What followed was astonishing. The burden that had clung to me for so long lifted. I felt light and peaceful. My parents didn't react with judgment or disappointment—instead, they embraced me with love and understanding. They reminded me that I was never alone.

That simple act of truth, though small, felt sacred. It was a lesson in surrender. A reminder that walking a spiritual path isn't about escaping hardship—it's about facing it with grace, honesty, and faith.

If even this humble act—opening my heart—was touched by my Guru's grace, I can only imagine what complete surrender might bring. It showed me that the Guru's guidance is constant, even in the quiet, unseen moments. It may not arrive with fanfare, but its presence is unmistakable, shaping, healing, and gently guiding us back to truth.

3.3 Ananda & Buddha: The Twin Paths of Bliss and Enlightenment

Ananda and Buddha were more than historical figures—they reflect two spiritual archetypes. Ananda, Buddha's cousin and disciple, once requested to remain in his Guru's presence. Though Buddha cautioned him, he relented out of compassion.

But the story isn't the focus here. What struck me deeply was a question my Gurudev once posed during a discourse: *"Do you wish to walk the path of Ananda, or the path of Buddha?"* That one question became a seed, quietly transforming my perspective.

The path of Ananda is one of closeness to the Guru—drawing light, wisdom, and grace through surrender and proximity. It's gentle, nurturing, and rooted in bhakti. The disciple walks with trust, letting the Guru illuminate the way.

The Buddha path, by contrast, is solitary—marked by intense tapasya, fierce independence, and deep inner struggle. It's a path of silence, effort, and awakening. The seeker walks alone, fueled by unwavering determination. If successful, they attain the ultimate truth and become a Buddha.

Later, I came across a story about Ananda during the Buddha's Mahaparinirvana. Despite lifelong service to his Guru, Ananda had not attained enlightenment. When asked why, Buddha replied: *"A spoon may stir the soup but cannot taste it."* Ananda was close, yet distant. He revered the form but missed the essence of it.

This shook me. It helped me realise that the Guru is not the body but a divine energy, like the wind: present, felt, but never bound. Like the sun: radiating light equally, regardless of distance.

Initially, I too believed that physical proximity would fast-track my growth. But Gurudev's question—*"Do you want to be Ananda or Buddha?"*—made me rethink. Physical closeness comforts the ego.

Fundamental transformation lies in inner connection, recognising the Guru as energy, not form.

Are these two paths separate? Not at all. They often meet. The devotion of Ananda can mature into the wisdom of Buddha. And even the most resolute seeker eventually leans on grace. Both are valid, both powerful.

This teaching helped me drop the false choice. I could walk with Ananda's bhava and also receive Buddha's clarity. One nurtures the heart, the other awakens the soul. Both belong to the same river, flowing from the divine.

When I reflected on which path I was destined for, I realised something more profound: *the path chooses you.* We think we're choosing, but it's our karmas, samskaras, and the grace of Guru and Ishta that desire for us.

I never consciously said, "This is my path." Instead, I was swept into a current where bliss and wisdom flowed together—surrender met awareness, and devotion gave rise to insight.

Why confine myself to one when the divine offers both? And truly, *who am I to choose at all?*

I am neither the doer nor the one who decides. When I try to make choices from a limited mind, I risk letting ego steer the journey. Instead, I've surrendered to divine will, trusting that the path unfolding before me is exactly what I need.

Letting go of the need to choose has freed me from the burden of comparison. I follow the guidance I receive—step by step, moment by moment—with faith that it will lead me home.

In my experience, bliss and wisdom are not opposites; they are companions. The bliss of devotion energises my practices; wisdom refines and deepens them. Together, they create a flow that sustains my journey.

Bliss gives me the strength to endure. Wisdom shows me how. One fills the heart with love and gratitude; the other lights the way with clarity.

If I were to describe my journey, it would feel like being carried by a river of grace. I am not rowing the boat—I'm simply flowing, nourished by waters of both Ananda and Buddha. In that flow, there's no need to choose. I remain open, receptive, and surrendered—and I see that Ananda and Buddha are not destinations, but the journey itself.

The Path of Ananda, deeply woven with bhakti, is personal and transformative. It's the path of surrender, where one seeks union through love and unwavering faith. Though blissful, this path is not without challenge, especially for those of us living amidst worldly duties.

Many, including myself, begin this path with more yearning than knowledge. The heart longs for the divine, but the mind fumbles with practice and scripture. Here, the Guru and sacred texts become lifelines. Bhakti teaches that this very longing is a blessing. Even without clarity, devotion can open doors that intellect alone cannot.

Living a worldly life and expressing deep devotion isn't always easy. We're not sannyasis—we have families, jobs, responsibilities. There's often a fear of being misunderstood. "What will people think?" But I've learned that this fear reflects others' limitations, not mine. Over time, I've balanced devotion with duty, knowing the divine sees my heart.

One of bhakti's greatest gifts—and challenges—is maintaining *bhava*, the devotional mood. At satsangs, we sing, dance, and weep in divine joy. Yet, once the event ends, many lose that connection. I try not to let it fade. Whether I laugh, cry, or sit in stillness, I let these become my worship. Others may see it as strange, but these are life's happiest moments, untouched by opinions.

Bhakti offers a bliss unlike anything the senses can touch. It turns even the mundane into sacred acts. This joy is not fleeting—it's eternal, born from the soul's embrace of the divine.

Devotion frees you from ego, the source of most suffering. When you surrender, you no longer need control. Peace arises not from proving anything but from trusting everything.

As Sanatana Dharma teaches, Bhakti is the most straightforward and tender path to the divine. Unlike the demanding routes of karma or jnana, bhakti is like a mother who takes your hand and walks you home.

The *Bhagavata Purana* recounts how devotion lifted souls like Dhruva, Prahlada, and the Gopis. Their stories remind us: divine love asks for no qualifications—just an open heart.

You don't need to be a scholar or yogi. Just be willing. I have no special skills. I began this path late, after 36. Even now, I struggle to remember shlokas or follow rituals perfectly. I make mistakes. I know this.

But does that mean I should stop? Not at all.

To manage these challenges, I keep a printed handout with all the procedures, shlokas, and ritual guidelines, following them precisely as instructed by my Gurudev. What once felt like a limitation now feels like grace. If I had memorised everything, ego might have crept in with the illusion of mastery. I remain humble and aligned with his guidance by staying anchored to the PDFS my Guru gave.

I'm at peace with the thought, "I don't know this." There's no burden of proving anything. I'm not here to display knowledge but to deepen my connection with the divine. This shift has made my practices more joyful and authentic. Do you see what I mean?

For me, Bhakti isn't about rituals—it's about being with the divine in every moment. When I eat, I offer the first bite. When I walk, I chant. I surrender it to my Guru and Ishta when I struggle, trusting they'll guide me. This remembrance keeps me rooted in devotion, no matter what life's storms bring. And the joy it brings is beyond description.

The Path of Ananda has taught me that the divine isn't something to be found—it's something to be lived.

The Path of Buddha, rooted in Jnana (wisdom) and self-realisation, is often seen as distinct, but my intention isn't to separate it from Ananda. Instead, I hope to show how they intertwine—and why the Path of Buddha begins with humility.

You may read of enlightened souls who seemed to awaken purely through knowledge or effort. But as we saw with Dhruva's story, their "beginning" was the culmination of many lifetimes of tapasya, devotion, and grace. We focus only on the final chapter and miss the invisible pages written across past births.

This is why I believe the Path of Buddha naturally arises from the Path of Ananda. Devotion dissolves ego, purifies the heart, and calms the mind, allowing true wisdom to emerge. Bhakti lays the foundation for Jnana.

Now, you might wonder why I've written an entire chapter on this if, as I've said, we don't really choose our path. The reason is essential.

Ananda and Buddha are not opposite paths chosen by different seekers, but complementary phases of one seeker's evolution. And it's not just that both can be embraced—eventually, both must be. One essential quality allows this integration, which I'll share later in the chapter. For now, stay with me as we explore how Ananda and Buddha prepare the seeker for the three primary yogic paths.

Bhakti Yoga – The Path of Ananda:
Through love and devotion, the seeker experiences divine bliss.
Bhakti softens the heart and draws grace effortlessly.

Jnana Yoga – The Path of Buddha:
Through inner inquiry and discernment, the seeker uncovers truth and

self-realisation. It demands depth, detachment, and subtle understanding.

Karma Yoga – The Bridge of Action:
Through selfless service, one purifies the ego and acts in harmony with the divine will. Karma Yoga harmonises the inner joy of Bhakti with the clarity of Jnana.

For those of us living amidst worldly responsibilities, these three become the pillars of our spiritual life. They help us integrate Ananda and Buddhi—bliss and wisdom—while navigating the cycle of samsara. And here's the deeper truth: Ananda and Buddhi are not separate. Real wisdom awakens bliss. Absolute bliss leads to deeper insight. Like two wings, they lift the seeker together.

There is one element I hold most sacred in all this: Bhava.

Without Bhava—without the emotional essence—no path can flourish. Without it, rituals are dry, knowledge becomes sterile, and devotion becomes performance. Bhava is the pulse of the soul that turns mantras into connection and worship into union.

Especially on the path of Bhakti, Bhava is the invisible thread tying us to our Guru or Ishta. It makes our efforts authentic, tender, and accurate.

Even Adi Shankaracharya, revered as a master of non-dual wisdom, acknowledged the power of Bhava in his teachings on Manasa Puja—the mental worship of the divine. His reverence reminds us that the heart must touch even the subtlest paths.

Manasa Puja, or mental worship, transcends the physical rituals we perform. It takes worship into the realm of the mind, creating a deeper connection with the divine. Here, Bhava becomes the driving force, making every offering—flowers, incense, water—a silent act of internal devotion.

As Shankaracharyaji taught, Manasa Puja is the highest form of dhyana. It needs no external materials or elaborate settings. It flows solely from Bhava. When the heart is full of devotion, the deity awakens within, making worship intensely personal and profound.

Now, consider Bhava in the context of the two paths—Ananda and Buddha.

On the Path of Ananda, Bhava is the lifeblood of Bhakti. Without it, devotion becomes mechanical. Bhava brings bliss into every mantra, every prayer, and every thought of one's Ishta or Guru.

On the Path of Buddha, Bhava appears differently. It becomes a reverence for truth, a love for wisdom, and an emotional commitment to self-realisation. Without Bhava, even Jnana remains dry and disconnected.

In truth, all spirituality depends on the concept of Bhava. Take Manasa Puja—it cannot exist without emotional depth. Bhava lifts rituals from routine into sacredness. It bridges the human and the divine, making the formless felt.

In my journey, Bhava has guided every step. Whether lighting a diya or chanting a mantra, Bhava transforms these into sacred offerings. It is Bhava that turns longing into love and prayer into presence.

If I've realised one truth, it is this: Bhava is the gateway to transcendence. Whether you walk the path of bliss, wisdom, or both, Bhava carries you forward. It allows you to feel the divine within and to move closer to liberation.

I must share a beautiful example, made possible only by my Gurudev's grace. The "Sadhana App" by Vedic Sadhana Foundation perfectly embodies Bhava in action. It gives anyone, anywhere, the ability to begin their spiritual journey, with no materials, special conditions, or cost. All that's needed is a willingness to act.

That's what makes it so powerful. The app removes every excuse we have for delaying Sadhana—no time, resources, or sacred space. My Gurudev has made the path so simple that even amidst worldly duties, one can connect with the divine as naturally as breathing.

This is Bhava made accessible. It's not about the form—it's about the feeling. The app shows us that the only requirement for spiritual progress is sincerity. And yes, you don't even need initiation to begin. Isn't that remarkable?

This offering is just one of many treasures from my Gurudev, and I'll share more of them later when I speak about my practices. But I had to mention it here, as it perfectly illustrates the essence of Bhava—the power to turn within and worship without obstruction.

Now, it's time to share the fundamental quality I mentioned, without which no seeker can transition from Ananda to Buddha. That quality is Vairagya—detachment.

Without Vairagya, one stays on the surface of the spiritual path, unable to dive deeper. It is the bridge that links blissful devotion with inner wisdom.

Return to the story of Ananda and Buddha. When Buddha said, "a spoon cannot taste the soup," he wasn't just making a metaphor—he was pointing to Vairagya. No matter how close one appears to be to the divine, without detachment from the ego, desires, and attachments, actual realisation remains out of reach.

As the verses explain:

"Though all through life the fool might wait upon the wise, no more Dhamma can he sense than spoon the taste of soup."

No matter how long he stays near wisdom, a fool cannot grasp it if his mind is clouded by attachment. Like a spoon that serves soup but never tastes it, the ignorant cannot absorb true wisdom.

"Though briefly one intelligent might wait upon the wise, quickly Dhamma he can sense as tongue the taste of soup."

In contrast, one who is inwardly detached quickly grasps the essence, just as the tongue instantly senses flavour. This discernment arises from vairagya.

For someone like me, whose heart overflows with devotion to my Guru and Ishta, the idea of detachment can feel contradictory. How does one detach from what they love the most? How can one distance oneself from the Guru's grace or the divine's loving presence?

The answer lies in understanding vairagya. Detachment does not mean withdrawing love—it means letting love flow freely, without expectation or clinging. It is not the absence of feeling but the purification of it.

Vairagya tests the maturity of our devotion. It calls us to release even subtle forms of possessiveness—not by denying love but transcending attachment. Loving the Guru and Ishta with a heart free from dependence opens the doorway to wisdom.

Swami Vivekananda's devotion to Sri Ramakrishna beautifully embodied this balance. His love was immense but not possessive. It was pure, rooted in surrender rather than ego. That is the ideal I strive toward.

I won't pretend I've mastered vairagya. The thought of detachment from my Guru's warmth or my Ishta's nearness still unsettles me. And yet, I know that true detachment doesn't sever the bond—it reveals its essence. In rising beyond forms, we begin to understand their eternal presence.

I remind myself often: the transition from Ananda to Buddha requires the courage to let go—not of love, but of the ego that clings to it. It cannot be forced. It must arise naturally, through grace, practice, and understanding.

Vairagya is not rejection—it is liberation. It is the ability to love fully without grasping, to surrender completely without needing anything in return. It transforms the sweetness of devotion into the clarity of wisdom.

This is why vairagya, to me, is not just a trait but the very essence of spiritual progress. It is the bridge between bliss and realisation, between heartfelt longing and liberating truth. It enables us to walk both paths—Ananda and Buddha—not separately, but as one.

Let this light of vairagya guide us forward. For in it lies the secret to living devotion and wisdom not as opposites, but as two expressions of the same divine truth.

3.4 Karma Sadhana: The Discipline of Action

Karma is one of the most profound and misunderstood concepts in spirituality. While it's often simplified as "cause and effect" or "what goes around comes around," Karma is far more intricate and deeply woven into the essence of life itself. At its core, Karma is not about reward or punishment, but about action, intention, and spiritual growth.

Even before I grasped its deeper meaning, Karma was present in my life through the living example of my father. As the eldest of three brothers and three sisters, he took responsibility for the entire family before marrying my mother. It was never a burden—it was his nature. He never hesitated or complained. It was how he lived.

My grandmother often spoke of those days. Working as an electrician in a small private company, my father earned just enough to meet basic needs. He repaired fans, tube lights, and other essentials to supplement this income, going door-to-door and charging just five rupees per job.

What touched me most was what he did with that extra income. Instead of keeping it, he used it to buy milk, tea, and sugar—so the whole family could share a cup of tea. For them, that cup of tea was a moment of togetherness, a quiet celebration in difficult times.

Even now, at the age of 73, my father's devotion to his family remains undiminished. He always put others before himself, often at the cost of his own comfort. My mother would sometimes question why he helped others so much, seemingly at the expense of his immediate family, but his sense of duty never wavered.

For him, his parents were divine—higher even than gods or saints. While my spiritual path has taken a different direction, I've always drawn deep inspiration from his sincerity and selflessness. He lived his truth without needing to convince others of it.

Looking back, I understand that he was living the core principles of Karma Yoga long before I knew the term. He worked without expectation, acted out of love, and performed his duties with unwavering dedication. Karma Yoga isn't always about grand sacrifices or spiritual rituals—it is often about silent, consistent service rooted in love and alignment with the greater good.

If this isn't Karma Yoga, then what is?

Swami Vivekananda often said that the attitude behind action matters more than the act itself. Karma is about intention—why and how we do what we do. Every act, when performed with awareness and sincerity, becomes sacred.

A common misconception is that Karma is only about punishment or reward, some cosmic ledger balancing our deeds. While cause and effect do exist, Karma is much more than consequences—it's about the awareness with which we live. It is a tool for transformation, not fear.

One of the first spiritual lessons I was taught was simple: "Do not harm any living creature." This belief, rooted in Sanatana Dharma and echoed in Jain traditions, shaped my early understanding of Karma. It helped me see all beings, no matter how small, as divine creations worthy of reverence.

Still, my path wasn't perfect. As a child, out of fear and ignorance, I killed insects. I didn't understand the depth of that principle. As my awareness grew, I realised the value of all life and the subtle harm caused by seemingly small actions. Karma is about what you do and who you become as a result of your actions.

Free will is perhaps the greatest gift granted to human beings. It allows us to think, feel, and act with conscious awareness. Every moment presents us with a choice, shaping our Karma. When faced with difficulty, we can respond with patience or anger. When given a chance to help, we can act with compassion or turn away in indifference. Each choice carries karmic weight.

But with this gift comes great responsibility. When we act in ways that violate truth or harmony, it is not destiny—our choice. Ignorance may influence us, but we are not helpless. Misuse of free will can bind us to suffering, while conscious, dharmic use can lead us toward freedom.

Let's take a simple example. Today, almost everyone owns a smartphone with internet access. We can watch uplifting spiritual discourses with a tap or fall into mindless distractions. The phone is neutral—our intent decides whether it becomes a tool for growth or an instrument of delusion. That is the essence of Karma: how we choose to use what's in front of us.

At the same time, free will exists within the framework of destiny. We are born into specific families with unique strengths and challenges, all shaped by our past karmas—our prarabdha. These form the circumstances of our current life, but don't dictate our inner growth. We still have the power to rise above them through hard work and mindful choices.

As the Bhagavad Gita (Chapter 3, Verse 35) beautifully says:

श्रेयान्स्वधर्मो विगुण: परधर्मात्स्वनुष्ठितात्।
स्वधर्मे निधनं श्रेय: परधर्मो भयावह:॥

"It is better to perform one's duty, even imperfectly, than to perform another's duty perfectly. Death in one's dharma is better than the fear of following another's."

This verse reflects the balance between destiny and free will. Karma may determine our outer roles, but how we carry them—with presence, devotion, and alignment to dharma—is our choice.

I have noticed this shift even in small things, like gently guiding a spider out of my room instead of killing it. This is not about fear of punishment or desire for reward—it is about respect for life, a deepening connection with nature, and a subtle evolution in consciousness. I see such small acts now as gestures of reverence toward Mother Nature herself.

Yet even this deeper awareness of karma is only part of the larger picture. The Gita (Chapter 3, Verse 15) offers another profound insight:

कर्म ब्रह्मोद्भवं विद्धि ब्रह्माक्षरसमुद्भवम्।
तस्मात्सर्वगतं ब्रह्म नित्यं यज्ञे प्रतिष्ठितम्॥

"All actions arise from Brahman, and Brahman arises from the imperishable. Therefore, the all-pervading Brahman is eternally established in yajna."

This reveals that Karma is not merely about what we do but about aligning our actions with the divine order. When our actions become selfless and offered in the spirit of yajna (sacrifice), they become sacred and liberating.

Another false belief is that Karma Yoga requires enormous efforts or dramatic sacrifices. In truth, it is about infusing small daily acts with sincerity and devotion. Whether preparing food, caring for a child, or fulfilling a simple duty—if done with awareness and love—it becomes a step on the spiritual path.

Before I met my Gurudev, I was deeply moved by Swami Vivekananda's teachings on Karma. His clarity helped me see how spiritual concepts could be lived daily. Even now, his vision echoes within me when I speak or write about Karma Yoga.

The word Karma comes from the root "Kri"—to act. But Karma isn't limited to outer deeds; it includes thoughts, words, and intentions. Every conscious or unconscious act leaves a subtle imprint on the soul, shaping our destiny and character.

The deeper truth is that Karma is not judgment. It is a law of alignment. The universe doesn't punish or reward—it reflects. Every action sows a seed, and each seed bears fruit. The quality of our inner life determines what grows.

Although, I have touched upon this earlier, it is essential to dive even deeper to fully understand how Karma unfolds, we must grasp its three primary forms: Sanchita, Prarabdha, and Agami.

Sanchita Karma is the vast collection of all karmas accumulated across countless past lives. It's like a warehouse filled with impressions and results of every action we've ever taken—stored, waiting. Most of this Karma remains dormant in the background, silently shaping the broader conditions of our birth, as well as our tendencies and inclinations.

Prarabdha Karma is the specific portion of Sanchita Karma that has ripened and is playing out in this lifetime. It includes the circumstances we are born into—our family, health, opportunities, and challenges. It's like an arrow already shot—it must complete its course. We cannot undo it, but we can choose how we walk through it. How we face our prarabdha—with resistance, fear, acceptance, or wisdom—makes all the difference in how it shapes us.

Agami Karma is the Karma we create in the present moment through our thoughts, words, actions, and intentions. It is the most immediate and decisive because it is in our hands. Through Agami Karma, we build the future, create new trajectories, and transform our inner world. It's like steering the wheel of a moving vehicle—even if we cannot change the road behind us, we can decide where to turn next.

By living consciously, aligning with dharma, and embracing the spirit of Karma Yoga, we cleanse the impact of past actions and plant seeds of clarity, peace, and higher evolution for what lies ahead.

As a Jyotish Shastra practitioner, I've seen how these karmic forces reveal themselves in people's lives. Carefully studying the birth chart—dashes, grahas, and bhavas—offers insights into challenges and inner strengths. But I've always chosen simplicity over extravagance when it comes to remedies.

Rather than suggesting expensive rituals or precious gemstones, I focus on what the person can do from within—because that's where true transformation happens.

For instance, if a chart indicates financial hardship, I often suggest acts of generosity, discipline in spending, or mindful service. These simple steps not only uplift the person but also begin to dissolve the karmic root of scarcity. Similarly, in cases of strained relationships, I recommend forgiveness, silent prayer, or practising gratitude. These shift the internal energy, which in turn transforms external dynamics.

Strengthening one's Agami Karma can soften the effects of difficult Prarabdha, and future Sanchita can be prevented from forming.

On a personal note, despite my deep involvement in astrology, I consciously avoid reading my chart or that of my close family. There are reasons for this decision:

First, I prefer to focus only on what is in my control. Much in life is shaped by prarabdha, and I've learned to trust the process instead of constantly trying to predict or alter it.

Second, I want to avoid planting seeds of fear. The mind has a way of latching onto possibilities, especially negative ones. Not knowing helps me stay steady and clear.

And most importantly, I surrender to the divine will. I walk with the faith that my Gurudev and Ishta Devata will guide me through all karmic tides. That trust, for me, is more critical than any astrological insight.

When understood spiritually, each type of Karma has its lesson. Sanchita teaches humility—it reminds us of the vast unseen weight we carry. Prarabdha teaches surrender and resilience—it asks us to walk with grace. Agami offers empowerment—the reminder that right now, in this very moment, we hold the key to our evolution.

Even if we cannot rewrite the past, we can shape the present. In doing so, we transform the future, not just ours but also that of those connected to us.

Arjuna's dilemma on the battlefield of Kurukshetra perfectly reflects our human confusion. Faced with a difficult duty—one filled with emotional conflict and moral uncertainty—he hesitates. What if his actions cause harm? What if his Karma traps him further? In response, Sri Krishna introduces the key principle of Nishkaam Karma—action without attachment to results.

From the Bhagavad Gita (3.9):

यज्ञार्थात्कर्मणोऽन्यत्र लोकोऽयं कर्मबन्धनः।

तदर्थं कर्म कौन्तेय मुक्तसङ्गः समाचर।।

"Action performed as a sacrifice for the divine does not bind. But action done with selfish desire causes bondage. Therefore, perform your duty with detachment, O Arjuna."

This verse embodies the essence of Karma Yoga: Karma becomes a bondage only when it is tied to selfish motives. When offered as yajna—a selfless offering—it becomes a path to liberation.

Sakam Karma, or desire-driven action, generates vasanas—deep impressions—that bind the soul to cycles of rebirth. Every action with longing or ego leaves behind a residue, reinforcing identity and attachment. This is the fuel of samsara.

Nishkaam Karma, on the other hand, purifies the mind. When we act without expecting results, our focus shifts inward. The act becomes meditation. It prepares us for jnana—actual knowledge—which ultimately leads to moksha, liberation.

In the Bhagavad Gita (9.27), Krishna says:

यत्करोषि यदश्नासि यज्जुहोषि ददासि यत्।

यत्तपस्यसि कौन्तेय तत्कुरुष्व मदर्पणम्।।

"Whatever you do—whether eating, offering, giving, or practising austerity-do—do it as an offering to Me."

This single teaching transforms all life into sadhana. When done with surrender and reverence, washing dishes, managing a business, and raising children become spiritual acts.

To walk this path, three internal shifts are needed:

- Perspective: See even small tasks as service to the divine or life itself.
- Intention: Let the motive be pure, not driven by fear, pride, or ambition.
- Surrender: Offer the fruits of your work without clinging to outcomes.

Karma Yoga is not an abstract ideal. It is a practice. One lived moment to moment. It is not about renouncing the world—it is about engaging with the world without being consumed by it.

Swami Vivekananda beautifully encapsulates this in *The Complete Works of Swami Vivekananda*. He writes that repeated actions and thoughts shape our character. Every ripple, every choice, matters.

"Each action or thought is like a ripple in the vast ocean of life. The more we act with awareness and discipline, the more we shape our character into a force for good."

Character is not fixed—it is forged in fire, shaped by consistency. And Karma is the hammer.

The difference between work and duty lies in the intent behind it. Work, done out of necessity or desire, can bind. But when it becomes dharma—a calling from the soul—it transforms. Krishna says in the Gita (18.47):

श्रेयान्स्वधर्मो विगुणः परधर्मात्स्वनुष्ठितात्।
स्वधर्मे निधनं श्रेयः परधर्मो भयावहः।।

"Better to do one's duty imperfectly than another's perfectly. Death in one's dharma is better than fear in someone else's."

Swadharma is not just our job or social role—it's our unique inner alignment. Living from that place, even if clumsy, is more sacred than walking another's path with perfection but no soul.

Vivekananda's teachings brought this alive for me. Karma Yoga, as he taught, is not about giving up action but about giving up attachment. It's not about being passive, but about being peaceful in action.

If done with awareness, every gesture becomes a spiritual one. Selflessness is the hidden altar on which these actions are offered. That's why, in Karma Yoga, the smallest service becomes divine.

Now, let's gently explore how this can be applied in real life, not just as a philosophy but as a practical application.

Begin each action with a pure and selfless intent. Serve without expectation. Reflect regularly—does this action align with my deeper values? Even a thank you should not be expected.

These aren't just ideals. They are tools for fundamental transformation. Karma Yoga teaches us that every act, no matter how small, has the potential to bring us closer to the divine when performed with humility, sincerity, and a sense of surrender.

The Bhagavad Gita teaches the same. Action isn't for personal gain but as an offering. In this offering, we find freedom.

The Isha Upanishad echoes this truth:

कुर्वन्नेवेह कर्माणि जिजीविषेच्छतं समाः।

एवं त्वयि नान्यथेतोऽस्ति न कर्म लिप्यते नरे।

"One should desire to live a hundred years doing one's duties. Only then can one live untouched by Karma."

So the goal is not to escape work, but to do it rightly, with the right bhava, and free of craving.

This is also what Krishna tells Arjuna during the Great War, right when the warrior's heart breaks. He tells him:

"Perform your duty, O Arjuna, with evenness of mind, abandoning attachment to success or failure. That evenness is Yoga."

This isn't limited to war. It's relevant to us when the heart hesitates, unsure if the action is right. Krishna's call is simple: act, but act without fear, without grasping at anything.

Swami Vivekananda brought this truth to life with a story that deeply touched me, and I'd like to share it now in my own words.

After years of meditation in isolation, a monk sat under a tree. Two birds fought above, and leaves fell. Annoyed, he glared at the birds—and they burned to ashes. Shocked by his newfound power, pride crept in.

Later, he went to beg for food. At one house, a woman asked him to wait calmly. His ego flared—how dare she? Her voice came from inside, "I'm not a bird you can burn."

Startled, he asked how she knew. She said her wisdom came not from austerity, but from sincere and selfless service. She sent him to a butcher to learn more.

The monk went, hesitant. But the butcher greeted him kindly, finished his work with complete dedication, and served his ageing parents lovingly. When they finally spoke, the butcher shared that spirituality lies in doing one's duty with love, humility, and detachment, not as an escape from life.

That story melted my heart. It revealed that Karma Yoga is not about renouncing responsibility but transforming it into worship. We grow not by withdrawing but by offering.

The woman and the butcher showed that:
- Dharma is living your truth, no matter how small or unrecognised the role may seem.

- Ego blocks growth, while humility opens the heart to divine knowledge.
- Work is sacred when it is done with love.
- Unattachment is not detachment but loving without expectation.

This story shaped how I see Karma Yoga, and I cannot emphasise enough how much it shifted my perspective. If this touches something within you, I urge you to read *Swami Vivekananda's The Complete Book of Yoga*. Its wisdom cannot be replicated—it must be experienced.

Even nature teaches the principles of Karma Yoga in profound ways. Consider the emperor penguin.

In the merciless cold of Antarctica, the female lays a single egg and carefully passes it to the male. He hoists the egg on his feet, covered with a flap of skin, and stands motionless through blizzards for two months, without food, while the female travels far to hunt and bring food back.

He doesn't complain; he doesn't walk away. He simply endures in love for life. He doesn't ask whether the chick will survive. He offers everything he has to fulfil his role.

That is Karma Yoga. Silent, still, enduring, and pure. No ego. No applause. Just the sacred fire of devotion and dharma.

In contrast, humans, blessed with free will, often seek convenience. Yet our choices can mirror the penguin's unwavering purpose if we align them with a conscious and service-oriented mindset.

So here is a simple practice I invite you to try:

Each night, reflect and write down three actions you performed during the day. Then ask:

- What was my real intention—selfless or self-seeking?
- How did it make me feel—light or burdened?

- If I had to do it again, would I make a different choice?

This small exercise is a mirror for the soul. It doesn't judge—it simply reveals. And with revelation comes realignment. Life doesn't give us a reverse button. We all have moments we wish we could undo. But Karma Yoga gives us something better—the power to move forward with awareness, to live gently, consciously, and meaningfully, and to leave fewer regrets and more love behind.

As you close this chapter, I invite you to embrace Karma Yoga not as a theory but as a way of life. Act with sincerity. Align with your truth. Let go of the result. That is the path, not of perfection but of conscious progress. Walk it with humility. Walk it with your heart.

3.5 Chatur Yoga Marg: The Fourfold Path of Yoga

In the previous chapter, we explored Karma Yoga—the yoga of action, which deeply resonates with householders navigating worldly life. But the spiritual vision of Sanatana Dharma extends far beyond a single path. It presents seekers with a rich, interwoven tapestry of disciplines, all pointing toward the same goal: the union of the Atman (individual soul) with Brahman (the Universal Soul).

Before diving deeper into these core ideas, I offer heartfelt gratitude to Swami Vivekananda Ji, whose clarity illuminated these timeless paths for modern minds.

Yogic philosophy teaches that the root cause of human suffering is avidyā—ignorance or forgetfulness of our True Self. This forgetfulness arises from three impurities of the mind, as described in Vedanta:

Mala: The impurity of selfishness and ego creates a false sense of separation.

Vikshepa: The restless, scattered nature of the mind—the infamous "monkey mind."

Avarana: The veils of ignorance that block awareness of our divine nature.

The Four Paths of Yoga—Karma, Bhakti, Raja, and Jñāna—are time-tested methods for dissolving these impurities and rediscovering oneness with all life. Each path addresses a particular tendency of the human condition, offering seekers a way to evolve through their nature.

Karma Yoga: The Path of Action

For those drawn to action and service, Karma Yoga purifies the heart by burning away mala. This path teaches us to act selflessly without clinging to outcomes. We move beyond the ego's demands by aligning our actions with divine will.

In Karma Yoga, even simple acts—such as feeding the hungry, caring for loved ones, or helping a stranger—can become sacred when they are offered without expectation. The beauty of this path is its accessibility; daily life becomes the field of spiritual practice. Mother Teresa remains a glowing example of a Karma Yogi whose entire life was an offering of selfless love.

Bhakti Yoga: The Path of Devotion

Bhakti Yoga is the path of love and surrender to the Divine. For those with soft, emotional hearts, Bhakti transforms longing into liberation. It softens the ego and awakens a sense of connection to all beings.

Devotional practices like kirtan, mantra chanting, puja, and heartfelt prayer are central here. Even everyday actions can be Bhakti when offered with love to one's Ishta Devata (personal deity). Cooking a meal or sweeping a floor can become acts of devotion. In Bhakti, no task is too small when filled with remembrance.

Raja Yoga: The Path of Meditation

Raja Yoga, also known as the royal path, is based on the Ashtanga Yoga system of Maharishi Patanjali. It addresses vikshepa—the restless and distracted state of the mind—by teaching inner control and stillness.

This path involves ethical observances (yamas and niyamas), pranayama (breath control), concentration, and, ultimately, meditation. For seekers who value structure and discipline, Raja Yoga provides a system for moving from chaos to calm, from external chatter to inner silence.

In today's world, even simple techniques like mindful breathing or mantra repetition can help centre the mind. Raja Yoga is for those ready to turn inward with discipline and depth.

Jñāna Yoga: The Path of Wisdom

Jñāna Yoga is the path of self-inquiry and higher knowledge. It is meant for naturally reflective, contemplative, and intellectually inclined seekers. This path targets avarana—the deepest layer of ignorance—by piercing it with the sword of discernment.

Through listening (śravaṇa), contemplation (manana), and meditative absorption (nididhyāsana), the seeker peels back illusion and comes face to face with the Truth: the Atman is none other than Brahman.

The key inquiry on this path is, "Who am I?" The answer is not a concept but a direct realisation that shatters false identity.

Although these four paths appear distinct, they are never isolated. They blend naturally. A Karma Yogi may experience Bhakti through love, a Raja Yogi may gain flashes of Jñāna in silence, and a Bhakta may begin serving through Karma. Each path supports the others, forming a holistic journey.

The Fourfold Path is not a rigid division but a graceful unfolding. It meets the seeker where they are—emotionally, mentally, and temperamentally—and gently guides them toward the same goal: liberation from the cycle of birth and death and reunion with the Self.

With this foundational understanding, we can explore how these paths intersect with other dimensions of spiritual philosophy, especially Ashtanga Yoga, which complements them beautifully. Let us continue this journey together.

Reflecting on my spiritual path, I find it impossible to walk just one. My practices have naturally woven together the threads of Karma, Bhakti, Raja, and Jñāna Yoga, creating an evolved harmony. I believe this integration unfolds uniquely for every seeker.

As a householder, Karma Yoga forms the foundation of my path. The principles of selfless action, which I've discussed earlier, shape my daily life and help me perceive divinity in even the most minor duties. But my journey does not end with action—it begins there.

Bhakti Yoga holds a special place in my heart. My Guru and Ishta Devata have guided me through this path of surrender and love. Bhakti has deepened my spiritual connection and offered comfort in moments of doubt. It reminds me, again and again, of the presence of grace and the sacred bond I share with the Divine.

My evolving awareness brought me closer to Raja Yoga, especially its contemplative practices. The eight limbs of Ashtanga Yoga have begun to shape my spiritual discipline. Though a beginner, I can feel their power to calm the mind and prepare the inner space for deeper self-inquiry.

Jñāna Yoga remains the most distant path for me. Its rigorous self-inquiry and discernment require a depth of intellectual stillness I have not yet cultivated. But I don't see this as a shortcoming. I trust it will unfold when the time is right, just as the other paths did.

One of the most humbling lessons I've received is that seekers don't need to choose their path consciously. It reveals itself, often silently, when the inner soil is ready. Whether Karma, Bhakti, Raja, or Jñāna Yoga, the one meant for you will draw you in, often guided by your Guru or Ishta Devata.

I still remember the early days of my seeking. I was curious, open, and hungry for meaning. Among the many paths I came across, Kriya Yoga stood out—its promise of inner transformation and higher states of consciousness stirred something within me. I was first introduced to the idea through a sacred book that is revered by seekers around the world. Though the path intrigued me, the depth of the practice felt distant and overwhelming at the time. I was just beginning, unsure where to go, constantly asking myself, "What next?"

Yet, as I've shared earlier in this book, life unfolds with divine precision. My path eventually led me to my Gurudev, who illuminated Bhakti Yoga. The way it all came together—the timing, the setting, the inner pull—was too aligned to be mere coincidence. I now understand it as divine grace, nudging me exactly where I needed to be.

Spirituality is never rigid. It is fluid, like a river that changes course but always flows toward the ocean. All four paths inevitably intersect.

For most seekers, the paths blend naturally, even unconsciously, enriching life from multiple directions.

At a particular stage, one path may dominate—not by effort but by inner necessity. That shift is not a decision of the intellect but of the soul. When it happens, the choice isn't ours anymore. It's the Divine choosing through us.

The convergence of these paths is a testament to the inclusiveness of Sanatana Dharma. Whether you resonate most with Karma, Bhakti, Raja, or Jñāna—or a blend of them all—know that your journey is unfolding perfectly. Walk it with sincerity, humility, and openness, and you will find that each step brings you closer to the eternal Truth that awaits within.

Let this understanding inspire you to embrace the richness of all yogic paths, knowing that they all lead to the same eternal destination: unity with the Divine.

For those seeking to discover their path among the four yogas—Karma, Bhakti, Raja, and Jñāna—I offer reflections based on personal experience, guided by the grace of my guru.

In the early stages of the journey, it's not necessary to dissect which path is the "right" one. Trying to decide intellectually often brings confusion or pressure. Instead, approach your search with an open heart and a willingness to surrender. Allow life—and the grace of your Guru or Ishta Devata—to unfold the answer.

In my case, I wasn't consciously seeking the correct path. I didn't sit and ask, "Should I walk the path of Karma or Bhakti?" My journey wasn't deliberate but intuitive—led by unseen hands rather than my calculations.

As shared earlier in this book, my life unfolded in a way that brought me to my Gurudev. I didn't plan it; it simply happened. I surrendered—with hope, faith, and no expectations. That surrender didn't come all at once. There were moments of resistance, complaint, and doubt, but even those moments were part of the process.

Surrender doesn't mean giving up; it means opening yourself to something greater than your ego. It means trusting the process, even when the path ahead seems uncertain.

This is much like meditation. Beginners often struggle with thoughts, and they're advised, "Don't fight them. Just notice, and gently return to the breath." Discovering your path works similarly. At first, you'll encounter many influences—some you'll resonate with, others you won't. You can try different practices, stick with some for a while, and then move on. That's natural. What matters is that you observe with patience, not judgment.

Your path gradually becomes clearer. For me, it was the presence of my Gurudev that illuminated Bhakti Yoga as my core practice. But this was not a conscious decision—it was a result of surrender and grace.

I'll share my practical steps in Part Two of the book in Section 5 *'Grihastha Sādhana: Spiritual Practice in Daily Life.'* These aren't just ideas; they're lived experiences. I hope they serve as both inspiration and guidance. Whether you're starting or deepening your journey, these practices will show how devotion and discipline work together.

This path is so compassionate because it doesn't require perfection. It welcomes you precisely as you are. You grow into it—gradually, organically. Your path is not something you must find; it finds you.

So I offer this: begin where you are. If a service calls to you, start there. Follow that impulse if you feel drawn to chant, meditate, or reflect. Be sincere. Let the Divine take care of the rest.

Eventually, your Gurudev or Ishta Devata will clear the way, just as mine did. Until then, walk with trust, curiosity, and an open heart. The journey itself is the destination, and every step brings you closer to yourself.

At this point, sharing the profound wisdom in our sacred scriptures is essential. These timeless teachings offer inspiration and clarity for the logical mind. And if you find specific ideas challenging to accept right now, that's perfectly alright. The mind is meant to question and evolve. This gradual unfolding is part of the path.

I'll draw from the Vedas, Upanishads, and other foundational texts to support your understanding. The Four Paths of Yoga—Karma, Bhakti, Raja, and Jñāna—are all deeply rooted in Sanatana Dharma, illuminated in the Bhagavad Gita, Upanishads, and other sacred works. Each is enriched by teachings, shlokas, and stories that have guided seekers for millennia.

The Bhagavad Gita presents Karma Yoga as a means to liberation through selfless action. In his dialogue with Arjuna, Bhagavan Krishna offers a powerful teaching:

Bhagavad Gita (Chapter 3, Verse 19):

"तस्मादसक्तः सततं कार्यं कर्म समाचर।

असक्तो ह्याचरन्कर्म परमाप्नोति पूरुषः॥"

"Therefore, without attachment, do your work as a matter of duty, for by working without attachment, one attains the Supreme."

This verse captures the essence of Karma Yoga—performing one's duty without expectation, aligning one's actions with divine will. Arjuna's inner conflict becomes the field upon which Krishna reveals that the right action becomes a sacred offering when detached from the outcome.

Bhakti Yoga expresses itself most deeply in complete surrender to the Divine. The Gita speaks of this beautifully:

Bhagavad Gita (Chapter 9, Verse 34):

"मन्मना भव मद्भक्तो मद्याजी मां नमस्कुरु।

मामेवैष्यसि सत्यं ते प्रतिजाने प्रियोऽसि मे॥"

"Fix your mind on Me, be devoted to Me, worship Me, and bow to Me. In this way, you will certainly come to me. I promise you this because you are dear to me."

The Gopis' unwavering love for Krishna symbolises the highest expression of Bhakti. Their surrender was so total that they transcended all limitations, embodying divine love. Ras Leela is a poetic metaphor for this union—Jiva merging into Paramatma.

Raja Yoga, rooted in discipline and meditation, is systematised through Patanjali's Ashtanga system. Its essence is captured in the Yoga Sutras:

Yoga Sutra 1.2:

"योगश्चित्तवृत्तिनिरोधः।"

"Yoga is the cessation of the fluctuations of the mind."

Sage Vishwamitra's journey illustrates the challenges and triumphs of Raja Yoga. Despite setbacks, his persistence in meditation ultimately led him to become a Brahmarshi.

Jñāna Yoga, the path of inquiry and discernment, leads the seeker toward Self-realization. The कठोपनिषद् offers this insight:

कठोपनिषद् | Verse 15:

"सर्वे वेदा यत्पदमामनन्ति तपांसि सर्वाणि च यद्वदन्ति।

यदिच्छन्तो ब्रह्मचर्यं चरन्ति तत्ते पदं संग्रहेण ब्रवीम्योमित्येतत्॥"

"The ultimate goal that all the Vedas extol, that all austerities proclaim, and desiring which people lead a life of Brahmacharya, I will tell you in brief—it is Om."

In the Brihadaranyaka Upanishad, Yajnavalkya's conversation with Maitreyi reveals that immortality is attained through possessions and knowledge of the Self.

Each of these paths stands distinct yet interconnected. As Bhagavan Krishna affirms:

Bhagavad Gita (Chapter 4, Verse 11):

"ये यथा मां प्रपद्यन्ते तांस्तथैव भजाम्यहम्।

मम वर्त्मानुवर्तन्ते मनुष्याः पार्थ सर्वशः॥"

"In whatever way people approach me, I reciprocate accordingly. Everyone follows my path in all respects, O son of Pritha."

This verse affirms that all spiritual paths ultimately converge. A seeker may favour one path, but inevitably, all four touch the heart in different moments, shaping a unified journey toward the Divine.

These shlokas, teachings, and stories don't just describe the four paths—they bring them alive. They show how each path can guide a seeker inward, aligning life with eternal Truth and divine harmony.

Though Karma, Bhakti, Jñāna, and Raja Yoga differ in method and mood, they all lead to self-realisation and union with the Divine. They reflect the diverse temperaments and circumstances of seekers, yet their essence remains the same. To understand how these paths can be more structured, we turn to Ashtanga Yoga as outlined by Maharishi Patanjali. While the Four Paths offer broad approaches to spiritual life, Ashtanga Yoga presents a systematic framework for harmonising body, mind, and spirit. This practical path complements and deepens the insights of the Four.

Ashtanga means "eight limbs" (अष्टाङ्ग), symbolising eight integrated steps that guide the seeker inward, from ethical living to complete absorption in the Self.

More than a checklist, Ashtanga Yoga is a unified methodology—purifying the body, mind, and soul through gradual, inward progress. These are the eight limbs:

Yamas (Restraints)

These ethical foundations regulate our relationship with the outer world, cultivating peace and reducing inner conflict:

- Ahimsa (Non-violence): Kindness in thought, word, and deed.
- Satya (Truthfulness): Honesty with integrity.
- Asteya (Non-stealing): Avoiding what isn't ours—tangible or subtle.
- Brahmacharya (Moderation): Channelling energy through restraint.
- Aparigraha (Non-possessiveness): Letting go of attachments and greed.

These principles support a life of simplicity and moral strength, reducing karmic burden and anchoring us in Dharma.

Niyamas (Observances)

Focusing inward, the Niyamas cultivate personal discipline and self-reflection:

- Shaucha (Cleanliness): Purity in body, thoughts, and emotions.
- Santosha (Contentment): Inner peace regardless of conditions.
- Tapas (Discipline): Willingness to undergo difficulty for spiritual growth.
- Svadhyaya (Self-study): Studying scriptures and the Self with sincerity.
- Ishvarapranidhana (Surrender): Offering all actions to the Divine, trusting its guidance.

Together, Yamas and Niyamas create a holistic foundation for harmony with the world and oneself.

Asana (Posture)

Contrary to the modern obsession with physical feats, Patanjali defines asana as a steady and comfortable seat for meditation. It supports inner stillness and focus, not performance.

Pranayama (Breath Control)

By regulating breath, we influence prana, our vital energy. Pranayama stills the mind, deepens presence, and bridges body and spirit.

Pratyahara (Sense Withdrawal)

Rather than suppressing the senses, Pratyahara gently redirects attention inward. It quiets external noise, allowing the mind to withdraw from distractions.

Dharana (Concentration)

With the senses turned inward, dharana trains the mind on a single point, such as breath, a mantra, or a form. It prepares the seeker for deeper absorption.

Dhyana (Meditation)

Dhyana is a sustained, effortless focus. The mind flows in unbroken contemplation, softening the boundaries between the seeker and the object of meditation.

Samadhi (Absorption)

In Samadhi, duality dissolves. The seeker becomes one with the object of meditation—pure awareness, untouched by ego, aligned with the Divine.

The beauty of Ashtanga Yoga lies in its holistic nature, connecting external discipline with inner transformation. The first four limbs—Yama, Niyama, Asana, and Pranayama—build a strong ethical and physical foundation. The remaining four—Pratyahara, Dharana, Dhyana, and Samadhi—are inward-focused, leading toward spiritual realisation.

Ashtanga Yoga becomes a practical roadmap, unifying these steps into a single spiritual discipline. It honours the systematic and personal nature of inner evolution and accommodates each seeker's unique rhythm.

Engaging with the eight limbs has been grounding and humbling in my journey. To be honest, I haven't yet fully entered the realm of

Pratyahara—the withdrawal of senses beyond their influence. My current efforts remain rooted in aligning with the foundational limbs, particularly the Yamas and Niyamas.

Living the Yamas and Niyamas feels like tuning into the cosmic rhythm. They aren't rules but guiding principles that bring clarity and direction. Practising Ahimsa (non-violence) and Satya (truthfulness) has transformed me. Each conscious choice to live by these values creates a quiet inner shift—a subtle but sacred alignment with something beyond myself.

At present, I am advancing toward the final level of a four-stage journey in the path of becoming a Yoga master. Having already completed three foundational and intermediate stages rooted in traditional Hatha Yoga and classical texts, I now find myself deepening into the final, most refined stage of this discipline. This is not for titles or recognition, but to honour a sankalpa I hold dearly—to make this body a sacred vessel of awareness, discipline, and selfless service. Alongside my work in Astrology and Numerology under Sri Hari Vedic Life, this Yogic path feels like yet another divine unfolding, guided by grace and anchored in sincere effort.

At Sri Hari Vedic Life, my core intention is transformation—not only my own but that of those who walk this path with me. Learning is not an occasional pursuit; it's my primary practice. It feeds both my evolution and the way I serve. Every lesson deepens my humility. Time and again, I return to the Truth that the only thing I truly know is that I know nothing. That awareness protects me from my ego, keeping me anchored and open.

This philosophy is the soul of Sri Hari Vedic Life. I am a lifelong student of life, spirituality, and the sacred sciences. With each step, my learning enriches my ability to guide others, allowing for an authentic, heart-level connection. I meet every seeker not as a teacher but as a fellow traveller.

Though I've taken yoga courses before, I now aspire to go beyond the basics—to live yoga as a way of being, not just through concepts, but through embodied Truth in harmony with divine principles.

As for which limb is most impactful, I don't believe one can be singled out. These limbs are not isolated practices but interwoven steps of one ascending path. Skipping or selectively practising them rarely works. Each one supports the next. Actual growth flows naturally when approached with sincerity and patience.

What I've come to realise is that the journey itself is the transformation. It's not about achieving perfection but allowing grace to guide us forward. The most crucial step is simply beginning. Yoga isn't just a physical or mental exercise—it's an invitation for the Self to meet the Self.

When you begin this journey, your body or identity does not take centre stage—it is your true Self. And in that unveiling, the beauty of yoga truly shines.

If you live a worldly life filled with responsibilities and challenges and wish to include Ashtanga Yoga in your daily routine, let me assure you—it's possible and more straightforward than it seems. I've been where you are. The journey begins with small, meaningful steps. This is what this entire book is about—making spirituality practical and accessible for people like us.

For me, it began with the first two limbs: Yamas (restraints) and Niyamas (observances). I didn't aim for perfection. I lived by these principles, incorporating them into daily life. Over time, they began transforming not just my actions but my perspective. I've shared before—I am no longer who I once was. These practices shift something deep within. You start to see the world—and yourself—with more clarity and calm.

Once your foundation is set with Yamas and Niyamas, the next step is dedicating just 30 minutes a day to your body and mind. Start simple:

Fifteen minutes of gentle movement—basic asanas or even stretches. Complexity is unnecessary—the goal is to connect with your body and gradually strengthen it. Combine this with conscious breathing to centre yourself and build mindfulness.

Fifteen minutes of meditation—sit and observe your breath. You don't need to force stillness; just be present. If your mind wanders, gently bring it back to focus. Initially, 10–15 minutes is usually more than enough. Over time, you'll crave this quiet connection with your inner Self.

This is how my journey with Ashtanga Yoga began. These simple, intentional acts created ripples that touched every aspect of life. In Part Two of this book, which covers practical spirituality, I'll share specific tools and techniques that have helped me. But for now, prepare yourself mentally. Commit sincerely—not out of pressure, but from a genuine desire to grow. If your heart is open, the transformation will happen naturally.

Every spiritual practice begins with effort and commitment. That's where Ashtanga Yoga becomes such a robust foundation. It offers a structured, progressive system that prepares us for whatever yogic path we pursue. Ashtanga Yoga weaves through all disciplines, harmonising body, mind, and spirit, making it easier to walk the path of Karma, Bhakti, Jñāna, or Raja Yoga.

As I progressed in Ashtanga Yoga, I noticed quiet yet profound changes in my life. I felt myself aligning with Dharma and the timeless teachings of Sri Krishna. This alignment brought inner peace, one that was not dependent on outer success or validation, but something deep within. It felt like I was being gently guided, step by step, toward something more significant.

Take the practice of Ahimsa (non-violence) from the Yamas. At first, we think of it as avoiding harm to others. But as I explored it further, I saw how it also means not harming ourselves, our body or mind. It means releasing self-criticism, overthinking, and the burden of unnecessary stress. It's about honouring our limits with gentleness and compassion.

Practising Asanas taught me not to push beyond what the body allows. Forcing the body into postures that it isn't ready for only leads to harm. As Patanjali said, True Asana is meant to be steady and comfortable. With patience and consistency, strength and flexibility emerge naturally. For some, this takes weeks. For others, it takes months or years. And that's perfectly okay. Every journey is unique. We must honour our path with humility and grace.

This mindset naturally complements all Four Paths of Yoga. In Karma Yoga, the discipline of Ashtanga Yoga instils mindfulness and detachment in our actions. In Bhakti Yoga, the internalisation of Yamas and Niyamas deepens devotion and surrender. In Jñāna Yoga, practices like Pratyahara and Dharana sharpen self-inquiry. In Raja Yoga, Ashtanga is the roadmap for meditation and union.

Letting go of rigid expectations and embracing the process is essential. Whether drawn to one path or exploring many, Ashtanga Yoga offers a universal toolkit. It doesn't seek perfection—only sincere effort and consistency.

Spiritual growth is like a flower blooming on a tree branch—naturally, when the roots are nurtured. Learn the truths, unlearn the myths, and stay open to the grace that flows through practice. Ashtanga Yoga doesn't just support the Four Paths—it enhances them, creating an inner union that transforms the seeker from within.

My Gurudev once said something about meditation that has stayed with me: "It's not important how long you meditated, but how effective your meditation was." Even a moment of stillness is progress. The next time, it may last longer. Slowly, through persistence, the mind learns. This wisdom has anchored my Ashtanga practice, reminding me that growth is gradual and perfection is never the starting point.

When I started practising Ashtanga Yoga, I asked myself after each session, "Am I better than I was the day before?" I considered it a success if the answer was yes. Some days I couldn't hold a posture. On other days, my meditation wandered. But I returned to the basics, reviewed my mistakes, and tried again. This self-correction became a source of humility and strength.

Starting this practice in my late 30s wasn't easy. The body resists, and the mind is full of doubts. But I drew inspiration from people who began at 60 or later, yet showed unwavering dedication. Watching them, I realised that age is never the barrier—mindset is. If they could do it, so could I.

This practice isn't about achieving visible perfection. It's about staying committed. Some days bring progress, others feel stagnant. But showing up matters. Every effort is movement, even when the results aren't noticeable.

Ashtanga Yoga gave me a framework for life—a rhythm of doing, refining, and sharing. Whenever I reach a point of clarity, I feel the urge to share it. This learning, living, and guiding cycle keeps knowledge alive in me and those I serve.

My most transformative moments haven't come from significant milestones, but from quiet victories: the first time I held a challenging pose, sat in honest stillness with my breath, or felt my life aligning with the principles of yoga. These are the sparks that keep me going. And now, sharing them, I hope to kindle a spark in you.

So start where you are. Don't let ideas about age, ability, or time hold you back. Begin. Do, repeat, and improve. Stay open to the teachings this path reveals. The journey itself becomes the reward.

As this chapter concludes, some of you, especially those familiar with this topic, may feel we've only skimmed the surface. And that's true. These paths—whether the Four Yogas or Ashtanga's Eight Limbs—are oceans of depth. Entire scriptures and lifetimes have been devoted to exploring them. It's impossible, nor was it my intent, to capture all their wisdom here.

My purpose was simply to introduce their essence—ignite a spark within you and help you recognise their place in your life. If this spark leads you to dive into scriptures, seek guidance from true masters, or integrate these teachings meaningfully, this chapter has fulfilled its purpose. Real understanding doesn't come from reading volumes but from living the truths they offer.

SECTION 4:
SAMATTVA YOGA: BALANCING DUALITIES

4.1 Shraddha & Samarpan: Faith and Surrender

Faith is not just a concept—it is a lived experience, a force that breathes through every moment. It is unshakable knowing that someone, something, a force greater than anything in the three worlds, is watching over me, guiding and protecting me, testing me so I may rise.

I don't need a dictionary to define faith—my life defines it. Faith has been like a silent companion, not loudly announcing itself, but always present, lifting me when my strength fails, whispering through my doubts, and reminding me that I am never alone.

That "someone" may differ for each person. For some, it is their Ishta Devata; for others, the formless Divine; for many, it is their Guru who lights the path when all seems uncertain.

For me, it is my Gurudev. He is the bedrock of my faith. In his presence, doubt fades, burdens ease, and direction becomes clear.

No spiritual path—Karma, Bhakti, Raja, or Jnana Yoga—can be walked without faith. It is the invisible current that allows movement on the path.

Even Jnana Yoga, rooted in knowledge, begins with faith—that the Atman exists within, that it is a fragment of the Supreme, and that the questions "Who am I?" and "What is truth?" are worthy of pursuit.

Without faith, the first step is impossible.

I don't speak this from theory. I speak from life.

Everything about how I lived, thought, and perceived the world changed the day I placed unshakable faith in my Gurudev. It felt like stepping into a world where fear held no place because I knew—He was there. Why worry?

"Tum Rakshak Kahu Ko Darna?"

("If You are my protector, why should I fear?")

This is not just a verse—it's the pulse of my faith, a truth I live by. When we surrender to that higher presence, no storm can shake us.

But faith is not instantaneous. It doesn't arrive fully formed. It unfolds slowly with time.

Initially, my logical mind questioned, "How can I trust what I cannot see?" But then, I began noticing signs and answers from unexpected places. That's when I realised that faith is not blindness; it's a deeper view beyond the eyes.

And once faith begins to solidify, it is put to the test. Repeatedly.

It's as if the universe whispers, "Do you still trust, even now?"

Every time, I emerged stronger because I came to see those tests not as obstacles, but as training that refined me and shaped me for something greater.

Even now, I walk through these fires not to burn but to be purified. With each test—whether I pass or learn—I know one thing: I am being brought closer to my path.

This is faith.

And if you walk this path sincerely, you'll feel it, too. It will bloom in your heart, just as it did in mine, in its own time. Until then, keep walking. Keep believing. Know this—He is there. Always.

Faith and unquestioning belief are often confused. But the difference is profound, and knowing that difference protects the seeker.

In the early stages of the journey, the difference between faith and naive belief isn't always clear, not because of ignorance, but due to a lack of inner clarity. When the longing for truth awakens, the heart becomes eager to grasp anything that feels like an answer. In that eagerness, it's easy to confuse faith with unquestioning belief.

I've never been someone who could unquestioningly believe in something unseen. My mind has always questioned and always sought clarity. That nature protected me from falling into unquestioning belief, but I've seen many around me struggle with this confusion.

That's why I feel called to speak on it—you might face it, too.

I don't want to give you a theoretical or scriptural explanation. I want to offer something practical that helped me make this distinction.

The first and most important thing I would tell any seeker is to learn to listen to your heart.

Even science now acknowledges the power of intuition—what we've always known as the "gut feeling." But long before science gave it a name, our Rishis taught us:

"The heart is the seat of the Atman. The Atman knows the path because it is already connected to the Divine."

The challenge is that we don't know how to listen. Our minds are too noisy and filled with doubts, fears, and the constant hum of external influences. That's why so many fall into unquestioning belief—they haven't yet learned to separate what's real from what only appears.

So, how do you know your faith is genuine and not blind?

Faith is selfless. Naive belief is transactional.

Faith doesn't ask for anything. It invites Surrender, patience and sincerity.

Unquestioning belief, however, often comes with demands, conditions, or hidden agendas.

Here's a simple check:

If you follow a path, teacher, or tradition, ask yourself, "What is being expected from me?"

If the answer is sincerity, discipline, or devotion, it's faith.

But if you feel pressured by constant monetary demands or obligations that don't feel right, pause and take a moment to observe. I'm not saying teachers shouldn't receive offerings or fees. That's not the point. The point is the intention behind it.

Imagine millions of seekers like you, each being asked the same thing. Multiply that expectation. Then ask:

"Does this still feel pure?"

"Is this truly a path to freedom—or just another transaction in the name of spirituality?"

Your heart will know.

People often ask me, "What if I don't have a Guru yet? How do I avoid blind belief?"

I always say—let Mahadev be your first Guru.

Pray to Him. Surrender to Him. Ask only this: that your faithful Guru finds you when the time is right.

That's what I did. And by His grace, I was protected from paths that weren't meant for me.

If I were to distil this entire message into one truth, it would be:

Faith empowers. Unquestioning belief entraps.

Faith frees you, grounds you, and aligns you with the truth.

Naive belief binds you to fear, dependency, and illusion.

So, as you walk this path, hold that distinction close. Whenever in doubt, seek Mahadev's guidance. He never leaves a sincere seeker unanswered.

Coming to surrender, if you asked me when surrender transformed my life, I'd tell you—it wasn't a moment. I don't "practice" surrender. I live it.

Every breath, thought, and action—I exist in Surrender.

To some, that may sound lofty or unattainable. But I'm not here to say what pleases. I'm here to speak my truth.

People often say Surrender is difficult. And I agree—but I also don't.

It feels challenging when you're still holding onto control, thinking, "I am the doer, the one in charge of my life." But the moment you realise you are never in control, to begin with, Surrender becomes the simplest thing in the world.

I first truly understood Surrender when I read *I Am That* by Sri Nisargadatta Maharaj. It didn't just introduce me to a new idea—it shattered my sense of 'I'. We live believing, "I am this body, this mind, this identity." However, even identifying with body and mind is an illusion on the spiritual path. The ego—this deep identification—is what blocks surrender.

You cannot surrender fully until you rise beyond this attachment.

That's why I return to this point again—because this is where true Surrender begins. It's not only about letting go of control; it's about letting go of the self-image we cling to. The "you" attached to a name, form, thought, and worldly role must dissolve.

For me, Surrender didn't come through effort. It came naturally, as grace. A blessing from my Gurudev.

When I stopped identifying with my ego self, Surrender happened. Not just as a disciple bowing to his Master, but also as one who realised nothing was left to hold onto. The one who surrenders is no longer "me" as a separate being but "me" as That.

This may seem abstract or difficult to grasp. But without breaking through the *Avarana*, the veil of ignorance, complete Surrender remains distant.

You may ask, "If Surrender is so transformative, how do I do it? How do I let go of ego?"

The answer is—you don't surrender. It happens. When resistance drops, the need to control fades, and the illusion of separateness dissolves; it arises independently.

But until it happens naturally, here's what you can do:

Flow with life. Let go of the need to shape every outcome. Don't fight circumstances. Just walk with awareness.

Watch your mind. It will resist—because it feeds on control. Observe that resistance without reacting.

Hope, but don't expect. Hope opens the heart; expectation binds it. Hope surrenders. Expectation clings.

Detach from results. Do your part, give what you can, and then let go. When attachment dissolves, Surrender begins.

The moment you surrender, you are free.

The biggest illusion is that we were ever in control. When you realise you are simply an instrument of the Divine, Surrender becomes effortless. In that Surrender, there is peace. There is liberation.

Don't overthink it. Let it unfold.

And when it does, surrender won't be something you practice—it will be something you live.

Surrender is often misunderstood. People think it means giving up, becoming passive, or abandoning life's duties. But that's a mistake.

Surrender isn't inaction—it's acting with complete trust in the Divine. It's not escaping responsibility—it's fulfilling it with detachment. It's not weakness—the most incredible strength- the ability to trust without fear.

For me, Surrender is not a practice. It is the way I live. It's in my thoughts, my words, my breath. It's how I exist.

When people hear about Surrender, they often ask, "How can someone reach this stage? What does it look like in daily life?"

Many friends, relatives, and even close family don't know about my spiritual journey. Because Surrender isn't something to be displayed or proven—it's an inner transformation. It quietly reshapes how you see life. You still wake up, work, and fulfil responsibilities. You still face challenges and uncertainties. But now, you no longer carry their weight.

You trust a higher force guiding each step, protecting you, and unfolding life exactly as it's meant to. So, you stop resisting. You stop forcing outcomes. You still act, but your actions become offerings to the Divine, not efforts for personal gain. You still face hardships, but with trust, not fear. You still experience uncertainty without being shaken, because you know you're held.

People think Surrender means doing less, pulling back, or becoming passive. But it's quite the opposite. On the path of truth, your work deepens, your responsibilities grow, and the burden disappears.

Now, your efforts aren't for success—they're for seva. Your work isn't for recognition—it's for dharma. And you stop obsessing over results because you understand they're not yours to control.

In today's world, we've forgotten who we are. We've become so attached to the body, the mind, and the idea of "I" that Surrender feels foreign—even impossible. But this isn't our true nature.

We were once so close to the Divine. Surrender was natural. Over time, as distractions grew, we drifted away. We began to think we had to control everything. That we must fight, resist, and take charge.

But Surrender isn't something new to learn—it's something ancient to remember. It's a return to our original state, a space where we trust more than we control, flow more than we force, and offer more than we expect.

That's why I always say that Surrender is not something I do. It is how I live. It's not a moment, not a declaration. It's not saying, "From now on, I surrender."

It's a process. A rhythm. A breath-by-breath letting go.

Some days, you'll struggle. Some days, you'll want to hold on again. But with every minor release, you'll trust a little more. And one day, without realising it, you'll look back and see—you've already surrendered. And that day, you'll be free.

At this point, I wish to introduce the final Niyama from Patanjali's Yoga Sutras: Ishvara Pranidhana. This is not just another spiritual term—it is the essence of Surrender, devotion, and trust.

For many, faith and Surrender may seem abstract, idealistic, and out of reach. But Ishvara Pranidhana grounds them. However, they transform surrender into a living practice, a way of being.

It is not passive or weak. It is conscious, active, and total Surrender. It is a realisation that there is a higher force—a divine intelligence, a cosmic rhythm—call it Ishwar, Brahman, Supreme Consciousness, or simply Life.

Once you truly understand this, you stop resisting, stop struggling for control, and no longer fight what is unfolding. You begin to flow, align, and surrender.

In Patanjali's Yoga Sutras, Ishvara Pranidhana is the final Niyama—the ultimate step. Master this, and nothing else remains. Why? When you fully trust the Divine and let go completely, your entire being becomes prayer. Every action, thought, and breath becomes an offering.

The Sanskrit term comprises Ishwara, which means Supreme Being, and Absolute Pranidhana, which means Surrender, devotion, and offering. Together, they mean complete surrender to the Divine.

But don't mistake this for renunciation or retreat. Ishvara Pranidhana is not about abandoning life. It is about embracing it fully, with every thought and action offered forward. It's not about doing less—it's about doing everything, but with Surrender.

Now, you may wonder, "Isn't this just faith?" Not exactly.

Faith is belief—trusting that the Divine exists and that a higher plan is in motion. Ishvara Pranidhana is beyond belief. It is the act of placing everything—your efforts, emotions, outcomes—into divine hands. It's not just trusting the river, but jumping in and letting it carry you. It's not just believing in fire, but walking through it without fear.

Faith is trust. Ishvara Pranidhana is union. It is offering yourself entirely—without fear, hesitation, or conditions.

Surrender is not doing anything. It is doing your best, but without fear. Acting—but without attachment. Facing life, but without resistance.

So, how does it look in daily life?

When you work hard but let go of anxiety about the outcome, that is Ishvara Pranidhana.

When you love someone deeply but don't try to control them, that is Ishvara Pranidhana.

When you accept loss without resentment, that is Ishvara Pranidhana.

When you achieve success but stay unattached, that too is Ishvara Pranidhana.

It is the highest form of action, free of fear, ego, or craving.

As the Bhagavad Gita teaches: "Whatever you do, whatever you eat, whatever you offer in sacrifice, whatever you give, whatever austerities you perform—do that as an offering to Me."

This is the heart of Ishvara Pranidhana: to live as if every act is a sacred offering, as if you are a vessel of divine will.

In meditation, it means sitting in silence without chasing any outcome.

In prayer, it means not asking, just bowing in love.

The next time you sit before your Gurudev or Bhagavān, remember:

You have nothing to give in the worldly sense.

But you have everything to surrender.

Ego. Anger. Lust. Laziness. Pride. Expectation.

These are the real offerings — and the only ones they truly await.

As Bhagavān Śrī Kṛṣṇa says in the Bhagavad Gītā (13.8–12):

अमानित्वमदम्भित्वमहिंसा क्षान्तिरार्जवम् ।

आचार्योपासनं शौचं स्थैर्यमात्मविनिग्रहः ॥

("Humility, sincerity, non-violence, forgiveness, simplicity, service to the Guru, inner and outer purity, steadfastness, and self-discipline...")

And so on, leading up to:

मयि चानन्ययोगेन भक्तिरव्यभिचारिणी...

एतज्ज्ञानमिति प्रोक्तमज्ञानं यदतोऽन्यथा ॥

("...constancy in spiritual knowledge, detachment, and exclusive devotion to Me — this, Arjuna, is true knowledge. All else is ignorance.")

These are the true flowers of the soul.

Offered not on a silver plate, but in the temple of inner transformation.

Daily life means living with intention, but without expectations.

Even in Yoga Asana, it means not forcing the body but softening it into the posture, not striving for perfection but letting the breath guide you, not chasing progress but being fully in the moment.

True yogis do not "perform" yoga—they surrender to it. They don't "do" asanas—they let them unfold. They don't "breathe"—they become one with the breath.

When you stop trying to meditate and simply allow meditation to happen, you have touched the essence of Ishvara Pranidhana.

This is where Karma Yoga and Ishvara Pranidhana merge. At work, we often wonder—will I succeed, be accepted, or achieve what I hope for?

Ishvara Pranidhana reminds us to work with complete sincerity but surrender the outcome. Pour your heart into your duty, but release all expectations. Give your best, but let go of the reward.

This is perhaps the most challenging practice—acting without attachment, loving without control, and living without resistance. But once you truly master it, you taste freedom. Ishvara Pranidhana is not just a discipline—it is a path to liberation. The moment you surrender, the struggle ends.

Joy or sorrow, success or failure—they become divine play. You remain unshaken, your peace untouched, because you've placed everything in the hands of the Supreme. Life no longer happens to you—it flows through you. That is true Surrender.

Faith and Surrender are not philosophical concepts for me; they are truths lived through the fire of daily life. I speak from experience—from moments when Surrender was my only option. I did not wait for certainty before walking this path. I've moved through doubts, financial crises, and failures—and still, I am writing this book in the heart of it all.

I don't know if this book will succeed. I don't know if anyone will read it if it's published, or if it will ever reach the world the way I hope it will. I'm not a seasoned writer like my Gurudev. I have no background in publishing or literary experience. And yet—I write. I show up. I do what must be done without concern for what will follow. Because right now, my duty is to write. That's all.

My only question is: Will this help someone? If the answer is yes, then I will write. That is faith. That is Surrender. And now, you hold this book in your hands—a living testament to that faith.

This is how Surrender becomes part of everyday life—not by waiting for perfect conditions but by acting despite imperfection. Surrender doesn't erase struggle—it transforms your relationship with it. Struggles may remain, but they no longer steal your peace.

Since I began walking this path, offering consultations while running a digital marketing agency that now teeters on the edge of collapse, I've seen one universal truth: everyone has problems. Regardless of wealth, status, or how perfect things appear, every soul carries a burden. The financially stable suffer in love. Those with success and relationships may face illness. Even the ones who seem to have it all often wrestle with inner chaos.

No one is exempt from suffering. So what shall we do? Keep complaining? Keep waiting for the perfect moment when all problems vanish before we surrender.

Or shall we remember the wisdom of our rishis, the grace of human birth, and the rare chance we've been given to seek something higher? Shall we recognise that liberation is not beyond reach, but waiting to be embraced?

As a child, I used to envy birds. They could fly freely and didn't have to study, work, or face life's pressures. But as I grew, I saw the truth. Even birds have their struggles—endlessly searching for food, building nests, protecting their young, and staying vigilant against predators. Their lives revolve around survival. But unlike us, they lack the opportunity to transcend suffering. They cannot break the cycle of birth and rebirth. We can.

And yet, instead of honouring this gift, we often complain.

Faith begins when you stop questioning why life is the way it is and start seeing it as an opportunity for growth. Surrender begins when you stop resisting and choose to walk forward anyway.

If you're struggling now, don't assume faith and Surrender are beyond your reach. They are forged in the fire of struggle. When you've done all you can, when the mind is weary, and no path is visible—that is the moment to release it into divine hands.

Trust that He knows. Trust that He sees. Trust that even when you feel lost, He is guiding you.

Faith and Surrender are the very heart of Sanatana Dharma, beautifully illuminated by countless stories and shlokas. While scripture has been interwoven throughout earlier chapters, this one calls for a unique story, perhaps the most defining act of Surrender ever recorded: Draupadi's Vastraharan.

In the court of Hastinapur, surrounded by kings and warriors, the Kauravas—drunk with power—had just rigged and won the game of dice. The Pandavas had lost everything, even their honour. Then came the cruellest blow: Draupadi was to be disrobed in full view of the assembly.

At first, she resisted. She pleaded with the elders—Bhishma, Dronacharya, even her husbands—but none came forward. She tried to defend herself, clinging to her saree. But human effort has its limits.

Finally, when all strength had been spent, she lifted her arms to the heavens and cried, "Govinda! Raksha! Raksha!" That one cry, born from total Surrender, transformed everything. Her saree became endless. No matter how fiercely Dushasana pulled, he could not succeed. He collapsed in exhaustion.

This is the essence of Surrender. So long as we believe we can manage it all ourselves, we are clinging to our ego. But when we accept our limits and offer ourselves to the Divine, we are uplifted in ways beyond logic. Draupadi's faith wasn't blind—it was rooted in experience, in the knowing that Krishna would come when called with a pure heart.

This is Ishvara Pranidhana: not weakness, not inaction, but trust in the Divine's infinite grace. We resist, fight, and worry—but once we truly let go, life responds with unimaginable support.

Sri Krishna gives the ultimate assurance in the Bhagavad Gita (18.66):

सर्वधर्मान्परित्यज्य मामेकं शरणं व्रज।

अहं त्वां सर्वपापेभ्यो मोक्षयिष्यामि मा शुचः।।

"Abandon all varieties of dharma and simply surrender unto Me. I shall liberate you from all sins. Do not fear."

This is Sri Krishna's final instruction to Arjuna. After revealing the essence of Karma Yoga, Bhakti Yoga, and Jnana Yoga, He tells Arjuna to let go of everything and surrender completely. It is the most direct path to liberation. No matter our mistakes or how lost we feel, Surrender remains open to us.

Another touching example of Surrender is the story of Shabari from the Ramayana. A humble tribal woman living in the forest, she was told by her Guru, Matanga Rishi, that one day Bhagavan Sri Ram would come to her. Every day for years, she cleaned her hut, adorned it with flowers, and picked berries for Him. She had no assurance, only faith.

One day, Sri Ram and Lakshman arrived at her doorstep. Overwhelmed, Shabari offered the berries she had lovingly gathered. But wanting only the sweetest for Him, she tasted each one first. Lakshman was shocked—how could tasted food be offered to the Lord? But Sri Ram smiled and embraced them joyfully, saying, "No food has ever been sweeter than this."

Her faith was unwavering, filled with love, beyond logic or formality. She never questioned or doubted—she simply surrendered, and the Divine responded with boundless grace.

This is what true faith does. It doesn't wait for proof. It simply knows.

From Draupadi to Arjuna to Shabari, our scriptures are filled with examples showing that faith and Surrender are never separate. Faith gives us the courage to surrender, and Surrender deepens our faith.

If Draupadi had lacked faith, she wouldn't have cried out to Krishna. If Arjuna had doubted, he wouldn't have embraced Krishna's guidance. If Shabari had questioned, she wouldn't have waited all those years. Faith lets us trust the unseen. Surrender allows us to release control. Together, they open the door to divine grace.

Throughout my own journey, I encountered moments of resistance and doubt. But each time I let go, I realised I was never walking alone. My Gurudev, Ishta Devata, and Bhagavan were always with me, guiding, protecting, and holding my hand.

So, if you're struggling with faith or Surrender, remember this: You're already being held. You are not alone, even if you don't see it now or can't yet feel it. The Divine has already embraced you. You have to open your heart and receive it.

This is Ishvara Pranidhana. This is the beauty of faith.

Did this reach your heart as deeply as it did mine? Because Ishvara Pranidhana isn't just philosophy—it's life.

4.2 Trishna Mukti: Freedom from Desires and Attachments

In Sanatana Dharma, desires are deeply linked to *Kama*, one of the four *Purusharthas* or goals of human life. Contrary to modern misconceptions, *Kama* is not limited to sexual longing. It includes all forms of sensory and emotional pleasure, appreciation of beauty, and deep human connection, whether expressed through art, music, nature, or relationships.

Kama translates to "desire, longing, or wish" and is referenced even in the most ancient scriptures.

In the Rig Veda (10.129.4), Desire is described as the first movement of creation:

कामस्तदग्रे समवर्तताधि मनसो रेतः प्रथमं यदासीत् ।

सतो बन्धुमसति निरविन्दन्हृदि प्रतीष्या कवयो मनीषा ॥

"Thereafter rose Desire in the beginning—Desire the primal seed and germ of Spirit. Sages who searched with their heart's thought discovered the existent's kinship in the non-existent."

Kama was the first spark, the initial impulse that set creation into motion. Even the *Brihadaranyaka Upanishad* echoes this truth:

"Man consists of Desire. As his Desire is, so is his determination. As his determination is, so is his deed. Whatever his deed is, that he attains."

Desires shape our *Sankalpa* (intent), which leads to *Karma* (action) and determines our destiny. If passion drives creation and transformation, how can it be called the root of suffering?

The truth is—desires themselves are not the problem. They are neutral. What matters is how we act on them. Depending on the path we choose, a desire can lead to Dharma or Adharma. Even in our prayers, we use words like *Kamana* (wish) and *Kampurti* (fulfilment), seeking divine blessings. Desire isn't inherently wrong.

Trouble arises when Desire overpowers our Dharma, blinds us, leads us away from the truth, or causes suffering for us or others. That is why it's said, "Desires are the root cause of suffering." Not because they exist, but because unchecked or selfish desires enslave us.

Looking back on my journey, I once had desires rooted in greed. I sold products people didn't need during my earlier years in digital marketing. I justified this as a business, but knew it was misaligned with my Dharma. That was a desire driven by ego and illusion.

Now, I have a different kind of desire. I dream of serving selflessly—not for name, fame, or even peace, but because it feels like the most natural expression of who I am. I wish to care for animals, especially cows and speechless beings with special needs. I want to create safe shelters where elderly homeless people can live with dignity and love. I envision Ayurvedic hospitals, holistic healing centres, and ashrams where true wellness is nurtured—physically, emotionally, and spiritually. I long for a home with a temple where I can perform Sadhana, Homa, and Yoga daily, plant trees, build nests for birds, pet cows, and create a sanctuary of peace and devotion.

These desires are not rooted in personal gain—they are grounded in seva, compassion, and something much larger than my own existence. They don't distance me from the spiritual path; they push me deeper into it. These desires are aligned with my Dharma. But I also understand: if I pursued them through unethical means, borrowed heavily, or compromised my values, even these noble intentions would turn into burdens. That is the real difference—between karmic bondage and karmic liberation.

Over time, these dreams have grown so vivid in my heart that they've begun to take form—not yet as institutions in the outer world, but as living visions within me. In moments of prayer, silence, or reflection, these names arise naturally—as if whispered by the Divine into my consciousness. I do not know when or how they will manifest, but I hold them with faith, love, and unshakable sankalpa. And so, I call them:

Sri Hari School – a world-class school for underprivileged children, offering wisdom, values, and education at no cost, because this is where I believe the real change begins.

Shyama Yoga Shala – a sacred space to teach traditional Yoga in its most undiluted and purest form, free from the dilution and distortion it has suffered under modern commercial and Western influences; a place where the original wisdom of the Ṛṣis can be preserved, practiced, and passed on as a living transmission of Dharma

Mahatmayam Senior Citizen Ashram – a dignified haven for the elderly with care, community, and spiritual support, including pilgrimages in their final years, because no one who has spent their life nurturing others should be left alone, unloved, or undignified in their final chapter

Pashupati Animal Shelter – a sanctuary for injured cows, disabled dogs, and every voiceless being in need of compassion, because true spirituality is measured not by how we treat the powerful, but how we care for those who cannot speak for themselves

Bhardwaj College – a higher education institution where students from Sri Hari School can study without the burden of tuition or societal limitations, because potential should never be caged by poverty, and every deserving student deserves the wings to rise

Atharva Ayurveda Institute & Healing Centre – a place for natural healing where no patient is turned away for lack of money, and Ayurveda is practiced with integrity and compassion, because healing should be a right, not a privilege, and the sacred science of Ayurveda must remain rooted in seva, not business

These are not fleeting ambitions. They are not business plans or projects for status. These are sacred imprints on my soul—non-negotiable truths I carry within me. And I know, with the grace of my Gurudev and the strength of my Sadhana, I will fulfill them in this lifetime.

That is the real difference.

Desires that align with Dharma and don't enslave us are uplifting. Desires that are blind, control, and pull us away from the truth are dangerous.

Here's something subtler to reflect on—even the Desire for Moksha can become an attachment. If we constantly obsess over liberation, thinking, "When will I be enlightened?"—that restlessness becomes a bondage.

True surrender is desiring without clinging, walking the path without being enslaved by the destination.

This is the secret: Desire but detached. Dream, but don't obsess. Want, but don't let your wants rule you.

Kama itself is not the enemy. Uncontrolled craving, desperation for results, and loss of Dharma breed suffering.

So, how do we live in this world and still feel content? Can we hold desires without becoming restless? These are the questions we must sit with.

We often say we want contentment, but do we? Or are we just seeking approval, validation, and a sense of superiority disguised as contentment?

There are two forms of contentment: one is real, rising from within. The other is imitation—an outward performance. Today, even minimalism has become a trend rather than a value. I once read an article about a celebrated entrepreneur known for his "minimalist lifestyle"—he wears the same colour t-shirt and jeans daily. But these "minimal" clothes cost thousands, and he owns many of each. Is that truly simplicity, or just luxury with a new label?

This is where most people falter. They aren't seeking contentment—they're seeking attention. The line between the two is paper-thin.

My personal role model for genuine contentment is Shri Ratan Tata. He was a man of immense wealth and influence, yet grounded, simple, and silent in his service. He doesn't seek validation. His life reflects quiet dignity, kindness, and a sense of purpose. His humility speaks louder than any brand could. That, to me, is true satisfaction.

But such contentment is rare.

Most people are caught in illusions, mistaking appearance for peace. I recall conversing with a friend who often makes expensive purchases—luxury watches, branded clothes, and high-end accessories. I asked him why. His answer stunned me. He said, "It makes me look rich, credible, trustworthy. People take me more seriously."

He isn't truly wealthy, but he's built an image. A large chunk of his earnings goes into maintaining that illusion, not to fulfil needs, but to project status. In reality, the brands become wealthier. He gets stuck in a cycle, trying to prove himself through material things.

And he's not alone. This is the story of many.

People don't want contentment. They want to be seen as content. They crave validation, admiration, and envy. And in chasing that, they sacrifice the very peace they claim to seek.

But here's the thing—we must learn from such people. Not to follow them but to understand what not to do.

I'm not saying you must never buy expensive things or enjoy a comfortable life. If something adds genuine value, aligns with your needs, and supports your path, then yes, invest in it. But don't let illusions dictate your decisions.

I've walked this path myself. I once believed success meant owning luxury, reaching financial goals, and earning recognition. But as I grew spiritually, I saw the truth—contentment doesn't come from the outside. It is a state of being, a shift in perception, an inner knowing of what truly matters.

Even now, I have certain material wishes—like owning a good, comfortable car. But this time, it's not about shine, status, or ego. I long for it because I want to give my parents the freedom and dignity they never asked for but always deserved. I dream of hiring a driver and handing them the keys—not just to a vehicle, but to their golden years. So they can visit temples, travel comfortably, go wherever their heart calls—without hesitation or worry. That's the purity I now associate even with the material things I desire. It's not about ownership; it's about offering.

Is contentment possible? Absolutely—but only through awareness and detachment.

Awareness of what matters and detachment from the need for external validation.

Contentment doesn't mean rejecting everything. It means being at peace with what you have while striving for what aligns with your life's purpose, or Dharma. It's living with purpose, not pretence. It means choosing what nourishes the soul, not what feeds the ego. It means fulfilling responsibilities without getting lost in unnecessary cravings.

This is absolute satisfaction.

There is also a deep confusion between love and attachment. Many believe love must include attachment—to love someone is to hold on and never let go. But is that truly love?

We hear phrases like "I can't live without you" or "You are mine." They sound romantic, but they reveal something deeper—are these words rooted in love, or is attachment masked as love?

The issue isn't just attachment—we've misunderstood what love is.

True love is vast, infinite, and boundless. It cannot be confined by control, expectation, or possession. The moment it becomes any of these, it is no longer love—it is transaction.

Earlier, I shared how I love my Gurudev. That love is pure, free of expectation, demand, or possession. It is devotion. It is reverence. That is true love.

However, in worldly life, what we call love is often characterised by dependency, infatuation, or a longing to be fulfilled by someone else. We confuse emotional need with divine connection. And from that confusion, suffering is born.

Why? Because attachment breeds expectation.

And when expectations aren't met, pain arises. A parent expects the child to follow their dreams—if the child chooses differently, it hurts. A partner expects specific behaviour—when unmet, it leads to conflict. A friend expects loyalty—when life shifts, the bond weakens.

At the heart of every broken heart is unmet expectations.

So ask yourself: is this love—or is it attachment?

Love does not cause suffering. Attachment does.

Have you seen a dog chasing its tail? It spins in circles, convinced it's chasing something outside itself. But the tail is already part of its body.

This is what attachment does to us. We chase joy outside, forgetting it already exists within. Like dogs, we run in circles, clinging to people, things, and relationships, believing we'll be whole only when we get what we want.

And when we finally "catch" what we were chasing?

Nothing changes because the chase is always an illusion.

That's what attachment is. A need dressed as love.

Think of a child clinging to a toy. If taken away, they cry as if the world ends. But a few years later, the same toy lies forgotten, replaced, and discarded.

This isn't love. It's attachment—temporary, intense, but fleeting.

As we grow, the objects of our attachment change—but the pattern stays the same. What was once a toy becomes a car, a relationship, a career, or a status symbol. We keep searching for something or someone to cling to.

But the truth is—nothing lasts. People change, circumstances shift, and life keeps moving. Without detachment, we fear loss, change, and the unknown.

Should we stop loving, then?

Not at all. The answer isn't to stop loving, but to love without attachment. Detachment doesn't mean indifference or emotional distance. It means loving freely, without the need to possess or control. It means caring deeply but without clinging. It means being fully present without fearing the future.

This is the path to true happiness—in relationships, life, and our spiritual journey. When we stop chasing, controlling, and expecting, we begin to experience, accept, and appreciate. That is true detachment. That is real love.

Detachment is often misunderstood as renunciation, but it's not about escaping life, responsibilities, or comforts. I've seen people who have renounced the world but remain attached to their identity, ideology, and pride. Wearing a robe doesn't make one detached. Living in an ashram doesn't eliminate inner desires. At the same time, a householder raising a family and fulfilling duties can be truly detached.

Detachment isn't about what you own or where you live—it's about the state of your mind.

Giving up everything externally isn't detachment—it's just another illusion. If that were the path to liberation, every poor person would already be enlightened. True detachment is doing your duties with sincerity without clinging to the outcomes. This is precisely what Bhagavan Sri Krishna teaches in the Gita. And who embodies Vairagya more than Mahadev?

"Main toh vairagi hoon, na mujhe sammaan ka moh, na apmaan ka bhay."

(I am a Vairagi—unmoved by praise, unshaken by insult.)

This line carries the wisdom of true detachment. When you are truly free within, praise doesn't elevate you, and criticism doesn't disturb you. You remain steady, unaffected, at peace.

For me, detachment doesn't mean rejecting all desires. I welcome them when they align with the Dharma, and accept them when they remain unfulfilled. I don't measure success by outcomes because my joy isn't tied to results. But how does one reach this level of understanding?

It begins with a simple shift in the mind.

Our actions, thoughts, and choices arise from the mind. If trained with care, it learns detachment. But this cannot be forced. Suppressed desires grow stronger. The detachment must evolve naturally, gently, and without pressure.

Let me share a personal example. In my teenage years, I was obsessed with powerful cars and motorcycles. The roar of an engine, the thrill of speed—it wasn't just excitement but a craving. I used to dream of owning high-end machines, imagining the day I'd finally ride them as a mark of success.

The same was true for technology. I chased the latest gadgets, top-tier phones, and advanced computers, believing they'd make me happy. But life has its way of teaching. Through hardships, struggles, and financial limits, I slowly realised a profound truth: the hunger for material things never ends.

Think about it—the first bite is blissful when you eat your favourite food. But as you continue, the satisfaction fades. Overeating can become discomfort. Desires are the same. They begin with excitement, but it's fleeting. Soon, something else catches your longing, and the cycle repeats. A lifetime is spent chasing what never truly fulfils.

When I began studying the Shastras, Puranas, Vedas, and Upanishads, I saw through this illusion. Luxury, fame, and wealth are distractions. Real fulfilment lies in spiritual growth. Reading my Gurudev's memoir, where he said all he sought from his tapasya was Maa's darshan, touched me deeply. What greater goal is there than Bhagavat Prapti?

That was when detachment awakened within me. Today, expensive cars, comforts, and possessions mean little. But I accept them. If they come, I will take them with gratitude. If not, I remain content. My peace no longer depends on whether I receive it or not.

Detachment, however, does not mean shirking responsibilities. I have a family, duties, and loved ones with different desires. It would be wrong to impose my detachment on them. Their expectations matter. It's my Dharma to honour them sincerely, even if my spiritual inclinations differ.

This is the distinction between true detachment and superficial renunciation. Detachment isn't about escaping the world—it's about engaging with it while staying inwardly free—doing all that life asks of us without being enslaved by outcomes.

I hope that the meaning of detachment is clear for those in the Grihastha Ashram by now. You don't need to leave your home, career, or family. You only need a shift in perspective. Live fully, love sincerely, serve selflessly, and detach gracefully. That is true, Vairagya.

Desires and attachments shape the human experience. They guide our joys and sorrows and determine whether we find bondage or liberation. Our scriptures—the Gita, the Upanishads, and the Vedas—don't ask us to suppress desires. They teach us to understand, refine, and eventually master them.

The Bhagavad Gita speaks to this with clarity:

कामक्रोधवियुक्तानां यतीनां यतचेतसाम् ।

अभितो ब्रह्मनिर्वाणं वर्तते विदितात्मनाम् ॥

(Gita 5.26)

Those free from Desire and anger, whose minds are steady and who know the Self, such sages attain liberation in this very life.

Krishna isn't telling us to destroy all desires. He asks us to rise above the compulsive cravings that rule us and the anger that arises when they go unmet. Fulfilment doesn't come from external possessions but from inner mastery. This is Vairagya—not withdrawal from life but release from the illusion that our joy depends on what we have or lack.

This is the balance—enjoy life, but don't cling. The world is for experience, not attachment. Suffering begins when we mistake temporary things for permanent joy.

There is a famous story about King Janaka, the ideal sthitaprajna, who remains unmoved by external events. Once, during a deep philosophical conversation with his Guru, a messenger shouted that his kingdom was on fire. While others panicked, Janaka sat still, mind immersed in the Self. When asked why he didn't react, he calmly replied, "Let the palace burn. It belongs to the world, not to me."

This is the pinnacle of detachment—not escaping duties but performing them with unwavering clarity, untouched by fear or clinging.

So, how do we walk this path in practical life? How do we remain inwardly still while managing duties, ambitions, and relationships?

The key is self-reflection. A sadhaka must watch the workings of the mind—how desires emerge, how attachments form, and how suffering begins when expectations are unmet. It's not about forcibly rejecting desires but about seeing them. Awareness brings mastery—we stop being ruled by our impulses and begin to guide them.

Desires, by themselves, are not wrong. Without Desire, creation wouldn't exist. But there's a difference between pure desires aligned with Dharma and cravings that bind us in suffering. I've spoken about my aspirations—to serve animals, help older people, build healing spaces, and live a life rooted in service. These are desires, yes—but not shackles. If they manifest, I welcome them. If not, I walk on with devotion.

This is the essence of detachment—not rejection, but refinement. We continue to live, love, and strive, but without the illusion that our happiness depends on outcomes. Desires may guide us, but attachments must not bind us.

When we reach this inner balance, we become free. We stop chasing happiness and begin radiating peace. This is the core message of our scriptures—a way to live fully in the world yet remain untouched by it.

4.3 Dhriti & Karuna: Patience and Compassion

Patience is often misunderstood. Some think it means quietly waiting, while others see it as enduring hardship with clenched teeth. But true patience is neither passive nor painful—it is a strength, a calm inner knowing that everything unfolds in its own time and that forcing or resisting only invites suffering.

In Sanatana Dharma, patience is more than a virtue—it is considered a form of truth, righteousness, compassion, and wisdom. It aligns us with the divine rhythm of the universe. It's not something to be practised occasionally, but a foundation for a higher quality of life. Through patience, we develop clarity, endurance, and spiritual maturity. Even Bhagavan Krishna considers it one of the divine qualities.

Patience is not waiting idly. It is mastery over the self. It's the ability to remain firm in dharma, no matter what's happening around us.

Take the example of Shri Rama. Despite being exiled, losing his kingdom, and losing Sita, he never faltered. His patience wasn't weakness—it was divine strength. He surrendered to the higher will without complaint. Similarly, the Pandavas endured exile and injustice without reacting hastily. They remained focused, trusting that dharma would triumph. Their patience was that of warriors—steadfast, disciplined, and dharmic.

In my own life, I've learned that patience is not about waiting for delays, but about trusting. I often felt restless in my younger days: Why aren't things happening? Why is life not unfolding the way I imagined? But as I progressed spiritually, I understood that patience isn't about waiting for change—it is about trusting the perfection of the present.

Like a flower that blooms in its own time, we cannot force spiritual growth. The more we push, the more we suffer. But when we trust and surrender, patience supports us. It's not inaction—it's alignment.

Today's world rarely values patience. Everything is fast—messages, entertainment, gratification. But when we become addicted to speed, we grow anxious and never truly at peace. Patience counters this. It helps us slow down, reconnect with our inner rhythm, and stay grounded in what matters.

I see patience as a spiritual force—the strength to endure, remain unshaken, and walk the path without rushing. It's not giving up. It's the courage to move forward without fear, to let life unfold in its divine timing, just like Rama, the Pandavas, and every realised being who walked this sacred path.

So, I invite you to reflect—what does patience mean to you? If you've seen it as mere waiting, look again. True patience is active trust. It's walking the path with stillness inside, surrender, and the wisdom to know that all is unfolding exactly as it should.

Life has repeatedly tested my patience, especially in relationships, family, and career. I've faced uncertainty, questioned everything, and stood at a crossroads with no clear direction. But if there's one truth life has revealed, it's this: things unfold in their own time, not when we want, but when they are meant to.

Earlier, I shared that my marketing agency reached a point where I had to decide whether to continue or let it go. It wasn't an easy decision. You can't make reckless choices with responsibilities and financial obligations at 36-37. You have to think about survival and those who depend on you.

My patience was tested as my agency declined, with clients leaving and projects fading. But instead of falling into despair, I used that time to grow. I immersed myself physically and spiritually in Jyotish, Numerology, Reiki, and Yoga. I deepened my sadhana and meditation and absorbed the grace my Gurudev blessed me with. I didn't abandon the agency, either. I continued serving my clients with honesty and integrity, fulfilling every commitment.

I wasn't just surviving—I was evolving. Looking back, I see how patience has carried me here.

In today's world of instant results, few understand patience. Everyone wants overnight success, but fundamental transformation takes time, especially in the quiet moments when you choose to keep going instead of giving up.

Let me share one story that taught me a lot. I once worked with a high-paying eCommerce client. I handled his entire digital marketing, including website, social media, and ads. Each month in our meetings, he would ask, "Where are my sales?" And I would explain, "Marketing builds awareness. Sales depend on product quality, pricing, and customer service. Marketing can't guarantee conversions overnight."

But he couldn't accept that. He wanted instant results from a single blog or social media post. I don't blame him—he had expectations. But the truth is, I made a mistake too. I took the project out of desperation, ignoring that our visions didn't align. I just wanted to earn, so I compromised my ethics and interests.

This continued for six or seven months until I finally told him, "I don't think I can serve you anymore. You need someone who can meet your expectations, and I'm not that person." That day, I understood—this was not my path. I was forcing myself into a world that no longer resonated with me. But this realisation didn't come overnight. It took time, reflection, and patience.

I continued working for survival, but built toward what I truly loved. Slowly, life began to shift. Things started aligning. That patience I held onto—that quiet, persistent faith—led me here.

As I write this book, I realise what patience is. It's not just waiting. It's growing while you wait. It's preparing while the path is being cleared. It's trusting that the light will come even in darkness if you keep learning, evolving, and walking. And when it does, you'll know—it was all worth it.

Many people struggle with patience, especially in today's fast-paced world of instant gratification. The real challenge isn't just about waiting—how and what we do during that time. Impatience stems from restlessness, desperation, and resistance to the natural rhythm of life. We want immediate results; when they don't come, we feel frustrated, stuck, or hopeless.

If you've ever visited an Ayurvedic Vaidya, you might've noticed how they approach healing. Unlike modern medicine, which treats symptoms, an Ayurvedic Vaidya focuses on the root cause. Similarly, impatience doesn't need direct suppression—it's a symptom of something more profound. To cultivate patience, we must look within and understand the forces causing our inner unrest.

One major contributor is fragmented attention. Most people struggle to focus on a single task because their minds are constantly distracted. To prove this, ask yourself—what did you eat for dinner last night? If it takes effort to recall, it's not due to a poor memory but a lack of focus or presence. Your mind was likely consumed by your phone, the TV, or wandering thoughts about the past or future.

This is where patience becomes difficult. We live either in regret or anxiety, rarely in the now. To develop patience, we must learn to be present in the moment. Rather than forcing yourself to be patient, train yourself to be mindful. Patience grows naturally when the mind is steady.

If you're in a challenging phase, working hard but not seeing results, or feeling lost, start by taking a step back to gain a better understanding. Ask, what is life trying to teach me through this delay? What lesson is hidden in this moment? Shifting your mindset from frustration to curiosity changes everything.

Also, reduce distractions. Don't overload yourself with multitasking. Be present. When you eat, just eat. When you walk, just walk. When you work, just work. The more you train your mind to focus, the more patience you will develop.

Remember that the past is memory, and the future is beyond your control. No amount of thinking will change what is destined. What you have is this moment. If you can make it peaceful and meaningful, you won't feel impatient—you'll feel aligned.

Patience isn't passive. It's trusting the process, surrendering to divine timing, and fully living the moment. The next time impatience arises, don't resist. Gently bring your attention to the now and ask, "What can I do to improve this moment?" That's where your power lies.

Patience and faith are inseparable on the spiritual path. If faith is your unwavering trust in divine will, patience sustains that trust through time. Faith collapses under pressure without patience, and without faith, patience has no direction. Patience is the actual test of faith.

Let me give you a scenario. Imagine being stranded in the middle of a vast ocean, your boat's engine dead, no land in sight, no help around, and all communication devices failing. You're left with nothing but time, endless waves of uncertainty, and a rising sense of helplessness. Now, imagine a storm brewing in the distance. You're alone, vulnerable, and entirely at the mercy of forces beyond your control.

Pause and reflect—what would you do? Panic? Shout for help even though no one can hear? Jump into the unknown waters, fearing what might lie beneath? Most would feel anxious, even terrified. And yet, in truth, there is nothing to do but wait. You can let panic consume you or surrender to the moment with patience, trusting that something—divine grace, inner strength, or sheer resilience—will carry you through.

I recall two films that reflect this union of patience and faith: *'Adrift'* and *'True Spirit'*. *Adrift* (2018) is based on the true story of Tami Oldham Ashcraft, who survived a violent hurricane in the Pacific. Her boat was wrecked, her fiancé injured, and she had to navigate alone across thousands of miles. No miracles—just patience, strength, and will.

True Spirit (2023) portrays Jessica Watson, a 16-year-old Australian who sailed solo worldwide. Facing perilous conditions and inner doubts, her only lifelines were patience, self-belief, and trust in the journey. I share these examples because faith isn't always about divine intervention. Often, it's the trust we place in ourselves, life's process, and our ability to endure. Patience is what sustains that faith during moments of uncertainty and pain.

Even in the Ramayana, we find this lesson. When Lakshmana was struck down in battle, Bhagavan Sri Ram, though the Supreme himself, didn't use divine powers to revive him instantly. He followed the natural course, calling a Vaidya and sending Hanumanji to fetch the Sanjeevani herb. Even God upheld the path of dharma, karma, and patience. This teaches us that faith does not mean passively waiting for miracles but acting sincerely and trusting the process.

This is real patience. It isn't inaction nor blind hope. It's the strength to walk forward with trust, even when results are slow. It's staying steady through trials, knowing that time and truth always reveal the path.

You may wonder why I suddenly referenced movies after drawing on scriptures. I understand that thought. As I write this, I continually place myself in your shoes. This book isn't meant for renunciates in Himalayan caves—it is for us, the Grihasthas. We live in the world, carry duties, raise families, and still long to walk the path of truth. And sometimes, it's a scene from a film that makes a lesson hit home. That's why I bring in such examples—to make ancient wisdom relatable to our lives today.

I could have mentioned many other films, but I chose just a few that beautifully capture the Spirit of patience and faith. One more worth mentioning is *The Walk* (2015), a biographical drama directed by Robert Zemeckis, based on the life of Philippe Petit, the French high-wire artist who, in 1974, fulfilled his dream of walking between the Twin Towers on a tightrope without any safety harness.

This film isn't just about an extraordinary feat; it's about unwavering faith, relentless patience, and surrendering to the process despite overwhelming odds. Petit's journey began as an impossible dream, but he nurtured it with dedication and determination. He trained for years, refining every detail, preparing for every challenge, and turning failures into learning opportunities. Even when others doubted him, even when fear loomed large, he clung to one thing—faith—faith in his vision, his practice, and his ability.

There's a moment in the film when he steps onto the wire. Everything else fades—just him, the rope, and the vast sky. That moment captures the essence of surrender. You do everything you can, and then you trust. You give your best; at some point, you must let go and allow life to carry you. That is patience. That is faith.

Just like Petit, we walk the tightrope of life. Doubts, fears, and trials will test our balance, but if we cultivate patience and surrender, we will walk steadily through it all. I included this film because even a story about a man walking between skyscrapers reveals the timeless spiritual truths of effort, trust, and letting go.

Compassion is another quality that is often misunderstood. Many see it as a weakness or people-pleasing. But genuine compassion is one of the highest strengths. It is not about being a doormat—it's about offering love with discernment. It's about giving with wisdom, helping with sincerity, and not being attached to appreciation or outcomes.

I remember a touching moment from Vrindavan. Sri Premanandji Maharaj was once approached by a man who said, "Everyone takes advantage of me. I can never say no." Maharajji gently replied, "Think of it this way—you're fortunate. You're of use to someone. That is a blessing, not a burden."

That insight left a deep imprint on me. We often feel depleted when others take from us. But what if we saw it differently? What if our ability to serve as a sign of grace? If someone benefits from our actions or presence, isn't that proof that our life has meaning?

Yet, compassion also requires clarity. My Gurudev is one of the most compassionate beings I've known, yet he is deeply disciplined. He gives endlessly to those who seek, yet guards his time with purpose. He once said, "I only have so much time. I must spend it to uplift all who walk this path." That, to me, is compassion in its most valid form—loving deeply, giving entirely, and staying rooted in dharma.

Seeing this, I realised genuine compassion isn't about being overburdened. It's about serving from inner strength, not obligation. It means knowing when to give and when to step back so your energy is not wasted but directed where it matters. Compassion isn't a weakness—it's one of the greatest strengths a person can possess.

Genuine compassion doesn't mean surrendering to the world's demands. It's extending kindness while maintaining balance. My Gurudev is the finest example of this. His service to society is rooted in unconditional love, yet he never allows himself to be consumed by others' expectations. I admire and strive to follow his ability to uplift countless lives while remaining grounded.

Compassion must be coupled with wisdom. When we give, it should be from a place of fullness, not depletion. A tree provides shade and fruits without asking anything in return, yet it stands rooted. However, a tree that overextends itself will break. Likewise, a compassionate person without inner stability eventually has nothing to offer.

Just as a Guru offers guidance without forcing wisdom, we must help others within healthy limits. Sometimes, the most compassionate act is to step back and let someone learn their lessons. Trying to shield others from their karma can hinder their growth. Compassion doesn't mean saying yes to everything—it means discerning when to help and when to allow space for others to evolve.

In my journey, I've found the best way to be compassionate without losing myself is to be detached with love, offering kindness without expectation and without becoming entangled in others' pain. I've also learned the value of setting boundaries. If I feel drained, I pause and realign. I remind myself that I can give only when I'm whole.

If you ever feel that compassion makes you weak, ask yourself: Am I giving from a place of strength or depletion? If it's the latter, take a step back. You don't have to carry the world on your shoulders. Genuine compassion is like a river—flowing freely, nourishing all it touches, yet always true to its course. It doesn't force itself nor allow itself to be drained.

We must live this balance: giving without losing ourselves, loving without surrendering our peace, and helping without abandoning our dharma.

Throughout my life, even the smallest acts of compassion have transformed moments for me and others. Compassion isn't always grand. Sometimes, it's a simple gesture: offering a seat to a mother or elder on a crowded bus, stepping back in line, tipping someone who works tirelessly, not bargaining with small vendors, and feeding underprivileged children. These are not just acts of kindness—they're silent prayers. The joy in their smiles, the gratitude in their eyes—these moments change something within you.

Even something as simple as saying sorry can dissolve tension and create peace when you're not at fault. The ego resists, but as your heart expands, compassion begins to flow as naturally as breath.

Yet, there are times when compassion meets helplessness. I've experienced moments where someone was in pain, but I had nothing to offer—no time, no money, no resources. In those moments, I turned to prayer. A sincere prayer is not inaction—it is the most powerful offering when nothing else is possible. I entrust their well-being to the divine, knowing that the universe operates in ways we cannot see.

This feeling of helplessness isn't limited to human suffering. I feel it when I see trees being cut down without thought. Trees are living beings, silent yet sentient. This is why I avoid using wooden furniture in my home. I'm not here to dictate choices, but for me, choosing alternatives like PVC brings a sense of peace. At least I know I'm doing what I can.

The pain deepens when I see cruelty toward animals—beings who cannot even speak for themselves. The suffering they endure is heartbreaking. What can I do? Again, I turn to faith. I surrender to Pashupatinath, Mahadev. He is the protector of all life. I trust He sees what we cannot, and justice will unfold in divine time.

Compassion is not about fixing everything. It's about doing what you can, with what you have, wherever you are—and surrendering the rest to the divine. When this shift happens inside you, your world changes.

Balancing patience and compassion begins with how we relate to expectations. Often, we think patience means waiting for something outside to change, or that acts of kindness should bring acknowledgement. But why expect anything at all?

Genuine compassion is not transactional. It's not something you offer, hoping for praise or return. If the expectation is even subtly attached, it becomes a disguised need for validation, rather than pure compassion. When your kindness goes unnoticed and you feel disappointed, it's a call to reflect.

That's where self-inquiry becomes vital. Was the act truly selfless, or was there a hidden desire for recognition? I don't mean to say we must deny our emotions or pretend disappointment doesn't exist. But we must become aware of the subtle avidya—those veiled expectations hiding even in acts of love.

With this awareness, you move beyond conditional compassion and fragile patience. You stop feeling restless when things change, or your care isn't returned. Instead, you grow into quiet detachment—not from love, but from needing anything in return.

This shift is transformational. Your love flows without exhaustion, and your patience holds without frustration. You give, yet remain whole.

You care, but you are not controlled. This is the harmony between compassion and patience, untangled from the burden of expectation.

Once you step into this space, the journey becomes lighter. Waiting becomes flowing. Giving becomes being.

How can a chapter dedicated to karuṇā — the divine flow of compassion — ever be complete without remembering Karuṇā Nidhān himself, Maryādā Purushottam Bhagavān Sri Rām?

There is one prasanga (Sacred Episode) from the Sri Ramcharitmanas that always brings tears to the eyes, regardless of how many times it is heard. I had first encountered it through the moving narration of Dr. Kumar Vishwas ji, and ever since, it has been etched in my heart. It is the episode where Bharata, along with Kaushalya Mata, Kaikeyi Mata, Sumitra Mata, and the entire Ayodhya Sabha, arrives at Chitrakoot, requesting Sri Rām to return to Ayodhyā and reclaim his rightful throne.

As Sri Rām sees the entourage approaching, his heart overflows—not with pride or hesitation, but with boundless love. Despite the pain of separation and the injustice done, his eyes soften, his voice mellows, and his feet rush forward, for he sees not court and politics, but his family—his aatma-bandhus- standing before him.

Sri Rām first walks directly toward Mata Kaikeyi. With folded hands and moist eyes, he bows down and touches her feet.

Kaikeyi, once radiant with regal confidence, now stands shattered within—her eyes swollen, her heart drenched in remorse. As Sri Rām bows, she cannot contain her emotions and collapses into his arms, sobbing.

"Mujhse aprādh ho gaya, Rām...

Aaj ek māta, kumātā ban gayi...

Mujhe kṣamā karo, putra."

Her voice trembles, soaked in regret. The woman who once demanded vanvāsa is now crushed under the weight of her own repentance. Yet what does Rāma do?

He lifts her gently, places his hand on her head, and says with a smile that could heal the deepest wounds:

"Mātā, mujhe sab gyaan hai.

Aapke mann mein kabhi dvesh na tha, na he āgyā mein galti thi.

Yah sab toh daiv-yog se hua hai.

Aap meri mātā thi… hain… aur rahengi."

He recounts a tender memory from his childhood:

"Mātā, when I was a child, I would see you in my dreams and cry to be in your lap. Kaushalya Mātā, with a smile, would carry me to your chamber and lay me beside you. Only then would I sleep peacefully. You are not separate from my love—you are a part of it."

Kaikeyi, overwhelmed, asks only one thing:

"Sab mujhe dūtī kaheṅ, dand deṅ—main sab sah loongi…

Par ek vinti hai—bharat mujhse na ghṛṇā kare…

Mujhe apnī māṁ samjhe…"

And Rāma promises—not only with words but with his heart—that Bharata will love her again, and that Ayodhyā will see her not as a villain, but as a mother redeemed through love.

Then comes the most poignant interaction: Bharata and Rāma.

Bharata—whose body is thin with austerity and eyes swollen from sleepless cries—falls at Rām's feet, not as a brother but as a repentant soul.

He weeps:

"Bhaiyya, tum van mein ho…

Sītā jī ne raj mahal tyāg kar ke van kṣetra chuna…

Aur main… Ayodhyā ka rājakumāra hokar bhi nirdhan ban gaya hoon.

Yeh sab mere karan hua hai…

Mātā ne āgyā di, par yah sankalp kyā main sehma paaya hoon?"

Rāma lifts him, embraces him tightly, and says:

"Bharat, yeh jo sab ghatnāyen huyi hain, yeh kisi vyakti ke kāraṇ nahi, yeh to vidhātā ke lekh mein likhī huyi kathā hai.

Jo kuch bhi hua, usme tumhara koi dosh nahi hai."

He consoles him not with logic, but with karuṇā, the same karuṇā that looks beyond deeds and directly touches the soul.

In that moment, Bharata finds peace—not in explanations, but in his brother's unconditional love.

Ramcharitmanas (Ayodhya Kāṇḍa):

"Rāma sakal guna nidhāna, karunā sugrīv samāna |

Jānī sabahim prīti kari, rāma bharata sanehi bakhāna ||"

"Rāma is the abode of all virtues, and his heart overflows with compassion.

He understands the hearts of all, and speaks to each one with deep love—with an affection that knows no bounds."

Jai Sri Ram.

4.4 Adhyatmik Sampada: Spiritual Wealth vs. Material Abundance

In my journey of observing life and understanding people, I've realised there is a deep confusion surrounding wealth, not just in modern society, but even among those who speak of spirituality.

Many people assume that wealth means having a large bank balance, a luxurious home, fancy cars, a prestigious career, and a high social status. Others, especially those inclined toward spirituality, believe that wealth is an illusion that must be abandoned in order to find peace.

Both miss the essence.

To understand the difference between material and spiritual wealth, we must revisit the statements in the Vedas about wealth.

The ancient Rishis understood human nature more deeply than any modern science. They didn't reject desires, nor did they glorify them. Instead, they offered a balanced framework—the four Purusharthas—to guide human life without falling into extremes as explained earlier.

Dharma (righteousness), Artha (material stability), Kama (desires), and Moksha (liberation) together form the holistic vision of life. Artha was never condemned. It was seen as necessary to live with dignity, fulfil one's duties, serve family and society, and uphold one's dharma.

The problem arises when Artha is pursued without Dharma. Then wealth, instead of supporting life, begins to consume it.

I've seen how many young people today resist spirituality as if it's a barrier to living fully.

And I don't blame them.

For centuries, spirituality has been misrepresented as suffering, denial, and giving up life's pleasures as if one must withdraw from the world to be spiritual. But this is a distortion.

Spirituality has nothing to do with what you own or where you live. You can be deeply spiritual in a palace and completely lost in a cave. The difference is within.

Being spiritual means living fully, without depending on external sources for joy. It's not about rejecting life, but about discovering the joy already within you.

Ask yourself—why do we chase wealth, security, and recognition?

At the root of it all is one reason: joy.

We study, work, earn, buy, and build—because we believe these things will bring happiness.

But have you noticed? Many people gain all they want, yet feel empty. Restless. Anxious.

Because in pursuing everything, they forgot to nurture the one thing they were truly after—joy.

Happiness is not something you get. It's something you create. You'll always feel unsettled if your joy depends on what happens outside of you.

But once you awaken joy within, no external storm can disturb you.

When friends or family ask me, "What's the difference between a spiritual person and a materialist?" I reply with this:

A materialist earns his food but begs for love, peace, and validation. He depends on others to feel complete.

A spiritual person, however, generates everything from within—his peace, joy, and fulfilment. If he must, he can beg for food. And if he chooses, he can earn that too.

That is the true meaning of wealth. At its core, wealth is neither good nor bad—it is a tool. Whether it leads to freedom or bondage depends entirely on how you use it.

So ask yourself: do you want to have everything on the outside and still feel empty within? Or do you want to be so full inside that no external force can shake your peace?

Because the richest person isn't the one with the most possessions—it's the one with the most inner joy. The choice is always yours.

In conversations—especially with those close to me—I've often been questioned about my struggles. "If you practice yoga, meditate, eat sattvic food, perform rituals, sadhanas, purashcharana, and read so much spiritual wisdom that you could earn a PhD—then why aren't you financially successful? Why, approaching 40, are you still facing obstacles? Why aren't you rich?"

I listen patiently—not because I'm offended, but because I understand their perspective. They see life only through the lens of the immediate and visible. They think spiritual practice should automatically remove all worldly problems. But life isn't a simple equation of practice that equals prosperity.

I answer in a way that speaks to their hearts, not just their minds:

"I'm like a fish taken out of the ocean. In my displacement, I've forgotten my home—the vast waters I once belonged to. I tried adapting to land, to air, to this foreign space. But no matter what I did, something inside always felt off. An uneasiness remained, no matter how comfortable things looked on the surface.

Now, I've found someone who knows the way back. My master is not here to lift and drop me into the ocean. He's here to guide me—to help me remember, teach me how to navigate the currents and find my way back. But I must swim. He shows the path, but I must walk it. If I truly surrender and follow, I will return to those waters one day. And when I do, the suffering and discontent I feel now will dissolve—like waves merging back into the sea."

Some still don't get it. They remain caught in the tangible logic of success and failure, as well as the pursuit of money and status. So I say:

"Back to your question—what am I doing with my life? I'm following my master's instructions to return to my source. Not to the 'self' you know me as, but to the eternal self, the pure consciousness that exists beyond all this worldly turbulence. My struggles are not signs of failure. They're the ripples of a fish trying to find its way home.

If you've understood this, then we're walking together. If not, you're just a step behind—and that's alright. You can follow me if you wish. Because you, too, are the same fish, struggling on land, forgetting your home in the ocean. If you feel the longing, the path is open. All that remains is for you to start swimming."

After reading about spiritual and material wealth, I'm sure a question might be lingering in your mind—one I once carried.

"Is it possible to experience inner joy?"

"What exactly is it?"

"Does it exist—or is it just a romantic idea?"

I used to wonder the same until one online video conversation changed everything.

Someone asked a beautiful, self-explanatory question, "Have you ever tasted sweetness?"

I nodded, "Of course."

"And how does sugar taste?"

"It's sweet," I replied.

"What is sweet?" he asked again.

I tried, "It's delicious... a pleasant taste."

But he gently pressed, "What *is* that feeling? Explain it without using the word 'sweet.'"

I couldn't. Eventually, I said, "I guess I'd have to give you some sugar so you can taste it yourself."

He smiled. "Exactly. Unless someone has tasted sweetness, no words can make them truly understand it."

That stayed with me. Isn't that what happens when discussing inner joy, peace, and fulfilment?

If you haven't experienced it, it sounds vague—maybe even unreal. But once you do, even for a moment, you realise it was always there, quietly waiting to be known.

Like most people, I believed material success would bring me peace. I thought that contentment would follow once I had money, status, and security. So, I chased it all—running harder, climbing faster. But the peace I longed for never arrived, and the calm I craved never stayed. It felt like I was climbing a ladder, only to realise it was leaning against the wrong wall.

Then, my Gurudev showed me the path I'd been blind to. He didn't "give" me peace—because peace isn't something to be handed over. Instead, he pointed me inward. He helped me realise that the sweetness I was searching for was already within me.

Earlier, I shared how sometimes I want to help someone but lack the resources. It's not personal desire that hurts me—it's the inability to serve. That ache has taught me something valuable: while inner joy is our greatest wealth, material means are necessary, not for indulgence but to support the Dharma.

That's why we work and earn—not because wealth is the end goal, but because it supports the higher path.

And this is where balance arises: material abundance guided by spiritual clarity.

Many people believe that material success and spiritual growth cannot coexist—that one must be sacrificed for the other. I once believed that, too. Haven't we all been conditioned to think that wealth and wisdom, prosperity and peace, cannot walk together?

But let's look beyond that belief. If you reflect deeply, you'll see that the evolution of individuals and humanity has never been shaped merely by external forces. It has always been guided by the whispers within, by the voice of the Atman.

The inner and outer worlds are not at war. They are reflections of each other, like the ocean and its waves.

I have never claimed to have attained complete spiritual wealth or material success. I'm still finding my way in the material world, and spiritually, I've only just begun. But that's precisely why I'm sharing this—not as a master but as a fellow traveller.

If anything you've read in this book has made you pause, reflect, or feel a shift, doesn't that prove the power of spiritual wisdom? And yet, I am still at the beginning of the journey. With the grace of my Gurudev, if I can write something that resonates even now, imagine what can unfold as I continue to walk.

The real question isn't whether material and spiritual success can coexist—it's how we align them. The answer is clear: nothing will remain out of reach once I deeply understand life's dos and don'ts. I'll be guided by the Vedas, anchored in Dharma, and led by a mind under my command, not the other way around.

When this inner order is established, material wealth no longer distracts—it becomes a tool, not a detour from Dharma, but a means to walk it more steadily.

The real threat isn't wealth—it's Ego.

I've seen many sincere sadhakas falter here. Even after acquiring knowledge, wisdom, and years of intense practice, the Ego silently reappears. I've written about this before, but it's worth repeating: this is where most people lose the game.

Life is like a game of Snakes and Ladders. You climb step by step, gaining clarity and spiritual insight, nearing the final square. And then

Ego, now disguised in the robes of your wisdom, whispers, "I have arrived." One moment of arrogance—and you slide down.

True spiritual wealth is not just about rising—it is about remaining grounded. It's about protecting your mind from derailment.

In the end, neither lack of resources nor intelligence causes failure—the unchecked Ego strikes when you're at your peak.

This is why spiritual wisdom is the foundation. It's not about rejecting the world but staying clear-eyed in it. Dharma doesn't demand poverty; it demands alignment.

According to the Vedas, material wealth isn't to be renounced—it's to be rightly placed. People should have enough to live with dignity, support their families, and uphold their Dharma without constant stress about survival.

Once that clarity arises—whether through conscious effort or inner realisation—every action begins aligning with Dharma.

In my case, I now practice Vedic Astrology, Numerology, and Reiki Healing and teach Yoga, Pranayama, and Meditation. But why?

Because now, there's a purpose.

I see people running from one astrologer to another, spending heavily on rituals, gems, and metals, desperate for relief. And yet, their problems remain—or worsen. Still, they search. Still, they ask for help.

When I see this, I can no longer stay silent. I know there's another way.

With the wisdom my Gurudev has given me, I offer simple yet powerful solutions—remedies that are not resource-intensive, extravagant, or limited by financial constraints. Instead, they are practical, accessible, and deeply compelling.

I don't ask people to accept fate—I guide them to face challenges with an open heart and a resilient mind. Through awareness and mindfulness, I help them actively transform their circumstances rather than passively endure them.

This is where knowledge truly matters.

When I suggest a remedy, I'm not just addressing current issues—I'm working on their Agami Karmas, shaping future karmic patterns. I offer treatments that involve selfless Dāna, sacred Darshan, and conscious actions, which shift their energetic blueprint. I now teach a course focused on this principle—how real prosperity comes through karmic alignment.

I also guide those overwhelmed by sorrow, anxiety, or inner chaos inward. Instead of waiting for outer circumstances to shift, I teach ancient Yogic tools, meditation, and Pranayama techniques to restore balance, clarity, and healing from within.

Ultimately, no gemstone, ritual, or external remedy can bring lasting peace unless one learns to master one's inner world.

This is the core of my work at Sri Hari Vedic Life.

Spiritual wealth plays its greatest role here. It helps align material pursuits (Artha Vyavastha) with Dharma. It ensures wealth is earned not through greed or harm but through honesty, compassion, and integrity.

As one moves towards spirituality, something subtle shifts.

Kindness and empathy arise naturally. Decisions are no longer driven by personal gain but by a sense of responsibility. We begin to act without attachment, trusting that what is truly ours will come and what isn't will disappear.

This is when wealth ceases to distract and becomes a tool for service. It is no longer the destination—it becomes a means to uplift, serve, and live rightly.

There are no alternatives to performing our duties. Just living in this world is a sacred obligation. None of us can escape it.

And that, in itself, is reason enough to act the way Bhagavan Krishna advised Arjuna—detached from results, devoted only to the action.

Material wealth is neither good nor bad—it is neutral. Whether it binds us or frees us depends entirely on our mindset.

Now, let me be honest.

If I had achieved material success early in my journey, I may not have turned to the spiritual path. If life had gone smoothly, I might have stayed satisfied in my devotion, but perhaps I would never have longed to seek a Guru who could show me the deeper truths.

Only through longing, struggle, and questions that refused to leave me did I begin to walk this path.

Would I have chosen this path if everything had been perfect? I don't know. Maybe not.

But that's just my story.

I've seen others who have immense wealth yet live with deep devotion. They are far ahead of me in spiritual growth. So, I don't believe that only struggle leads to awakening.

For some, it's not wealth that disturbs them. It might be relationships, health, or something else beyond their control.

And that's what I've come to understand—at some point, every human being is brought to a place where they are compelled to look beyond the material world.

At some point, everyone begins seeking answers, which is how most of us find the path of truth. Once we realise that the material world alone cannot fulfil us, we seek something higher, something eternal and beyond suffering. Whether that search begins from pain or wisdom, it leads us back to our true nature.

Material wealth is not a barrier to spiritual growth. It becomes a problem only when pursued without a sense of Dharma or when it fosters attachment and blindness. But when wealth supports Dharma, when one is free from greed and rooted in inner awareness, Artha becomes a means to liberation, not bondage.

This is why we learn all this—to live in the world without being bound by it.

Let me be clear—when we first enter this world, we don't understand concepts like spiritual or material wealth or the balance between the inner and outer. We don't even know that a choice exists between the two. As our desires awaken, the mind is naturally drawn to comfort, indulgence, and instant pleasure. Discipline or self-inquiry doesn't arise unless the mind is trained.

And the mind does not easily surrender that control.

You may wonder what I mean. So let me ask you—have you ever enthusiastically taken out a gym membership? How many days did you go? Did you even use 20% of what you paid for?

This isn't just about the gym. It applies to anything that demands discipline.

Yoga starts with excitement, but it then fades. Meditation begins well, feels good, and then stops. Self-growth always seems like a good idea—until the mind tricks you into quitting before any transformation truly begins.

Isn't that your story?

It's mine, too. I face this battle daily. Yes—even now. Even after all I've learned and experienced, my mind resists.

This is precisely what I want you to understand.

The mind does not want you to grow. It resists anything that demands effort or long-term consistency. It craves comfort. The spiritual path, especially at the beginning, is not always comfortable.

Because this is not a temporary shift—it is a lifelong transformation.

Our thoughts, habits, and desires are etched into us like carvings in stone, years, decades, or even lifetimes deep. Through spiritual practice, we try to rub the sandpaper of awareness against that stone to smooth away the false and the limiting.

But here's the tricky part—it's not just stone. It's also fragile.

If you rub too hard, it cracks. And once broken, there's nothing left to fix.

This is why transformation must never be forced. It must be slow, steady, and wise. Too much pressure creates resistance. Too little, and the mind slips back into old habits.

Does that mean transformation is impossible?

Absolutely not.

If someone asks, "How can you be so sure?" my answer is simple—I have evidence. I don't need to create theories. Our scriptures, saints, and sages have already proved this path through their lives. And more than that, I have my Guru.

My Guru has lived the truth of the Vedas, the Upanishads, the Bhagavad Gita, and the teachings of Sanatana Dharma—not partially, not philosophically, but fully and unquestionably. When he says something, I take it as the Gita itself. I have no reason to doubt him—not in this world or any other.

I'll share the practical aspects of this transformation in part two. But for now, all I ask is this—believe. Believe that change is possible and that you can reprogram your mind. That the path is open. Because the moment you think, you've already taken your first step toward victory. And that is where the journey truly begins.

When it comes to understanding wealth, nothing shaped my perspective more than the wisdom of Sanatana Dharma and the teachings of realised masters. The Vedas, Upanishads, and Bhagavad Gita illuminate the concept of Artha—material prosperity—in a way that is far deeper than today's world, which often reduces wealth to money, possessions, and social status.

Modern success is often measured by what one owns or displays. But Sanatana Dharma views wealth as a balance—a harmony between

Dharma (righteousness), Artha (prosperity), Kama (desire), and Moksha (liberation).

A verse from the Bhagavad Gita deeply transformed my outlook:

त्यक्त्वा कर्मफलासङ्गं नित्यतृप्तो निराश्रयः |

कर्मण्यभिप्रवृत्तोऽपि नैव किञ्चित्करोति सः || (Bhagavad Gita 4.20)

"One who renounces attachment to results, who is ever content and self-dependent, though fully engaged in action, does nothing at all."

This revealed to me the secret of true prosperity: not to abandon wealth or work but to detach from obsession with results. When wealth is pursued with purity and in accordance with Dharma, it uplifts. When chased through Ego and greed, it enslaves.

Another story that reshaped my understanding is of King Harishchandra, as written in the *Devi Bhagavatam retold* by Sri Ramesh Menon. Harish Chandra was a great and just ruler. But when divinely tested, he gave up everything—his wealth, power, and family—to uphold the truth. Even in his lowest state, he remained true to Dharma. Eventually, his perseverance was rewarded, and his former glory was restored.

This story teaches that wealth gained through truth serves a higher purpose. However, wealth born from deceit and attachment eventually brings downfall.

One of the most eye-opening teachings I received from my Gurudev, especially during my Sri Suktam Sadhana, was understanding Lakshmi and Alakshmi. Lakshmi is known as the goddess of prosperity and fortune. But what many overlook is that wealth has a shadow—Alakshmi. Where there is greed, arrogance, and misuse of wealth, Alakshmi enters. She brings conflict, loss, restlessness, and pain.

Lakshmi graces those who earn wealth through Dharma. Such wealth brings peace and joy to the individual and society. But when wealth is gathered through greed or selfishness, it becomes a curse—Alakshmi.

That's why, in Vedic traditions, Dharma is the foundation. A house built on righteousness stands strong, while one built on greed eventually collapses.

One of the most powerful realisations for me was that wealth is not something we own but something we are entrusted with. The Rishis never viewed wealth as a personal possession—it was a divine resource meant to serve a higher purpose. Used with detachment and wisdom, wealth uplifts. When used with Ego and hoarding, it leads to suffering and separation from truth.

This changed everything for me. I understood that I was only a caretaker. Wealth, when handled with humility, can heal lives and create harmony. When misused, it creates inner emptiness.

Thanks to the teachings of Sanatana Dharma and my Guru, I no longer see wealth as mere money. Wealth is not just about wealth; it's also about wisdom, health, peace, meaningful relationships, and a life rooted in Dharma. Wealth becomes a problem only when pursued mindlessly with attachment. It is not ownership—it is a sacred responsibility. How we use it determines whether it becomes a blessing or a burden.

Most importantly, my Guru taught me that the highest wealth is self-realisation. Once a person knows their true divine nature, everything else becomes secondary. They may still earn and live in comfort, but they are no longer bound by it.

I aspire not to reject wealth but to master it, align it with Dharma, and use it for service, not bondage. That is true wealth.

We must shift from external possession to inner mastery to understand the balance between material and spiritual wealth. Wealth itself is neutral. It can be uplifting or destructive, depending on how we hold it, with greed or with detachment.

One of life's greatest illusions is the idea of ownership. We claim "my house, my wealth, my success," yet none of it goes with us. The

Kathopanishad teaches this beautifully through Nachiketa's dialogue with Yama. When Yama offers riches and pleasures, Nachiketa says:

"Oh, Yama, these are temporary and fleeting. No wealth can give true fulfilment. I seek that which is eternal."

This is not a rejection of wealth but a recognition of its impermanence. Detachment does not mean discarding wealth—it means not being possessed by it.

People often think detachment means giving up desires, but the mind is naturally drawn to engagement. It is not desire that binds us—it is attachment.

A detached person can enjoy wealth without feeling pride, work hard without fear of failure, own a lot, and remain free. This is not easy, but it is the way of the wise.

Both material and spiritual wealth have their place. The real question is not whether we should have wealth or not, but whether we can manage it without being managed by it.

True mastery is engaging with the world while staying free within.

This is the balance we must strive for.

In my experience, karma plays a profound role in shaping both material and spiritual wealth. Every action we perform—whether in this life or previous ones—creates ripples that manifest as the circumstances we face today. Some call it destiny, others luck, but at its core, it is simply the unfolding of the karmic seeds we've sown over time.

I believe the struggles I've faced in business, career, and finances are deeply rooted in past karma. For years, I felt stuck in survival mode, unable to make progress despite my sincere efforts. I questioned, I complained, and I felt helpless. But over time, I saw that even my suffering was part of the karmic path I had to walk.

Some might ask, "What does karma have to do with wealth? Isn't that just about effort and opportunity?" But the deeper I've gone into spirituality, the more I've realised everything is interconnected—including wealth. Karma shapes our thoughts, thoughts shape our actions, and actions shape results.

If one has accumulated good karma through dharmic choices, material success may come naturally, not as a reward but as a consequence of alignment with truth. On the other hand, someone driven by greed or dishonesty may find that no matter how hard they work, true prosperity—inner or outer—remains out of reach.

Spiritual evolution also follows karmic patterns. Some people are naturally drawn toward wisdom and peace, while others remain trapped in material pursuits. Past karmas shape this, too.

A common misconception is that karma binds us helplessly to our fate. People say, "If karma decides everything, aren't we powerless?" The answer is yes and no. Yes, past karmas shape our present. We cannot erase what has already been done. But no, we are not helpless. Karma is not a fixed destiny; it's a dynamic force shaped by our actions today.

We may not undo the past, but we have full power over the karmas we create today. And these karmas determine the quality of our future.

Understanding karma is key to mastering material and spiritual prosperity. When our actions are rooted in Dharma and selflessness, we shift the karmic momentum in our favour. Life becomes lighter, more aligned, and more fulfilling—not just financially but emotionally and spiritually.

Many of my students and clients ask, "If karma already influences our lives, how can we reduce its negative effects?"

The answer lies in Agami Karma—the conscious action of the present moment. No matter how spiritually I grow, I cannot undo the past. But I can shape the future by aligning my actions today with wisdom and Dharma.

When someone asks me during a Jyotish consultation, "How do I change my fate?" I tell them, "Do the right karma today. Surrender the results to the Divine. Accept your struggles with grace. Let every obstacle become a step toward your higher evolution."

Only a small fraction of people can truly receive and apply this advice the first time. However, it remains the only path to lessen suffering and create a prosperous future in inner and outer wealth.

If you ever feel caught between choosing a materially successful life or a deeply spiritual path, don't view them as opposites. That division is a mental construct.

As Grihasthas, we are not meant to abandon one for the other. Our honest Dharma lies in balancing both—living a life where material success and spiritual evolution support each other, rather than competing against each other.

4.5 Kshama & Kritagyata: Forgiveness and Gratitude

As we move forward on the journey of balancing material and spiritual life, we encounter two of the most transformative forces in human experience: gratitude and Forgiveness.

Gratitude shifts our perception, dissolves negativity, and attracts abundance. Forgiveness, on the other hand, frees us from pain, resentment, and karmic burdens. These are not just feelings but energies that shape our consciousness and influence our karmic path.

For me, gratitude didn't begin as a deep realisation. It started as a simple habit—a routine of saying "thank you" to the universe. At first, it felt mechanical, something I did because I had heard it would help.

But slowly, something changed.

What started as an effort became easy. I no longer had to remind myself to be grateful—it became my natural response. It wasn't just about acknowledging blessings, but about seeing life through a different lens - living from a place of acceptance and surrender. Gratitude stopped being a practice and became a state of being.

This shift touched every part of my life:

My thoughts became lighter, less caught in lack or complaint. I noticed what was already abundant.

My actions reflected more patience and humility. Seeing life as a gift naturally brings care.

Most of all, my reactions changed. Frustration and anger softened. I began to trust that even challenges held hidden blessings. I stopped asking "Why is this happening to me?" and started asking "What is this teaching me?"

Gratitude, I've realised, is not just a virtue or practice. It is a weapon— a powerful one. It destroys negativity, dissolves ego, and cuts through the false self. Ego survives on dissatisfaction, on comparison, on craving more. But gratitude says, "I have enough. Life is whole."

Gratitude purifies. It cleanses the mind, the emotions, and even karmic impressions. Most beautifully, it becomes a quiet, effortless path to the Divine. Sometimes, the deepest spiritual progress doesn't come from penance or intense spiritual practice—it comes from a heart filled with gratitude.

When you are genuinely grateful—not just in words but in your very being—you're already moving toward the Divine. You are already aligned with wisdom, peace, and joy.

Gratitude has reshaped my path. It was never something I consciously set out to master, yet as I reflect, I see clearly—it was the bridge that carried me through my doubts, difficulties, and delays in my spiritual journey.

I began this path later in life, not in childhood, when the mind is more agile and memory is sharper. I started sadhana and rituals when the grasping power had already begun to slow. It wasn't easy to accept.

I struggled. I tried forcing myself to memorise shlokas, prayers, aartis, and stotras. I would sit for hours, repeating them over and over, but the words refused to settle in my mind. My head felt too full, cluttered with years of worldly noise.

And then came the self-doubt.

When I listened to fellow sadhakas effortlessly reciting the glories of the Devatas and Devi Maa, I felt small. I asked myself—

"Why can't I remember these divine hymns?"

"Why is it easy for them but so difficult for me?"

"Am I lacking devotion? Am I not worthy?"

I was rigid with expectations, trying to force my mind to obey, resisting what was instead of embracing it.

That resistance created suffering.

And that is where gratitude gently entered, not as a grand realisation but as a quiet shift. One day, I stopped complaining and simply accepted my limitation.

I said to myself, "Yes, I struggle to memorise. Yes, I began late. But does that mean I stop? Does that make my spiritual journey any less meaningful?"

And with that surrender came gratitude.

I felt thankful that I even knew these practices existed.

Thankful that my Gurudev had brought me to this path.

Thankfully, I could still read, chant, and receive the essence of these sacred verses—even if I couldn't remember them by heart.

That simple shift changed everything.

I, who once couldn't read Sanskrit properly, now read with ease from PDFS and printouts. My pronunciation, once hesitant, is now firm. I can even sing with bhava, with devotion, as if these sounds have always lived inside me, waiting to be remembered.

How beautiful is that?

Is that not grace?

The verses are still tricky. My memory hasn't become sharper overnight. But my inner stance changed—from frustration to humility, from resistance to reverence. And that allowed grace to flow.

This is just one way gratitude has shaped my path. There are many others, where simply choosing to be grateful, rather than resisting life, opened the doors to peace and progress.

I chose this example because it is deeply personal, and because it proves something vital:

Gratitude is more than just being thankful; it's a genuine appreciation for something or someone. It is about becoming open—open to grace, open to learning, open to life as it is.

In the end, spiritual growth isn't measured by how much we memorise, but by how much we feel, absorb, and realise the Divine within us.

I can say this with certainty—not because I read it, not because someone told me, but because I lived it.

There are times when gratitude feels impossible, when pain is heavy, when the mind is exhausted. When nothing feels fair and the idea of saying "thank you" feels absurd.

In suffering, our instincts don't turn to gratitude. The mind wants to escape, to resist. And yet, that is when gratitude becomes its most potent.

Because gratitude isn't denial, it's not pretending that everything is fine. It's the courage to find even a flicker of light when all you see is darkness.

And before we move ahead, there's something else I must introduce: forgiveness.

Are you still with me?

Because this matters.

Gratitude and Forgiveness walk hand in hand.

Gratitude softens the heart.

Forgiveness cleanses it.

Gratitude lets us embrace life as it is. Forgiveness enables us to release what weighs us down.

When we are in pain, when life feels unfair, and the heart is heavy with resentment, gratitude may seem out of reach. But forgiveness? Forgiveness is the doorway that leads us there. It clears the mind, creating the space for gratitude to rise.

Before we delve deeper into forgiveness, let me first reveal a truth that is often misunderstood about gratitude. Many think gratitude is about feeling happy or positive. But it's not. Gratitude is not an emotion—it's a recognition.

It's recognising that even pain has a purpose. That every struggle is shaping us in ways we may not yet understand. That no experience, no matter how harsh, is meaningless.

There were times I told myself, "There is nothing to be grateful for right now." But looking back, I see clearly—every hardship was a doorway. A doorway to strength, to clarity, to growth. Gratitude doesn't deny pain—it helps us rise above it.

Some truths can only be learned through difficulty. Peace is best understood after restlessness. Strength, after weakness. Surrender, after a battle you cannot win. And gratitude, in the moments it feels impossible, you choose it anyway.

That's when it becomes more than a virtue. It becomes your being. And that's when life begins to shift.

Bhagavan Krishna said, "I am in each atom, in the smallest of particles, and they are in me." These words, present across the Gita and Upanishads, had always been there. But until my Gurudev spoke of them, they remained concepts—not living truths.

They say that knowledge becomes wisdom only through experience or grace. And when my Gurudev explained this, I felt the truth, not as a thought, but as a realisation.

In that moment, I saw Bhagavan everywhere—in every atom, every moment, every joy, every sorrow. Every experience, thought, and feeling carried His presence.

If the Divine is present in all, how can anything be evil?

This changed everything.

"If every moment is infused with Bhagavan, then every moment is perfect in itself." Even my struggles, my losses, my setbacks—they were divinely arranged. Not just good—they were necessary. And from that day on, I began to feel deep gratitude, not just for the blessings, but for the burdens too.

Because if He is present in all, then even our suffering is sacred.

How merciful is Bhagavan, to shape us through experiences—even when we fail to see the lesson in them?

I've noticed something in people that reveals the power of perspective. Some constantly complain. Their food is never good enough, their homes are never comfortable, and their work is never fulfilling. Even nature, in all its majesty, becomes a target for complaints.

If summer is too hot: "Oh God, why this cruel heat?" If winter is too cold: "Can't you be kinder?" If it rains: "When will this wetness end?"

But do they ever pause to consider that the world isn't designed to cater to their convenience? That nature isn't obligated to meet their moods?

Where I live in Rajkot, Gujarat, we experience harsh summers, cold winters, and heavy monsoons. But what of it? Are there not people thriving in far more extreme climates?

In Cherapunji, it rains almost year-round. In Rajasthan, temperatures often soar above 50°c. In Ladakh, the cold is nearly unbearable. Yet life continues. People adapt, survive, and even flourish.

It's not the seasons that make life difficult—it's our mindset. It's not the external that causes suffering, but our resistance to it.

This is where the wisdom of the Bhagavad Gita becomes transformative. When you begin to see everything as Bhagavan's will, problems turn into purpose.

Instead of asking, "Why is this happening to me?" you begin to ask, "What is Bhagavan showing me through this?"

When the sun blazes, you say, "This too is divine." When the rain pours endlessly, "This too is grace." And when life turns upside down, you trust, "If Bhagavan is in every moment, then this too is here to guide me."

From here, gratitude flows effortlessly—because now you're no longer resisting reality, you're flowing with it. And to flow with life is the highest form of grace.

To know whether gratitude attracts abundance, we must first understand what abundance truly is. Most people think of it as something external—something to earn, chase, or collect. But abundance isn't something we reach; it's something we recognise.

This truth is hard to grasp when life seems to withhold what we long for. But struggling to accept it doesn't make it any less accurate. Abundance is not about quantity—it's about awareness of the blessings already present.

Imagine standing in the middle of an ocean with just one glass of fresh water in your hands. That single glass becomes invaluable, while the vast ocean around you cannot quench your thirst. But instead of cherishing the glass, the mind obsesses over the sea, lamenting what it cannot have. We mourn what's missing instead of honouring what we hold.

This is how most people live. Their eyes are set on the unreachable, and in doing so, they miss the miracle of what already surrounds them.

Nature teaches abundance in its purest form. The same air breathes life into both the wealthy and the poor. The same sky shelters kings and beggars. The sun shines for all. The trees stand tall through storms, asking for nothing, giving everything—shade, oxygen, and stability. They protect the Earth without seeking recognition.

If nature exists in such generous balance, why do we feel deprived?

Because we look at what's absent instead of what has been offered, we chase what we lack, forgetting to bow before what we already possess.

You may think these are just philosophical ideas, but this is the only way I've truly grasped the essence of abundance. It isn't something found in riches or possessions—it's something realised within. And no, I'm no teacher of these truths. I'm only sharing what I've lived. In moments of solitude, when I reflect deeply, I often hear a voice within whispering, "Jai, you're the luckiest person in the world. Why are you sad?" That voice—my inner self—reminds me that I've already been given everything I need, and more.

To live in abundance, one doesn't have to be rich or powerful. One simply has to embrace being alive, recognising that life itself is the greatest treasure. But something powerful happens when we embody gratitude. It's often said that what you stop chasing comes to you. This isn't a poetic idea—it's something I've experienced. When we loosen our grip on our desires and stop treating life as a struggle for more, what we once chased often begins to flow toward us effortlessly.

That's why I believe gratitude is the gateway to abundance. When we're truly grateful, we stop living in a state of lack. We no longer cry over what we don't have. Our vision clears, and we begin to see the immense blessings already surrounding us. In that state, abundance naturally expands—not because we're demanding it, but because we're finally aligned with it.

This doesn't mean we stop working toward our goals or become passive. That's not Santosha. True contentment doesn't mean letting go of effort or ambition; it means being fulfilled by the journey, regardless of the outcome. It means working sincerely, giving your best, and receiving whatever comes as a blessing. When you detach from results, whatever you receive feels like a bonus, and bonuses are met with joy, not expectation.

The more profound realisation is that while gratitude attracts abundance, by the time we reach that state, we no longer cling to it. Whether something comes or not, whether we gain or lose, we remain at peace. If abundance arrives, we welcome it. If it doesn't, that's perfect too. Because in gratitude, every breath is a gift, every moment is enough, every experience sacred. When you live this way, what is left to long for?

To truly feel gratitude, we must first understand what it is not. It is not blind acceptance or passive contentment that halts growth or ambition. If gratitude becomes an excuse for stagnation, it isn't gratitude—it's avoidance. That's why simply saying "thank you" without emotion, or forcing ourselves to feel grateful when we don't, is hollow and ultimately disempowering.

Genuine gratitude is something else entirely. It doesn't hold us back— it lifts us. It isn't passive—it burns bright like fire in the soul. It is not a practice of stillness, but a force that inspires movement—forward, upward, inward.

Before moving forward, there's something deeper we must acknowledge. Gratitude does not mean renouncing desires. This is a crucial balance. Many people, in their early spiritual journey, mistake desires (kāmanās) as obstacles to growth. But that's not true. My Gurudev, Swamiji, once said something that stayed with me forever— a person with no desires is like the dead child of a monkey. In some species, when a baby dies, the mother still carries its body, unwilling to let go. The child no longer grows or evolves, yet the mother clings to it. This is what happens when we force ourselves to abandon all desire—we lose our vitality, but we continue with the motions of life.

Mother Nature is not cruel. She doesn't create without purpose. Every being is born with a dharma, a role in this cosmic dance. To live without aspirations is to move through life like a lifeless form. Nature will still carry you, for she is a mother, but you will not truly be alive.

Misunderstanding gratitude as passive contentment—where one extinguishes their fire while trying to appear grateful—only leads to stagnation. Genuine gratitude doesn't kill your ambition. It fuels it. It awakens a deeper purpose. Once you realise that life itself is a gift, your actions naturally align with something more significant. Your efforts become offerings. They stop being about personal success and begin to fulfil your dharma.

That's when you start recognising the difference between forced and genuine gratitude. As I've grown, my desires haven't disappeared—they've expanded. But they're no longer self-centred. They arise from service, from dharma. And so, even the most minor victories feel profound. I celebrate them because they belong to a purpose greater than myself.

Feeding an underprivileged child a ₹50 meal can feel like a divine act—not because I feel noble, but because I recognise how blessed I am to be the vessel through which nature serves. That's the secret. Gratitude isn't about donation or virtue-signalling. It's about seeing yourself as part of an excellent flow and feeling immense thankfulness that you were chosen to participate.

When gratitude comes from that space, it's effortless. It becomes as natural as breath.

Gratitude, without doubt, is a form of devotion. It's not just about saying "thank you" or seeing the good in life—it's a way of surrendering to the divine, without demands, without conditions. Many saints describe gratitude as the purest form of bhakti. A grateful heart doesn't protest, doesn't seek—it bows down in silent reverence to the grace already present.

When I practice gratitude during meditation, my mind stops clinging to desires. It doesn't resist or struggle—it rests in contentment, in awareness, in the peaceful acceptance of what is. I could explain this even further, but for now, the essence remains this: gratitude is devotion in its purest form.

But here is where my journey took a different turn. Gratitude didn't come to me naturally. I mentioned this earlier, and I'm repeating it because I know how many seekers struggle with this. It's one thing to hear teachings about gratitude—it's another to *live* it honestly. And that's one of the reasons I'm writing this book. For me, gratitude wasn't a sudden enlightenment. It was a gradual unfolding, deeply woven into many aspects of spiritual life—purpose, karma, devotion, faith, surrender, ego, desires, expectations, detachment, contentment, and more, which I've shared. It will continue to be shared in the coming chapters in part two.

There were times I'd read the words of great masters and feel they were speaking a language I couldn't yet understand. Their wisdom on devotion, surrender, and gratitude sounded profound, but I couldn't fully absorb it. Still, I followed—not out of understanding, but out of faith that one day I would. And they were right. Every word was accurate. The issue wasn't their teachings—it was the gaps in my foundation. I lacked certain inner understandings that would allow their wisdom to settle.

This is why I felt called to write this book. Because I know that experiencing gratitude isn't as simple as hearing about it, nor as impossible as it sometimes feels. The challenge lies in finding the missing threads—the subtle truths that turn spiritual ideas into lived experiences.

For me, that missing thread was my Gurudev. The day I began truly *understanding* him—not just hearing his words, but letting them shape how I think and live—everything started falling into place. Suddenly, the teachings of other enlightened beings also began to make sense. Before that, their words had felt distant. But when my Gurudev's wisdom became my foundation, I saw how they were all saying the same truth in different ways.

So when I say that gratitude is devotion, I don't mean it as a practice to be remembered. I mean it as a shift in your very being. I never practised gratitude in the sense of setting reminders to say "thank you". It simply became part of me—woven into my breath, my thoughts, my choices. It wasn't something I did—it became who I was. And when that happens, when gratitude flows through you without effort, it becomes true devotion. It ceases to be a concept and becomes the very essence of who you are.

And now, we arrive at something vital—gratitude as the bridge between material and spiritual wealth. As I've said, it's not just an emotion. It's the root of joy, the lens through which all of life transforms. When we talk about balance—between Artha and Moksha—it is gratitude that keeps us grounded, centred, and aware.

When you begin seeing life through the lens of gratitude, something profound shifts. You no longer live in lack. You stop seeing yourself as a victim. You stop postponing happiness until some future goal—material or spiritual—is achieved. You begin to notice that abundance was always present. You see blessings that were hidden in plain sight. Complaints fade. Thankfulness arises, not as discipline, but as a spontaneous expression of joy. And when that shift happens, your entire relationship with life changes.

There have been so many moments where I've laughed at my old self—at the way I used to think, the burdens I carried, and the endless complaints I made. Gratitude doesn't just change how you feel—it transforms how you think, respond, and live. Imagine how beautiful life becomes when your thinking shifts completely. When you no longer drain yourself with drama, when family issues stop weighing you down, and arguments no longer feel like battles. You begin letting go with ease. You start seeing grace even in hardship. You walk through life lighter, freer, no longer bound by unnecessary suffering.

This doesn't mean challenges vanish. There will still be tests of patience and difficult times. But when gratitude is your foundation, you stop seeing these as burdens and start seeing them as passing waves on the surface of your deeper self. Gratitude reminds you that you have enough. That you *are* enough. And from that knowing, the endless worrying and grasping start to fade.

This is how gratitude completes the circle between material and spiritual life. As householders, we're not renunciates—we live in the world, fulfil duties, raise families, and pursue careers. But gratitude elevates our experience of this path. It turns us into householders who lead with awareness, who become sources of calm, clarity, and quiet strength for those around them.

I've seen this in my own life. People who knew me in my more restless years are amazed at the change. They notice how my behaviour has softened, how I meet difficulty with calmness I once lacked. Some friends even reach out when they're overwhelmed — not because I have the power to fix their lives, but because they sense I've found a different way of seeing.

But I say this with complete humility. I claim no power, no remarkable ability. I often tell them, "I'm not doing anything special. I'm not a saint. I'm not a miracle-worker. I'm just an ordinary person." The only difference is that I've walked this path. And even that wasn't by my doing—it's all the grace of my Gurudev.

His wisdom flows like the morning mist—gentle, constant, unconditional. Whether I gather it or not, it keeps falling. I've held onto as much as I could, within my limits. But the credit is not mine. It is his grace, his presence, his light. I am just a reflection, a vessel through which that grace expresses itself.

This, too, is gratitude—knowing nothing belongs to you, yet feeling the joy of having everything.

Before we move ahead, let us pause and go deeper into the second great force—Forgiveness.

To me, forgiveness is not just letting go—it is a deep cleansing of the soul, a purification of the mind, a release of the heart. It's not only about moving past resentment; it's about making space for something greater. Imagine a glass filled with murky water. If you want to fill it with something pure, the first step is to empty it. You cannot pour in clarity while it still holds poison. Forgiveness is that emptying. It is the surrender of all that weighs you down, all that distorts your peace. Only when you've fully released bitterness can love, gratitude, and grace begin to fill you.

People often misunderstand forgiveness. They think it's about letting someone off the hook, about doing a favour to the one who hurt them. But forgiveness is never about the other person—it's about you. It's about freeing yourself from resentment, from the weight of old wounds, from the suffering that lingers long after the pain was caused. Holding onto anger doesn't punish the person who wronged you—it punishes you. It walls off your heart, clouds your mind, and drains your peace. But the moment you forgive—not just in words, but from the depths of your being—you experience a lightness that words cannot describe.

Have you ever held a plank pose? In yoga, we call it Utthita Chaturanga Dandasana. Your body trembles, your breath tightens, and your strength is tested. And then you let go. That one moment of release, of surrender—it's one of the closest physical experiences to what forgiveness feels like for the mind.

Now imagine carrying anger and resentment not for minutes, but for months or years. How heavy the mind becomes. How much energy gets trapped in clinging to pain that serves no purpose? And now imagine what it feels like to say, "I don't carry this anymore, finally." That relief, that peace, that quiet joy—that is the gift of forgiveness.

Forgiveness is not weakness—it is strength. It's the decision to stop suffering, to free yourself, to make room for something purer than the pain. When you truly empty yourself of resentment, you become a vessel for gratitude, clarity, and joy. Forgiveness isn't just a decision—it's an evolution of the soul. And once you taste its freedom, you'll wonder why you carried the weight for so long.

I wasn't always this way. Forgiveness was once foreign to me—something I never even considered. I held onto every slight, every insult, every wound. I stored them all, no matter how small. And because of that, I carried an invisible weight that only grew heavier with time. Looking back, I can see how much of my energy was lost in resentment.

When I started earning, I developed a false sense of independence. It was the small-mindedness of a teenager who suddenly had money and thought he needed no one. But even before that, I had always been a bit emotionally distant. In school, I had good relations with classmates but no deep connections. I never had that one close friend who stays with you through life—the kind that laughs with you decades later, reliving old memories. I know such friendships exist. I've seen them. But I never had one.

And I know why.

It's because I never forgave. I held onto every slight, every emotional bruise. I let them shape how I saw people, how I approached relationships. I didn't let things dissolve. I held on.

Because of this, my life became smaller, more isolated. And I had no idea how deeply trapped I was in my inability to forgive.

There's one incident from my childhood that shows how unnecessary most of our anger truly is.

I remember wanting a pair of shoes that lit up when you walked. It was a big deal for me. I begged my parents for days, but they kept refusing. Then one day, my father's friend came over. I took the chance to complain. "Uncle, Mom and Dad won't buy me my favourite shoes." He convinced them, and eventually my mother got them for me. I was overjoyed.

But this is where the real story begins.

We went to visit some relatives, and I wore those shoes for the first time. There was someone I wanted to impress, a childish desire. At their house, everyone removed their shoes at the entrance. But I didn't. Not to be disrespectful, but because I was proud and lost in excitement.

Suddenly, I heard a loud voice.

"Don't you have any sense? Why are you wearing shoes inside my house? Even your parents removed theirs! You're such a careless child!"

The words hit me like a slap. I froze. I hadn't even realised what I was doing. But instead of apologising, I quietly stepped outside. I didn't remove my shoes. I just refused to go in.

My parents called me. I didn't respond.

That was it. I never revisited their home. Not once.

Looking back, I see how ridiculous that was. At that age, it felt like a profound insult. But now, I understand. Today, if someone walked into my puja space wearing shoes, I'd feel bad too. I may not shout, but I'd feel what they felt. Their approach was harsh, but the intention wasn't wrong.

That's what life teaches. Most of the things we carry—anger, resentment, hurt—are as small as this. At the time, they seemed huge. But as we grow, we realise they weren't significant at all.

Still, people hold onto such incidents for years. I was one of them. I treated my grudges like treasures, protecting them, feeding them with my thoughts. And what did I gain? Only heaviness.

But life has its way of teaching.

Over time, something shifted. I began to see how much energy was wasted holding onto things I couldn't change. There is no reverse button in life. So what's the point in carrying it?

That's when I began letting go.

Today, if I saw that same relative, I could offer a full Sashtang Dandvat Pranama—not out of duty, but with true humility.

That's what forgiveness does. It doesn't just lighten the mind—it sets you free. It helps you see life not as a pile of past wounds, but as a journey, where every person and every moment help shape who you are.

That is the real power of forgiveness—not just for others, but for yourself.

The link between forgiveness and karma isn't just philosophical—it's deeply practical. Every thought, action, or reaction is a form of karma. Choosing to forgive or hold onto resentment, to release or to cling—these, too, are karmas. And like all karma, they shape not only your outer world but also your inner world.

Looking back, I see a pattern in my karmic tendencies. I held tightly to knowledge, skills, and advantages. I was selfish in ways I didn't even recognise. If I knew something, I'd keep it to myself, thinking that sharing would strip me of my uniqueness.

In some ways, this belief had truth. I had developed skills that set me apart.

I excelled at product presentations, was skilled at handling client objections, and was convincing during test drives that often led buyers to choose my brand. I had a natural way of connecting with people, especially in my mother tongue. These made me feel valuable.

Beyond sales, I had other strengths as well. I was good with computers, setting up LANS in corporate offices. I understood operating systems and gadgets better than most. In school, I excelled in theory but struggled in math, accounts, and statistics. Still, wherever I went, I had an edge. But I saw my knowledge as something to protect, not share.

If a colleague or friend asked for help, I hesitated. I thought, "If I give this away, what will I have left?"

Then life taught me a lesson I wasn't ready for.

Despite all I held on to, when I needed help, no one came forward to help. And why would they? I had spent years giving nothing. I had kept everything to myself. And now, life simply mirrored that emptiness.

This is karma. It isn't an instant trade—do good, receive good. It's not "I help you, you help me." It's subtler. Karma reflects who you are. You receive what you live.

That realisation hit hard. I had clung to what I thought was value, but in doing so, I blocked myself from receiving anything more significant.

The day I understood karma was the day I realised that others didn't cause my suffering—it was self-created. Not because of what happened to me, but because of how I lived, thought, and held onto things that were never meant to be hoarded.

And today, look at me.

I'm not just sharing my knowledge—I'm giving everything. I'm writing this book, openly revealing my mistakes, my past ignorance, and even the most personal lessons I've learned. I'm not hiding my strengths or my flaws.

Why?

Because I now understand that true wealth—material or spiritual—comes not from keeping, but from giving.

Forgiveness is the same.

To forgive is to release. It's to let go of karmic weight. It's to open up to something greater than what you lost.

Each time we hold onto resentment, we carry karmic baggage. Every time we cling to an insult, we tighten the chains of suffering. But when we forgive—not just in words, but profoundly—something shifts.

We become beautifully empty.

And in that emptiness, we become open to grace.

Forgiveness isn't a favour to the one who hurt you. It's a gift to yourself. It's how you break the cycle of pain. It's how you transform karma—not by erasing the past, but by choosing how you live now.

And that, truly, is liberation.

Self-forgiveness is not just an act; it is essential to spiritual growth and evolution. It is the foundation of inner peace, the key to breaking free from the past, and the path to embracing life as it unfolds in the present.

Forgiveness is often misunderstood as something we extend only to others. But what about the wrongs we've done to ourselves—the choices we regret, the pain we caused through our ignorance? This is where Ahimsa, the principle of non-violence, reveals its deeper truth.

Ahimsa is not limited to refraining from harming others—it also means not harming oneself. Yet many of us carry wounds of self-inflicted suffering: guilt, shame, regret. We judge ourselves harshly, replaying past mistakes over and over. If we truly understand Ahimsa, we see that clinging to guilt is just another form of inner violence.

I've carried that weight too. I've been ignorant, careless, and blind to the blessings and people in my life. I've hurt others, sometimes unknowingly, and even now, memories of them return as reminders of how far I've come. There are times I feel I did them wrong. And yet, I ask myself—what can I do now?

I cannot change the past or rewrite history. So, what is the purpose of endless regret? It has no end. Once you fall into it, you keep losing. You start with one thing, then another, and soon your whole life is caught in a web of "what ifs" and "if onlys." But regret changes nothing—it only robs you of the present.

We all make mistakes, and we all wish we'd chosen differently at times. But what matters now is how we respond. Do we keep making the same mistakes, or do we use them as opportunities to grow?

Self-forgiveness doesn't mean being careless or ignoring consequences. It means accepting what was, learning from it, and choosing not to let it define you. Holding onto guilt destroys not just your past—it also robs you of your present and your potential.

That's why self-forgiveness is so vital. If we carry guilt, we miss the life unfolding before us. And in truth, this breath is all we have.

Forgiveness isn't always a choice of the mind. Sometimes, it's the heart that holds on. Some wounds cut so deep, some betrayals ache so sharply, that even when we understand forgiveness intellectually, the emotions remain raw. The pain resists logic.

I've been there. I've felt that resistance. I knew forgiveness was the path, yet I couldn't walk it. The hurt was too real. And that's when I realised—true forgiveness is not a decision. It's a process. A slow, sacred healing of the heart.

Despite all this, I still take these moments as my tests. Because in the larger scheme of life, if we don't learn to forgive, we cannot truly grow. You cannot cultivate kindness, humility, or inner peace while clinging to grudges. You cannot walk the path of bhakti or surrender with a heart heavy with resentment. Divine love cannot fill a heart that's still closed.

These are life's realities. That's why life is called a journey of pain. We've all suffered, felt betrayed, heartbroken, and disappointed. And yet, we wake up each day wanting to live, to grow, to feel more fully. What does this tell us?

It tells us that forgiveness is not about the past—it's about the future. It is a conscious choice: do I carry this pain forever, or finally set it down and walk forward, lighter, freer?

And sometimes, we are the ones who caused the pain. We're not always the victims. Sometimes, it's our words or actions that hurt others. When guilt arises, when that awareness becomes too loud to ignore, we must also learn to forgive ourselves.

When I find myself in such moments, I simply apologise. Not always face-to-face. But silently, sincerely, by surrendering the guilt to the Divine. I say:

"I know I caused pain. I'm not proud of it. I feel the weight of my actions. Bhagavan, if you, who are infinitely kind, can forgive me, please do. I don't want to carry this guilt anymore."

And something shifts. The burden eases. The heart opens. Because forgiveness is not for others—it's for us. And once that's understood, forgiveness no longer feels forced—it becomes natural.

We often speak of "forgive and forget," as if the two go hand in hand. But our minds are not designed to forget. They remember—especially the pain. The betrayals, the insults, the wounds—these etch themselves deeper than joy ever could.

So if we cannot forget, can we truly forgive?

The answer doesn't lie in erasing memory, but in choosing what we give weight to. When someone says, "Forget it," they don't mean delete it from your mind. They suggest—stop feeding it, stop giving it control.

In that sense, forgetting becomes just as vital as forgiving. Because what good is forgiveness if you still let that pain shape your emotions, control your responses, haunt your peace?

Think of it like prioritising tasks in life. We sort what's urgent and what's not. The same must be done with the mental burdens we carry. Ask yourself, "Is this still important? Is this truly worth holding onto?"

Most of the time, you'll find it's not. It's just emotional clutter, unnecessary weight. And once you recognise that, letting go becomes easier.

This is why forgetting, not in the sense of erasing, but of deprioritising, of choosing not to give something space in your mind, is just as vital as forgiving. But I understand this isn't easy. This is where Abhyasa, consistent practice, becomes essential.

Like everything else in spiritual life, forgiveness and forgetting don't happen instantly. Just as you don't master yoga in a day, or build a strong mind overnight, you don't suddenly wake up free of resentment. It takes time. Depending on your temperament, past, and self-awareness, it may take longer or shorter. But what matters is your willingness to begin.

Because the more you practice forgetting, the lighter you become. The more you practice forgiving, the freer you feel. And when you finally let go of something you once thought was impossible to release, you'll look back and wonder why you held it so long.

Forgiveness is never truly about the other person—it's always about you. Every aspect of spirituality is about you. Healing, evolving, and awakening—all begin and end within. The world outside is only a mirror, a trigger, a stage. But the transformation always happens inside.

I've seen this unfold many times.

I refrain from sharing details from my consultations, as I deeply respect the trust placed in me by those who seek guidance. However, the essence of one particular conversation felt important to include here—not for storytelling, but for the clarity it may offer to you, dear reader. With her kind permission, and without disclosing any personal information, I'm sharing a brief overview of the situation, solely to support the understanding of what follows.

Recently, I was consulting with a woman who came to me for her astrological and numerological charts, hoping to resolve the difficulties in her life. As she described her problems, I recognised something I once saw in myself—a refusal to let go.

She was carrying everything. Past hurts, betrayals, painful memories—she had stored them all. The suffering wasn't just from the past; it was ongoing because she wouldn't let them go.

She resisted the idea of forgiveness. To her, the people who had wronged her didn't deserve it. And I knew then—I couldn't change her through advice. I had to help her see her offering.

So I asked her gently, "All these emotions—this pain and bitterness—who are they harming? Are they affecting the people who hurt you in any way? Or are they only hurting you?"

She went silent, then whispered, "I am harming myself. They don't even know what I'm going through. They don't care. But I suffer every single day."

I said, "Exactly. That's the point. You're holding on to poison, hoping it punishes them—but it's only destroying you."

She sat still, thinking. Then she asked, "But how do I move forward?"

I told her, "The past is already over. These memories are only imprints now. The only thing that's real is this moment. And in this moment, you have a choice—carry the pain or set yourself free. Don't worry about the future—it's not in your control. Don't cling to the past—it's gone. Just live this moment without bitterness, without grudges. Live as if you're the happiest person in the world. Just try it for one day. Then two. Then three."

She agreed.

A week passed. One day, while riding through heavy traffic, I kept receiving multiple calls. Thinking it might be urgent, I pulled over, removed my helmet, and checked—she had called. I rang her back, wondering if something was wrong.

As soon as she answered, her voice held something new—lightness. Freedom. Joy.

She said, "I feel completely relaxed. I feel free. I don't need any more remedies—I already found my relief."

I smiled. I knew exactly what she meant.

Before coming to me, she had already consulted several astrologers and numerologists and tried numerous remedies. Many of them were not only expensive but also impractical—difficult to follow, and disconnected from her reality. Despite her sincere efforts, nothing seemed to bring lasting change.

When she came to me, I didn't offer a long list of rituals or remedies. I simply recorded a short, guided meditation—personalised for her—and asked her to practice it for just ten minutes a day, whenever it felt comfortable. That was all. Nothing else. No yantras, no elaborate rituals, no conditions.

And she did it. Just that. And the shift she experienced was profound.

Are you seeing the real difference? Sometimes, the most powerful transformation doesn't come from doing more—it comes from going within.

This is the power of forgiveness.

We believe forgiveness is a kind act toward others. But honestly, it's the greatest kindness toward yourself. Holding onto resentment chains you to the past. You keep drinking poison, hoping someone else suffers. Forgiveness breaks those chains. It cleanses and liberates. And when you finally let go, you don't just move on—you rise.

Forgiveness is not weakness. It is a strength. But people often confuse forgiveness with reconciliation. They assume forgiving someone means allowing them back into your life, acting as though nothing happened. But that's not true.

Forgiveness and boundaries don't need to be balanced, because when forgiveness becomes your nature, there's no calculation left. Saints don't forgive with effort; they forgive by default, just like Gautama Buddha.

There was once a man who constantly insulted Buddha. No matter how often it happened, Buddha never reacted. One day, in frustration, the man asked, "I've insulted you for years. Why don't you get angry?"

Buddha smiled and replied, "If someone brings you a gift, and you refuse it, to whom does it belong?"

The man said, "It still belongs to the one who brought it."

"Exactly," Buddha said. "I never accepted your hatred—it still belongs to you."

That is true forgiveness. You reach a space where others' negativity no longer touches you. Forgiveness isn't forced—it becomes who you are.

But does it mean allowing that person back into your life?

Not at all. Forgiveness does not require trust. It doesn't mean letting someone repeat their behaviour. It's not about excusing others—it's about freeing yourself.

You can forgive and still draw boundaries.

You can release resentment when you decide that someone no longer belongs in your life.

Forgiveness is for your peace. Boundaries are for your self-respect.

When you evolve, when wisdom deepens, you stop worrying about what others think. If they think you're weak, let them. If they think you're naïve, so be it. It no longer matters.

The "old you" who cared about others' opinions is gone. The "new you" walks a higher path.

And if a thought like, "What will they think of me if I forgive?" still crosses your mind, it's a sign—keep walking. You're not there yet. Your path leads beyond such thoughts.

In Sanatana Dharma, forgiveness is not just a virtue, or a duty, or a mark of wisdom. It is the natural state of a being aligned with truth, with dharma, with the divine flow of life.

Think about it. Do the trees hold a grudge against the one who cuts their branches? Does the river stop flowing for someone who once polluted it? Does the sun withhold its warmth from those who curse the heat? No. Nature follows its dharma effortlessly.

Forgiveness is that same effortless state. A space where no resentment is stored, no past wound nurtured. In our journey toward self-realisation, holding onto anger or pain is like carrying unnecessary weight on a long pilgrimage. The more you have, the harder it becomes to carry. Refuse to let go, and you may never reach your destination.

This is why forgiveness isn't just a choice—it's the only way forward.

If forgiveness is natural, why does it feel so hard?

Because we've drifted from our natural state, we've covered ourselves with ego, false identity, expectations, and attachments. These layers of avaranas make forgiveness seem like a lot of work. But really, it's holding on that requires effort.

So when someone asks, "Is forgiveness a virtue?" I say, it's beyond virtue. Virtue is cultivated—this is uncovered. It already exists deep within us.

If asked, "Is forgiveness a duty?"—I say it's beyond duty. A duty is an obligation. Forgiveness flows when you realise clinging to pain only wounds you further.

And is forgiveness wisdom? Wisdom leads to it, but forgiveness isn't wisdom—it is the fragrance of wisdom. Like a lotus that does not try to be fragrant—it simply is. When wisdom blossoms, forgiveness becomes its effortless scent.

Forgiveness, as I understand it, isn't just part of spiritual growth—it is the way to live. It is the breath of peace, the state of a liberated being, the gateway to divine union.

And when forgiveness comes—not just from the lips or mind, but from the depths of your being—you feel a lightness, a freedom, an inner vastness that words can't describe.

The remorse—or the lack of it-isn't the other person's concern.

This must be understood deeply. Forgiveness is not about them—it is about you. It is not about whether they acknowledge or regret—it is about whether you wish to be free.

People struggle here because they treat forgiveness like a transaction. "They must deserve it." But who decides that? And if they don't ask for it, must we carry resentment forever?

If you've truly walked far on this path, this won't even be a question.

The one who's matured in understanding does not wait for apologies or regret. They simply let go of the past and move forward.

Let's look at it clearly—if someone wrongs you and feels no remorse, who suffers?

Them? No. They're unaware.

You? Yes. Because you hold the pain.

So, who is being punished?

That is the irony. The one who refuses to forgive is the one who suffers the most. The person you haven't forgiven may not even know the weight you carry. But you do. You feel it. So why let it poison your life?

Why give their past actions power over your present peace?

Forgiving someone who is not sorry does not mean their actions were acceptable. It only means you are choosing peace over pain. You're freeing yourself.

And if you need a starting point on this path of forgiveness, begin with gratitude.

Now, are gratitude and forgiveness complete without each other?

No, absolutely not.

Think about it—how can you be truly grateful for life if your heart still holds resentment? Gratitude is light, openness, and expansion. Resentment is heaviness, constriction, and resistance. They cannot coexist.

If you're sincerely grateful for the present moment, for the grace around you, how can you continue to cling to old wounds?

And forgiveness, without gratitude, remains incomplete. Forgiveness without gratitude feels like an obligation, something done just because it's "right." But when forgiveness is born from gratitude, something deeper happens. You begin to see the hidden blessings in your pain. You recognise, "This experience made me stronger." You understand, "This suffering deepened my wisdom." You accept, "This pain became my greatest teacher."

When forgiveness merges with gratitude, it ceases to be about "letting go"; it becomes a transformation. And in that transformation, you realise something profound: you were never forgiving *them*. You were freeing *yourself*.

There is a beautiful shloka in Sanskrit Subhashitani:

क्षमा बलमशक्तानाम् शक्तानाम् भूषणम् क्षमा।

क्षमा वशीकृते लोके क्षमयाः किम् न सिद्ध्यति॥

Forgiveness is strength. For the weak, as well as for the strong, it is an ornament. Forgiveness conquers all. What can one not achieve through forgiveness? What can a wicked man do to someone who holds peace as a sword? Fire on barren ground extinguishes itself. Virtue is the highest good. Forgiveness is the greatest peace. Knowledge brings the deepest satisfaction, and benevolence is the trustworthy source of joy.

This shloka reminds us that forgiveness is not a sign of weakness—it is a sign of immense strength. Retaliation is easy. But to forgive, to rise above the wound, takes a power far greater.

As I mentioned earlier, although Kaikeyi was the reason for his exile, Rama never blamed her. Upon returning from exile, victorious, he bowed before her with the same love and respect.

Why?

Because Rama's heart was vast, he understood what most fail to see—his exile was not misfortune. It was divine design. Without it, the great battle of Dharma would never have been fought. Without it, his divine example would not have been revealed.

So, in his heart, there was no bitterness—only gratitude.

That is the ultimate truth: everything has a purpose. Even pain. And when you realise this, forgiveness becomes effortless. Gratitude arises naturally. You stop seeing life as happening *to* you and start recognising that everything is happening *for* you.

This, to me, is one of the highest revelations of Sanatana Dharma. Forgiveness and gratitude are not separate. They are one.

They also shape our karmic patterns. Karma is not an external force deciding our fate—it is the vibration of our thoughts, actions, and reactions. What we think is what we become. If anger, ego, and resentment fill our minds, our karmas reflect that. However, if we approach life from a space of forgiveness, gratitude, and humility, our karmas naturally align with dharma.

Every action begins with a thought. If that thought is rooted in bitterness, the karma is impure. If that thought is born of love, surrender, and clarity, the karma is transformative.

That is why I say: forgiveness and gratitude are not just emotions—they are karmic instruments.

If you're struggling with resentment, it only means one thing: you're still growing. Keep walking.

Resentment is not failure—it is a sign of growth. If you're struggling, it means you're aware of the problem. And awareness is always the first step toward transformation.

But forgiveness is not about speed. It's not something to force within a day, a week, or even a year. It unfolds when the heart is ready.

So be patient with yourself. The fact that you're struggling means you're already on the path. Keep trying, keep observing, keep surrendering. One day, you'll wake up and realise that the resentment no longer grips you.

And in that moment, you will smile—because you'll know you are free.

If someone feels ungrateful or lost, I'd say that's a natural state, too.

Do not mistake it as failure. Feeling lost is the first sign that you're searching for something more. Feeling ungrateful means you're beginning to question your current view of life.

And that's a good thing.

Because the moment you become aware of your ungratefulness, you've already moved toward gratitude.

Many people live their entire lives without realising what they already have. But if you are even asking, "Why am I ungrateful?" or "Why do I feel lost?"—you are already searching.

And the one who searches constantly finds.

So, embrace this phase. It's just a passing storm, and beyond it, there is clarity.

Start small. Find just one thing to be grateful for today. It doesn't have to be profound. It could be the air you breathe, the food on your plate, or even the ability to read these words. Hold onto that one thing, and let it grow.

Soon, you will see—you were never lost. You were preparing to be found.

If there's one truth I've learned, it's this—life flows with ease when we stop resisting. The more we cling to pain, the heavier we become. The more we try to control, the more we suffer. But the moment we let go—when we surrender to gratitude and forgiveness—we experience something rare: lightness, freedom, peace.

Gratitude is not just about saying thank you—it's about seeing the divine in all things. Forgiveness is not just letting go of hurt—it's freeing ourselves from burdens we were never meant to carry.

Together, they become the most powerful spiritual practices.

So, as we close this chapter, take a deep breath and ask yourself—What can I let go of today? What can I be grateful for right now?

It's not about forcing anything. It's about opening your heart to the quiet joy of being.

Because when you truly embrace gratitude and forgiveness, you'll realise—the universe was always kind to you. It was simply waiting for you to notice.

Silence ends with sacred sound.

ॐ सर्वे भवन्तु सुखिनः
सर्वे सन्तु निरामयाः ।
सर्वे भद्राणि पश्यन्तु
मा कश्चिद्दुःखभाग्भवेत् ॥
ॐ शान्तिः शान्तिः शान्तिः ॥

ANTAR YATRA – THE INCOMPLETE JOURNEY

When you reach the end of something, it is natural to ask, "Is this complete?" But if you have truly walked with me through these chapters, you already know—the answer is no.

What you hold in your hands is not a conclusion. It is a threshold.

We have explored the origins of the soul, the whisper of dharma, the illusion of ego, the weight of family, the nectar of bhakti, the fire of karma, and the dance of dualities. You now know how the world deceives, how the mind entangles, how even devotion can become diluted, and how easily we can forget who we are.

You've tasted the fragrance of the path, but the fruit is yet to ripen.
You've seen the sky, but you have not yet learned how to fly beneath it.
You've awakened… but you've not yet learned how to live awake.

This book—the first part of *Saṃsārik Yogī*—was meant to open your eyes. The next one is meant to open up your life.

There is a point in every journey when reading is not enough, when truth must be tasted in silence, when theory must fall to its knees before practice, when devotion must reach your hands, your tongue, your food, and your discipline.

That point is now.

In the pages ahead—pages not in this book, but in the **second part**—we will step down from the mountain of knowledge and walk barefoot into the valley of practice. We will enter the kitchen, the bedroom, and the timeline of your life. And there, we will meet the divine not in poetry or philosophy, but in breath, in posture, in prayer, in service, in simplicity.

The truth is: *You cannot become a Saṃsārik Yogī just by reading about it.*

You become one when:

- Your food becomes prasad.
- Your family becomes your temple.
- Your silence becomes deeper than your speech.
- Your discipline becomes gentler than your desires.
- And your surrender becomes stronger than your suffering.

In **Part Two**, we will dive into:

- The yogic lifestyle for the modern householder
- The purification of body, speech, and mind
- The role of time, karma, and death
- The subtle mysteries of seva, humility, dharma, and inner awakening
- The final unveiling of the Atma Yatra

But none of this can unfold if you stop now.

This book is not a flame on its own. It is only the matchstick. The fire is waiting. But only if you strike it.

I know this journey is not easy. I know your mind will say, "I've read enough." I see the world will pull you back with deadlines, bills, and distractions. But I also know this: if your heart stirred even once while reading these pages, if you felt even a single tear well up without reason, if your breath paused at even one sentence, **you are ready**.

And if you stop here… the journey will not be complete.

Do not let this become another book you finish and forget. Let it become a doorway. And then… walk through it.

Part Two is not a sequel. It is your *sādhanā manual*. Your mirror. Your breath. It is the second half of your spiritual heartbeat. I am not asking you to buy another book. I'm asking you to fulfil your calling. If this first half felt like home, then Part Two will feel like the temple within it.

So before you close this book, I ask only one thing: Pause.

Place your hand on your heart. Take one deep, honest breath. And ask yourself...

"Have I just read something sacred? Or have I become it?"

If the answer is the second, I'll meet you again— in the silence of the next page, in the discipline of the next dawn, in the surrender of the next offering. We began this path together. Let us complete it together.

With folded hands and a full heart,
Jai Om Dave

A Personal Letter to You

Dear Seeker,

If you're reading this, it means you made it to the very end.

Not just through the pages, but through every pause. Through the silences between the words, through the emotions you couldn't name, through the truths that perhaps made you uncomfortable. And for that, I bow to you.

I don't know your name. I can't tell your story. But I know your essence. And I know one thing for sure: you didn't arrive here by accident.

Perhaps this book found you in a moment of quiet desperation.

Perhaps it arrived as an answer to a prayer you didn't even know you had whispered. Or maybe you simply followed a silent pull—one that defied logic, but made your soul feel... seen.

I wrote this book not as a teacher, not as a guru, and certainly not as someone who has mastered the path. I wrote it as a fellow traveller. Someone who has stumbled. Who has fallen. Who has doubted every step. And yet, who kept walking—because stopping would have been more painful than continuing.

This is not a book I planned. It is a book I was given. Given by grace. Given by pain. Given by surrender.

I am not the source of this wisdom. I am only the witness.

The vessel. The servant.

Dear reader...
You are not alone.
Not in your fears. Not in your confusion. Not in your longing.

I may never meet you.
But I wrote these words for you.
For the version of you that lies awake at night wondering, "Is this all there is?"
For the version of you that smiles for others but weeps in silence.
For the version of you that is done pretending to be okay when your soul is begging for truth. And for the version of you that is brave enough to look within—even when it's hard, even when it hurts.

You have walked with me through the first part of this journey.
You've seen where we come from, why we suffer, and how we forget. You've remembered what it means to be aware, to be devoted, to act in dharma, to walk in faith.

But beloved... don't stop here. Don't leave this journey unfinished.

The second part of this book is not just a continuation—it's a transformation. It is where thought becomes action. Where sādhanā begins.

Where spiritual truth finds its breath in your body, your food, your silence, your discipline, your home.

If this first part opened your eyes,

The second part will help you live with them open.

You may still have doubts. That's okay.

You may still feel unworthy. That's okay too.

I did too for a long, long time.

But here's what I've come to know with certainty: The divine does not wait for perfect people. It walks with the sincere, the broken, the flawed, and the willing.

And so, if there's even a single spark inside you right now,

Don't walk away from it.

Fan it. Follow it. Trust it.

Because you have no idea what kind of fire it may become.

Thank you for reading. Thank you for feeling. Thank you for trusting me with your inner space. I do not take that lightly.

That Maa Jagadamba holds you close. That Sri Hari showers you with unshakable faith.

And I pray...

That wherever you go from here,

You carry not just my words,

But the *light behind them.*

We'll meet again—in the second part of this path. Until then, keep walking. With courage. With love. With surrender.

You are not alone.
You have never been alone.
And you never will be.

With my whole heart,
Jai Om Dave

ACKNOWLEDGMENTS

With folded hands and a heart full of surrender, I offer my deepest gratitude to the Divine Grace that made me a medium for this sacred work and allowed me to walk the path of a *Saṃsārik Yogī*. I bow down to Maa Jagatjanani Jagadamba, Sri Hari, and Mahadeva — the many forms of the One, the source of all that exists. It is only by their mercy that this book could manifest. Whatever value it holds, it is their blessing alone.

My eternal reverence and *Sashtang Dandvat Pranam* to my beloved Gurudev, Pujya Om Swami ji. As I have shared throughout this journey, every insight, every moment of clarity, and every ray of awakening that has touched my heart has flowed from His divine presence. He is my guiding light, my eternal refuge, everything to me. Words will always fall short of expressing the love and surrender I hold for Him. My only prayer is to walk His path, to serve as His reflection, even if only in the smallest way. Gurudev, you are within me, and I am simply trying to become worthy of your grace.

To my parents, my father, Mr. Nayan Dave, and my mother, Mrs. Padmini Dave — *Sashtang Dandvat Pranam*. It is said that even if one gives away their entire body, it cannot equal the sacrifices made by parents. Your love, your patience, your unwavering support — emotionally, mentally, financially, and spiritually — have been the soil in which this seed could take root. I am grateful beyond words that Maa Jagadamba chose you as the vessels through whom I came into this world.

To my wife, Charmi Om Dave, and my beloved daughter, Rudri Dave — thank you. For your quiet strength. For the unspoken patience. For walking beside me even through the darkness. In the life of a *Grihastha*, there can be no greater blessing than a family that supports his sadhana without complaint or demand. From the depths of my soul,

I thank you both for being the unseen light behind every visible step I've taken.

To Sadhviji, Sadhvi Vrinda Om ji — your writings shaped my bhava. The books *Om Swami: As We Know Him*, *The Rainmaker*, *Book of Faith*, and *Bhagavan and Bhakta* transformed my reverence for Gurudev into something more—a love so deep that it redefined who I am. Without your words, I may have remained only a respectful disciple. Because of them, I became a surrendered one.

To my *Gurubhai*, Parakh Om Bhatt — you were the divine instrument through whom I met my Gurudev in this lifetime. You know what your presence has meant in this journey. I carry your gesture in my heart forever.

To my teachers at the Hatha Yoga Institute — Himanshu Sir and Anchal Ma'am — thank you for teaching me Yoga in its purest form. From the *Patanjali Yoga Sutras* to the *Gheranda Samhita*, your instruction helped me realise the real depth of Yogic life. I will always carry your guidance with reverence.

To Mrs. Khushboo Shokeen, with deep reverence, I offer my heartfelt gratitude for introducing me to the profound sciences of Numerology and Reiki Healing. Your teachings didn't just equip me with techniques—they gave me the foundation to serve, to teach, to guide, and to heal. Today, as I walk forward as a mentor and spiritual educator in these sacred disciplines, I carry your blessings with me.

Without your wisdom, this path would not have unfolded the way it has. Thank you, truly, for being a luminous part of my journey.

To the beautiful community of fellow devotees and disciples:

Meeraji — for sharing my words across Wildr and beyond. Sheetalji — who saw something in me before I saw it myself. Vaniji — a source of constant guidance and encouragement. And there are many more in the community who have helped me in many ways. Your presence, support, and kindness helped my voice reach hearts I could not have reached alone.

To my friends — Naimish Shilu, Ghanshyam Ramani, Samir Borisagar, Pranav Tala, and many more — thank you for believing in me, especially when I did not believe in myself. In the worst phases of my life, your faith was a flame I carried in the dark. Every time one of you said, "You'll crack it, bro," something inside me chose not to give up.

To Ddeepika Om Sharma, a fellow devotee walking the path of our beloved Gurudev and Bhagavan Sri Hari, thank you from the depths of my heart. Your kind decision to create the cover design for this book, not as a professional service, but as an offering of faith and love, touched me more than words can say. In a world where most offer their skills for reward, you offered yours in silence, with sincerity. Your devotion, your intuitive understanding, and your artistic grace have not just framed this book—they have become part of its soul. I will forever carry your gesture as one of the most beautiful blessings this book has received.

And finally, to you, *dear reader*.

Your trust, your time, and your silent companionship are the soul of this work. Without you, these words would simply be ink. If they touched your life in even the smallest way, then my offering is complete. You, dear reader, are the very soul I wrote this book for — even before I knew your name.

May Maa Jagadamba and my Gurudev shower their grace upon you. May your path be lit with faith, steadied with discipline, softened with love, and blessed with divine courage. And may you, too, become a light for someone else one day.

Pranam,
Jai Om Dave

www.ingramcontent.com/pod-product-compliance
Lightning Source LLC
LaVergne TN
LVHW041909070526
838199LV00051BA/2553